NEWBON, BLOODY HELL

NEWBON, BLOODY HELL

A Life in Sports Broadcasting

GARY NEWBON

FOREWORD BY BARRY HEARN OBE

\B^b\

Biteback Publishing

First published in Great Britain in 2023 by
Biteback Publishing Ltd, London
Copyright © Gary Newbon 2023

Gary Newbon has asserted his right under the Copyright, Designs and Patents Act 1988 to be
identified as the author of this work.

ISBN 978-1-78590-8-163

10 9 8 7 6 5 4 3 2 1

A CIP catalogue record for this book is available from the British Library.

Set in Minion Pro

Printed and bound in Great Britain by
CPI Group (UK) Ltd, Croydon CR0 4YY

FSC
www.fsc.org
MIX
Paper | Supporting
responsible forestry
FSC® C171272

This is for the Newbon family past and present and all those who made my career possible.

CONTENTS

FOREWORD

It seems as if I've known Gary Newbon for ever – it certainly feels like it! Some people think that if Gary was a bar of chocolate, he would eat himself, but there's far more to this icon of sports broadcasting than meets the eye, and when you've read this book you will I'm sure agree that the man is a one-off.

I grew up mad on all sports and master of none of them, but throughout his career Gary has been involved in so much of the sporting world that he has become synonymous with many great memories and brilliant moments across a huge range of sports. His wicked sense of humour and fearless pursuit of pivotal moments live long in the memory, and somehow he became a major focal point in the crazy world of TV sport.

We crossed swords on numerous occasions. Some of those were difficult; for instance, when he refused to allow ITV to record an undercard fight featuring 'Baby Jake' Matlala, the world flyweight champion, because he had advertising on his trunks. He refused to budge despite a barrage of abuse from yours truly, but I did have the last laugh when the main event lasted less than one round and

ITV hadn't recorded the excellent title fight because of a 3in. x 2in. logo on his shorts!

But mostly we got on well in the mad world of sport, usually seeing the funny side of things, like when Chris Eubank's opponent Ron Essett was in the ring while Chris was still in his dressing room, waiting for his trainer to finish a shower, or when I wouldn't let Eubank in the ring after his entry music ('Simply the Best') was sabotaged. Newbon nearly had another stroke trying to keep to ITV's transmission times. But that was Gary Newbon – dedicated to his employers (thirty-six years with ITV and fourteen with Sky) and desperate to air the very best show he could.

He has had a remarkable broadcasting life with some amazing episodes, most of which are captured in this book. I can assure readers that they are all more or less the truth and some have given me a chuckle, as I read about Gary getting into a right mess and somehow emerging with a smile on his face.

Sport is such an important part of our lives and it makes memories that live with us for ever. Gary has played his part and lived the life and in doing so has established himself as a true icon of broadcasting.

I am proud to know him as a friend and I hope I can maintain the level of enthusiasm he has shown for the past fifty years.

Enjoy his memories; they are guaranteed to leave you with a smile on your face.

Barry Hearn OBE
September 2023

INTRODUCTION

I laughed a lot while I was writing this book. I know you shouldn't do that when you're telling stories about yourself, so I hope you find them funny as well. They are all true tales. When I look back over my fifty years of TV sports presenting, I cannot believe some of the things I got up to and the events I got mixed up in. It is time to share them.

The title of my book might puzzle you. Why *Newbon, Bloody Hell*? It was inspired by my most famous interview, which was with Sir Alex Ferguson after Manchester United's dramatic 2–1 European Champions League final win over Bayern Munich. Both United goals came in stoppage time when the game and treble trophy haul looked lost. On the final whistle, as he was struggling to take it all in, Sir Alex said to me, 'Football, bloody hell.' He then paused to recover and said, 'But never give in!' It was a golden time for broadcasting and newspapers and many of the strokes I needed to get ahead would not be acceptable today.

My opening chapters are about two successful football managers who played incredibly important roles in my career – Sir Alex Ferguson and Brian Clough. These were two of the sporting personalities that had the biggest impact on my career. The other two were boxer Chris Eubank and footballer-turned-TV-star Jimmy Greaves.

I will chart my journey from a £5-a-week apprentice journalist to years of a privileged and fulfilled life in television. I had disappointments along the way as well. During my thirty-six years with ITV and fourteen with Sky Sports, I experienced much to recall. Those years included seven World Cups, three Olympic Games and many football and boxing championships, both at home and around the world. I covered other sports too, including speedway, motorcycling, darts, snooker and greyhound racing.

My life was about covering and interviewing the biggest names in sport. Three times I interviewed Muhammad Ali. On seven occasions I interviewed Pelé. In fact, I was lucky enough to speak with a range of legends, including Carl Lewis, Mike Tyson, Lennox Lewis, Sir Garry Sobers, Sir Geoff Hurst, Jonah Lomu, Lord Coe, Lord Botham and so many others. There were many events and stories – the terrorist outrage at the Munich Olympics; sitting on Aston Villa's substitute bench at a European Cup final. I was Clough's minder the night he called Jan Tomaszewski a clown. One day I wondered about even including a young unknown Arnold Schwarzenegger on my TV show. Eventually I did show Arnie, but I refused to have my photo with him, telling everyone that they would never hear of him again. Oops!

One proud achievement was persuading the Queen Mother to let me make a documentary on Her Majesty's interest in horse racing.

I once had to ask Sebastian Coe to run 600 yards to my car soon after he won an Olympic gold medal.

I have fond memories of helping an unknown neighbour on his way to becoming a Formula One world champion.

I have enjoyed a career that many people would have loved to experience. I am still working flat out – it is what I do – but I have reinvented myself in different roles. I will never retire. I love it too much. Sadly, there are close friends who I have shared great experiences with who are not here to read this book. I still mourn their passing. Friends like the first million-pound footballer Trevor Francis, who I first interviewed when he was fourteen years of age; veteran actor Roy Dotrice, a bundle of naughty fun who passed at ninety-four; and above all my wonderful parents, Jack and Preeva Newbon, and my much-loved younger brother, Ian.

Why have I written this book? By the time it is published, I will be heading towards seventy-nine. Moving up the bench of life! I hope you enjoy some of my memories and tales and can smile and laugh along the way. If so, it has been well worth the effort.

CHAPTER ONE

THE CHARISMATIC BRIAN CLOUGH

Two of my most famous interviews were with two successful football managers to whom I owe a lot. The first was Brian Clough, who kissed me in front of millions of ITV viewers after his team, Nottingham Forest, suffered a heavy defeat at Everton. The second was with Sir Alex Ferguson, at a moment in which he was almost shell-shocked after Manchester United scored two stoppage-time goals to beat Bayern Munich 2–1 to win the European Champions League, complete the treble and eventually reward Sir Alex with a knighthood. And he provided me with a famous quote! Alex came halfway down the long Nou Camp tunnel for me right on the final whistle and said: 'Football, bloody hell,' and after a pause added, 'But you never give in!' The second quote became the name of the documentary on his life, which was masterminded by his son, Jason. Memories of working with Sir Alex form the next chapter.

Back to Clough. Forest had just played badly at Goodison Park and lost 4–0. Trevor East, ITV's head of sport, had told me that I had just thirty seconds at the end for the live interview as the play-ers came off. It was a Wednesday night on 4 April 1990, and we were tight up in front of *News at Ten*. This was not a sports channel with hours to fill. Before the game I went to see Clough, who invited me into the Forest dressing room. I was asked what I wanted, so I said I needed a very tight interview with him at the end of the match. After asking 'win, draw or lose?' (I said: 'Yes please'), Clough prom-ised he would do it. Just before the final whistle, Trevor said to me: 'Are you sure he'll do it?' I said I was positive. Clough was reliable and always kept his word.

What actually happened was Clough's team were very poor, and Everton beat them convincingly. I tried to make it easy for Clough, suggesting that Forest had played badly because they had a League Cup final coming up. Clough replied, 'Only Albert was sure of a place on the coach to Wembley.' I challenged Clough: 'You don't have an Albert.' Clough explained, 'Yes we do, he's the driver!' That stung me, rather stupidly, and I upped the aggression in my line of questioning. As I kept pushing Clough, the manager realised I was going way over the thirty-second limit, and my floor manager Stan Harding was going berserk, until eventually Clough rescued me by saying: 'Because our lot are a bunch of pansies like you and me!' and promptly gave me a huge kiss!

It threw me completely! On the night, the tabloid sports editors sent their match reporters round to ask me if Clough was drunk, but I explained that he just loves me! I am told Northern comedi-ans had a cruder version of events!

Clough is still talked about today and attracts the biggest laughs when I tell stories about him in after-dinner speeches. Per-sonality-wise there has never been anyone like him in football.

Liverpool's Jürgen Klopp, with his lovely smile and energy, is the closest in the modern game. People often ask me who would be No. 1 on my interview list. That should be a difficult choice, knowing all those I have been able to talk to on television, and many have been very good, but the top of my list? Brian Clough. He was a remarkable man – egotistical, genius, arrogant, bombastic, outrageous, funny, quick but at times, perhaps in contrast, very kind. I was 'on his patch' (the Midlands) and he really looked after me with access, interviews and trust.

He certainly understood the media and how to make headlines. He knew what he was doing. I once knew the vague details of a story, and Clough could have told me the whole thing, but he didn't want to. I asked him: 'Would you tell me in confidence, Brian?' He declined, saying: 'If you do not use it now, then you may in ten years' time.' Another lesson for me. What Brian achieved at both Derby County and Nottingham Forest was simply remarkable. He was of course most effective as a football manager when he was partnered by Peter Taylor. Clough was the leader, bossy, powerful. Taylor was the spotter of talent and, at times, a calming influence on Brian's excesses. They were to fall out over the financial spoils of their relationship and neither was effective in football managership on their own. Their breakup was such a shame.

But back to the many great days. Cloughie was brilliant but unpredictable to interview. But he would always attract a TV audience.

When I first came to Birmingham City in 1971 there was a big social club at the ground where you would see the likes of rock stars Jeff Lynne from Electric Light Orchestra or Roy Wood from the Move mixing with the other Blues fans drinking and talking pre-match. The lunchtime TV football shows on the BBC and ITV would be drowned out until someone yelled 'Brian Clough is on the telly', and you would then almost hear a pin drop. What was he going to say? Something outrageous? Who would he slag off? He was never dull; he certainly had it.

I started to interview him when the former England football captain Billy Wright became my boss at ATV, after signing me from Westward TV in Plymouth. The former Wolves and England captain was head of sport and outside broadcasts at the Birmingham-based TV centre. He was a lovely, modest man who never chose to remind you how famous he was at that time. But administration and appearing on TV to preview the Saturday games were certainly not his strength. On the latter, Billy struggled with words and names and regularly messed it up. The one thing I did not like Clough for was that the night before home matches he would assemble his players at the Midland Hotel in Derby, and part of the routine was to have a laugh at Billy. He deserved more respect. But, they had a point.

As much as I loved the man, I did eventually persuade the other bosses to keep Billy off the screen, apart from presenting awards and the like. Otherwise, Clough was great for me, providing regular interviews as Derby won the 1971–72 league title.

Clough and Taylor began their managerial partnership at Hartlepools United before moving to Derby County, where they soon took the Rams from the Second Division to winning the Football League title.

At the Baseball Ground stadium, Clough's office was right next to the directors' room – ironic, because he was soon to deeply dislike them. There was a long corridor from the manager's office to the home dressing room. He had a phone connection to that dressing room from it. One rare day Clough was the only person in the stadium apart from the apprentices cleaning up in the dressing room. Clough suddenly rang down to the youngsters. He asked: 'Do you know who this is, young man?' One apprentice answered: 'Yes. It's the manager, Mr Clough.' Clough replied: 'Good lad, now I would like a pot of tea with some milk, plus some biscuits.' Back came the question: 'Mr Clough, do you know who this is speaking?' The reply: 'No.' The young lad then exclaimed: 'Then f*** off!' Furious at this, the manager sprinted down the corridor, but the apprentices had all run out of the ground!

Clough, a regular pundit on ITV, was aware of London Weekend Television trying to keep me out of the loop at times, so he insisted that I did all the interviews 'on our patch' as he did when at Nottingham Forest. I will always be grateful for that, because it gave me invaluable network exposure; I was making my mark.

One of Cloughie's main characteristics was that he was very outspoken. He verbally attacked Leeds United as a dirty team and clashed with their manager, Don Revie. The memory of these attacks did not serve him well when he eventually lasted just forty-four days at Elland Road.

It goes without saying that he was far more successful at Derby, where his title win landed the club a place in the European Cup. He had assembled an exciting team with players like Roy McFarland, Alan Hinton, Archie Gemmill, John O'Hare, Kevin Hector, his faithful captain John McGovern from Hartlepools and Colin Todd. Before I arrived in December 1971, he had made two inspired signings – Willie Carlin from Leicester and Dave Mackay from

Spurs, and the Tottenham manager Bill Nicholson had asked Hayters Sports Agency to cover their end of the move. I was at Hayters at the time and was asked to do it.

Before he made the move to Derby, Mackay had been intending to return to Edinburgh and his boyhood club Heart of Midlothian, but one day Clough turned up at White Hart Lane to see Nicholson and said: 'I have come here to sign Dave Mackay.' This was an insight into how Clough and Taylor operated in those days: no nonsense. Incredibly, Clough persuaded Mackay to come to the Baseball Ground, and he went on to become such an influence on his teammates in the early days of Clough and Taylor's tenure. Mackay led by example; he did not talk a lot but showed how to do it, and when he gave advice, every player listened. Carlin in midfield cajoled and pushed the players. The two of them were so important in the formative years of the Clough era.

Carlin in midfield would play in front of Mackay, so that any opponents would have to get past him before Dave, who would play at the back with McFarland. Roy in turn would face the opposing centre-forward.

Mackay was getting towards the end of his playing days and his last season was the first time, after a long and aggressive career, that he played a full league season.

Mackay was also a great leader, and McFarland says that he and the other players learned so much. Mackay used to tell them that they should try things and that they could do it.

I was to get close to Mackay in his managerial days. An easy man to deal with and a schoolboy hero of mine when I used to travel to Spurs from my Cambridge home during the school holidays.

With Mackay ready to go, Clough and Taylor set their sights

on the nineteen-year-old Tranmere Rovers defender Roy McFarland, who was to captain Derby in their league championship year of 1971–72. McFarland was aware of Bill Shankly wanting him at Liverpool and, naturally, he was excited at that prospect. However, Clough and Taylor had other ideas. Taylor first saw McFarland in a season opener at Torquay, where Roy confirmed to me that he had a shocker against an experienced centre-forward. Taylor was to tell him later that he was attracted by McFarland's unwavering effort and commitment. The next game was at home. Unknown to Roy, Clough and Taylor had already agreed terms with Tranmere.

After the match, McFarland and his cousin went for a post-match beer, and he got home at 11.15 p.m. He went straight to bed but was woken two hours later by his mother telling him that, absurdly, there were two men downstairs who wanted to talk to him. Those two men were Clough and Taylor. Dressed only in his pyjamas, Roy listened as they informed him, between sips of the tea that his mother had made them, that they were there to sign him. Roy, confused, turned to his dressing gown-clad father for advice, which he received in the form of: 'Well, if they're this keen, I'd join them.'

Roy asked them for the weekend to think about it, but in their classic, direct style, they said no. It had to be done there and then. Taylor slid the form over and sat next to Roy, telling him to take his father's advice and sign, which he did. Tranmere played their home games on a Friday night so the next day, with his cousin, McFarland went to watch Liverpool win 5–0 at Anfield. Aghast, he turned to his cousin and exclaimed: 'What have I *done*? I've just made the biggest mistake of my life!' But if you asked him today, McFarland would tell you, as he did me, that it was not a mistake. It changed his football career for the best, with trophies and England caps to spare. And it was all down to Cloughie's midnight visit.

Another of these stories is how Clough slept on Archie Gemmill's sofa to make sure he signed him the next morning after 'selling' the midfielder the move to the Baseball Ground. That was then. I do not think Clough ever got to like the new world of football agents. My great friend Jon Holmes, the best in the business, had a rough experience at a meeting with Clough as Gary McAllister's possible move to Nottingham Forest failed to happen. Clough was similar to Sir Alex Ferguson in that, besides being winners, they had time and kindness for many people. I was a recipient of that kindness from both of them. When Derby played Slovan Bratislava at home in their European Cup campaign, Clough showed the kind side of his nature.

It involved my father Jack, who, as a youngster, loved cricket and boxing but had little interest in football. However, like many of his generation, that changed when England won the 1966 World Cup. We were a Cambridge family. In the Second World War my father had survived forty operations in a Handley Page Hampden, the RAF's slowest plane. It was so dangerous that only 8 per cent achieved that survival rate and they disbanded the model in the early 1940s. Ironically, I had first seen Clough in person playing in the stadium on the road I was raised: Milton Road, the home of non-league Cambridge City. He had taken part as a Sunderland player in the early '60s in a testimonial for Norwich City manager Oscar Hold and was still in his playing gear when standing on a seat listening to the presentations in the social club. I was a City supporter and stood underneath him when he stood on a bench seat. I was too much in awe to ask for his autograph. A big thrill...

Little was I to know that years later I would be interviewing him regularly while I worked for Billy Wright.

But anyway, back to this European match. I asked my dad if he would like to join me on the touchline, and he gladly accepted. Before the game, I introduced him to Brian. At the end, he beckoned in our direction: 'Come with me to the dressing room.' I moved forward. 'No, not you – your father, Jack.' They went into the Derby dressing room and I was left stranded for ages! I was soon looking at my watch, worried about running out of time before the highlights show in London. Cloughie had shown my dad around, introduced him to all the players and even asked him about the war and the family business that my parents built from scratch. He also explained the sayings on the wall: 'The greatest crime in football is to give the ball away' and 'God did not invent grass to keep the ball in the air!'

Eventually they both emerged, to my relief. Clough said: 'Jack, I now have to do some work with your son.' And turning to me he observed: 'By the way, Gary, I much prefer your father to you!'

Brilliant words. My dad, who was 5ft 7in, suddenly felt 6ft tall. I will always appreciate the way Clough treated him. Sadly though my dad, having survived the war, died from a heart attack when he was just sixty-two years old in 1982. I used to talk on the phone with him every day. I so miss him.

That Derby European Cup run ended in the semi-finals. They lost 3–1 in the first leg against Juventus in Turin. Archie Gemmill and Roy McFarland were booked – targeted because they were both on a yellow from a previous round and were therefore suspended for the return leg in Derby. It felt like the referee was against Derby all night.

Our commentator Hugh Johns and I had been sent over to watch the game as we were covering the second leg. We were joined by my close friend Lorenzo Ferrari, who at the time ran the most famous Italian restaurant in Birmingham. Hugh, one of the greatest voices in the history of TV sport, thought I wanted his job, which I did not! We had adjoining rooms in the hotel and spent the night emptying the two mini-bars while I convinced him there was nothing to worry about. We bonded from then on, and I was honoured to give the eulogy at his funeral in Wales in the summer of 2007, after he died aged eighty-four.

Back to the Turin first leg tie. We joined Clough and Taylor outside the Derby dressing room after the match. They were raging, instructing Lorenzo to tell Juventus and the referee what 'cheating bastards' they were and worse. Lorenzo tells me he had to put a softer spin on it. The media travelled on the team plane and Clough, still upset at this new experience of cheating, spent most of the flight going up and down the gangway, pouring us all drinks.

The home match finished 0–0. The day before, we had visited Clough at the Baseball Ground in his office. Lorenzo had brought his great friend Giampiero Boniperti, a Juventus legend. He had played his entire career at Juventus from 1946 to 1961 and was now president of the Turin club. He did not speak English, so Lorenzo asked Clough if Boniperti could see the pitch. Clough, still angry, said: 'No, tell him to f*** off.' Lorenzo explained to his great Italian friend: 'Mr Clough apologises, but he says it is not possible today as the groundsman is working on it and has locked the entrance.'

Clough learned a lot from that experience that was to stand him in good stead when he went on to win back-to-back European Cups with Forest. He took teams to four European semi-finals – two he won; the two he lost had seemingly biased referees. The other one was the 1983–84 UEFA Cup semi-final, when several highly debatable refereeing decisions went against Forest. It was later revealed that the referee, Guruceta Muro, had received a big 'loan' from the Anderlecht chairman, Constant Vanden Stock. When this emerged in 1997, Anderlecht were banned for one year from European competition. This was no consolation for Clough and Forest.

It ended badly for Clough and Taylor at Derby. The Derby chairman Sam Longson wanted Brian to cut down on his TV and newspaper writing commitments in London. Cloughie did not want to and the fallout began with the other directors encouraging the chairman to 'cut back on' Clough's excesses. I was being fed exclusive updates. Clough was convinced it was the chairman or someone outside the club with a vested interest. Actually, it was a senior member of staff. Clough did not hold it against me as he knew I was just doing my job, but his subsequent dislike of the chairman and directors was born from his fallout with Longson. My recollection is that he was persuaded by a director that if both Taylor and himself resigned, it would be a double deal, in that they would be reinstated and Longson would go. But sadly their resignations were accepted and they were not reinstated. Clough was furious. He watched an interview I did with the chairman explaining the situation, and when I reached Clough for a comment he exclaimed: 'You have just been talking to the reason!' He then used his fingers, gun-like, to 'fire' at the camera. It all fell into place.

The players led demonstrations and protests, but to no avail. There was no return. In 1975 his former Derby captain Dave Mackay and his assistant Des Anderson led the Rams to another league title. But the decline eventually followed and recent seasons have been disappointing at their modern stadium, Pride Park. There is a statue at the new ground of Clough and Taylor; Derby history owes much to them. Taylor went to Brighton to be joined later by Clough, who then went solo for a disastrous forty-four days at Leeds where players like Billy Bremner, who had been insulted in Clough's Derby days, never accepted him.

After Derby, Clough continued his work with ITV and for the vital 1974 World Cup qualifier against Poland at Wembley. I was Brian's ITV minder and was instructed to keep him away from drinking. I failed! Clough found out about a BBC drinks party happening before the match in the Wembley Hotel, and we were soon invited in there. I thought Brian was fine when we arrived at the ITV gantry for live coverage, but what followed caused headlines and is often recalled in articles about him. He was part of ITV's 'pundits' panel' at Wembley. We got there in good time.

The Polish goalkeeper was Jan Tomaszewski, and he stood between England and the win they needed that night to qualify for the 1974 World Cup. He made a series of vital saves that limited England to the 1–1 draw. Poland went on to finish third in those finals and he went on to be named best goalkeeper. He also played a crucial role when Poland won the silver medal at the 1976 Olympics. However, on the night of the game at Wembley, Clough described Tomaszewski as a 'clown'! He couldn't have been more wrong! Both Clough and Tomaszewski made a huge impact that night, for contrasting reasons.

After ITV came off air, we both walked up and down the pitch, the stadium now deserted. We were desperately disappointed that England would not be in West Germany. He never got the England job. Some at the Football Association seemingly felt they could not handle him. When Taylor and Clough had earlier been in charge of the youth players at an overseas tournament, they had waited some while on the team coach after the match before Clough ordered the driver to go and left the FA party stranded! It was criminal that Clough and Taylor never got the job and, despite two semi-finals and quarter-finals England have yet to win the World Cup again. Maybe Gareth Southgate will change that.

After that Wembley night with the Polish draw, I lost touch with Clough for a while (apart from interviewing him in a Solihull music venue). During that time, he was briefly at Brighton and Leeds. But he bounced back to the big time with Nottingham Forest from 1975 to 1993, and when Clough was reunited with his outstanding assistant Peter Taylor, the trophies began to flow. Let me get the major ones out of the way: First Division title 1978; European Cup 1979 and 1980. Four Football League Cups: 1978, '79, '89 and '90. Unfortunately, they never won the FA Cup, despite reaching the final in 1991, but Clough was awarded Football Manager of the Year 1978 and an OBE for his services to football in 1991. (Clough described it as 'other buggers' efforts'.)

When we think of successful footballing managers, the likes of Bob Paisley at Liverpool, Sir Alex Ferguson at Manchester United and Pep Guardiola at Manchester City come to mind. But these managers were working with *big* English clubs. Clough and Taylor achieved their success at Derby County and Nottingham Forest, who, with respect, were hardly huge clubs. At Derby, Clough and Taylor took the team back to the First Division, which they won. With Forest, they won the Football League title in 1978 after being promoted from the Second Division the previous year, and they then immediately won back-to-back European Cup trophies. That achievement was quite staggering and will probably never be repeated by a club the size of Forest. Clough was the abrasive leader who, when attempting to sign good players, would say to them: 'Show me your medals,' knowing of course that they had none of note. Taylor was the steadying influence and a fine judge of player. His son-in-law, John Dickinson, worked with me at ATV and then Central TV. I remember John telling me that he went with Peter to watch a prospective signing at Cambridge United. They left after two minutes with Taylor saying: 'He can't play... Not for us!'

Not that it was always sweetness and light for me.

One Saturday around 1980, I woke up on a Saturday having lost my voice. Katie told me that I couldn't possible go to work and do my *Star Soccer* show (highlights of some of the Midlands Saturday-afternoon matches). I told her that I was not letting anyone else do it! The first person I bumped into at the City Ground was Clough, who said: 'Morning.' I could hardly croak a reply and was asked what my problem was. When I told him that I had lost my voice, he said: 'Two and a half million people in the Midlands will be absolutely thrilled with that news.' And he promptly walked away! But he did later send the club doctor round to dose me up.

In the mid-'70s, I had formed the Midlands Soccer Writers club, which was based at Lorenzo's restaurant in Birmingham. As it developed, I persuaded my ATV bosses to let me stage the Midlands Player and Young Player of the Season Awards. We used one of our studios to put on a dinner jacket show with the media, managers, players and public figures like Jasper Carrott.

Clough did the honours in the second year, with Trevor Francis of Birmingham City winning the Young Player Award. When Trevor joined us on the stage, he had his hands in his pockets.

Clough said: 'You are a very talented young man. Now, if you would kindly take your hands out of your pockets, I will present you with this trophy!' Another Clough moment to remember! Mind you, we had to stop Trevor's manager Willie Bell sticking one on Clough in the bar afterwards! Willie, normally a lovely man, was very religious, so that was out of character for him. Sadly he died in 2023 in the USA from a stroke, aged eighty-five. As did lovely Trevor from a heart attack, aged just sixty-nine.

Much later of course Clough made Trevor the first million-pound footballer, and he went on to score the only goal in the European Cup final. I did a TV interview with Trevor when he was aged fourteen in Plymouth. He was the star of the Plymouth schools and was being watched by all the leading scouts. I was twenty-three and had just got my first job in TV with Westward TV. I do not know who was more nervous!

I followed Trevor to Birmingham. He had signed his Blues contract on the desk of my future wife, Katie, in the ATV newsroom. I was to join ATV later. Trevor split his time between his homes in Solihull, where I live, and Spain. We were close friends with regular phone calls and meetings when he was in Solihull. Like so many I was shocked and saddened by his death. Trevor was a lovely, approachable man who was very private. He was lost for a long while after his wife Helen passed away following a long and brave battle with cancer. He was a private man with a limited circle of friends at his own choice. I was lucky to be included.

I was at the Munich final as an observer for Trevor's finest moment. Trevor told me about the bizarre events the night before the game. Clough and Taylor called the players to a team meeting in their hotel. The squad assumed it was to tell them the team. No such luck. Indeed, they were not to know until well into the following morning. Clough kept ordering copious amounts of German wine. At one stage Archie Gemmill stood up, only to be asked by Clough where he was going. Gemmill explained he was heading for bed. 'No, you are not,' ordered Clough. 'Sit down!' Trevor told me that two of the selected team needed pills from the physio on the morning of the final after suffering slight hangovers. Clough was certainly unconventional.

Before Forest's European success, my ATV producer Trevor East had the idea of pairing Clough and myself once a month live in the studio on a Friday. Trevor went to see Clough and said it would be like David and Goliath. Brian said he would love it. Trevor asked him how much he wanted: 'Trevor, I want as much as I can get.' Point taken. The programmes were worth every penny.

Around that time, I was also told I had £7,000 spare on budget and to make a cheap series. I found seven highlights of the best matches of the '70s and '80s and offered Clough £5,000 to shoot a series with me in one afternoon called *Cloughie's Golden Oldies*, in which we looked back on the games. We did it in the Forest trophy room. He never saw any of them, but I briefed him about the games before every take. He was simply brilliant, producing lines like: 'I gave Coventry a million pounds for Ian Wallace and it is a testament to my ability as a manager that I did not get the sack for that signing.' But his pay-off line was the best. I thanked him at the end of the last 'programme', and he turned to the camera and commented: 'The biggest bouquet should go to the cameraman for managing to get both your head and mine in the same shot.' There will never be another like him.

There were some outrageous stories in those European runs too

– particularly the first one, in 1979. The European Cup was expanded and Forest drew Liverpool, with all their big players, in the first
round. It was a sign of things to come when Forest won their home
leg 2–0 and drew 0–0 in the second leg.

Next up were AEK Athens, with the away leg first. When we arrived in the Greek capital, the home supporters stoned the Forest
team bus. Glass flew everywhere. Clough, understandably, was very
angry. At the mandatory press conference the next day, a Greek
journalist revealed they had discovered that Forest were offering
their players a smaller bonus to beat AEK than they did to beat Liverpool: 'Why is this?' Clough's reply: 'So we can pay the referee as
much as your cheating bastards will.' Thanks, Brian. Being unpredictable, he then invited the Greek media to join us all for lunch.
One other Greek reporter asked if he might interview Forest's star
goalkeeper, Peter Shilton. Clough's response: 'As long as you promise not to ram his fingers in the lift on the way down.' Thanks again,
Brian. Forest won the match, and on the terraces behind our post-
match interview burned a range of small, controlled fires. Brian:
'They are lighting fires in my honour.' I decided not to correct him
by mentioning that was how they burned all the rubbish left by the
spectators out there.

Moving on to the semi-final. Forest play Cologne in the home
leg. It finishes 3–3 with the headlines that a Japanese sub has sunk
Forest: Yasuhiko Okudera scored in the eighty-first minute. ITV
covered this match, and I really thought that the three away goals
would be enough to knock out Forest for the away leg. At the end
of the post-match interview, I put that to Clough, who said: 'I hope
no one will be stupid enough to write us off.'

Taylor asked me to place a bet on Forest winning the away leg.

I got 7/2 for Forest to win, so Ladbrokes were agreeing with me. So, the match. Ian Bowyer scored the only goal. Peter Shilton made a wonderful save. Afterwards I put my head around the Forest dressing room door (those were the days) and Taylor asked: 'Did you get on [the bet with Ladbrokes]?!' I told him yes, and he was pleased. He then said that Brian was on the pitch. He was in fact walking around the running track outside the pitch, on his own in the now-deserted stadium. He beckoned me over. Putting his arm through mine, he said: 'After the 3–3 home leg, when I told you I hoped no one would be stupid enough to write us off, you dropped your microphone and Brian Moore in London fell off his studio stool. Now you both know what I was talking about. I'll see you at the airport.'

There were just a handful of trusted media in those days. Clough would give the press interviews, wonderful ones for both TV and the radio. Headlines all the way. Then he would say: 'Right, put your pens and microphones away; we're going out for a drink.' And we did. Everything else just finished for the day. Sadly those golden days are over! The arrival of social media, mobile phone cameras, mass media and 24-hour rolling news has brought a different world, one with little trust.

So, to the first European final. There was big disappointment for Archie Gemmill and Martin O'Neill, who were both returning from injury and therefore failed to make the team.

Martin is one of the cleverest players I have known, and one of the funniest. He was a law student in Northern Ireland who gave it up for football. He has always been a brilliant speaker. He was probably too clever for Cloughie, even though Martin still loves to talk about him; he recalls Cloughie with some affection. In one

18

interview Clough told me: 'John this and Archie this, but our No. 7 [O'Neill] may not be as clever as he thinks.'

I was present on a stage when O'Neill talked about a long stint in the reserve team; he said that he asked Clough about it. 'Why do you keep playing me in the second team?' Reply: 'Simple answer, Martin – I don't have a third team.' Genius!

But there was a soft side to Clough. On 2 February 2002, I suffered a stroke soon after leaving the Lowry Hotel in Manchester on my way to Old Trafford, to cover United. More on that in another chapter. I made a full recovery, but when I got home a week later, one of the many letters waiting for me was from Brian. He had simply written: 'Get well soon. We love you – Brian and Barbara.' I will always treasure that. Clough had a big heart for people in trouble and a full-throated commitment to the causes he believed in, like the Labour Party. He was a lifelong socialist. He also turned up to support the miners on their picket lines, as well as donating money to the trade unions.

But it was not always sweetness and light. Clough had a lengthy struggle with the demon drink, which affected him and the club. Years earlier he had fallen out with Taylor over the spoils of money. Taylor had left Forest to go back to Derby and, unknown to Clough, who was on holiday at the time, signed John Robertson. They never spoke again.

I went to Taylor's funeral in 1990 and Clough and his wife entered the church at the very last moment. We were pleased about that. I think Brian, a decent man under it all, was full of regret. Brian stopped drinking eventually when he needed a transplant. He recovered and one lovely summer's day I invited Brian and Barbara to lunch at their favourite spot, the Dovecliff Hotel near Burton on Trent. No cameras, no notebook, no agenda apart from an opportunity to thank them both for their support and kindness. We spent three memorable and happy hours there, including one final story from Barbara: when Brian was in a northern hospital waiting for the transplant, he was woken very early by the loud noise of a helicopter landing outside his room. He called for the surgeon and gave him a right telling off until he was told: 'Brian, that helicopter has brought your new organ.' Brian gave me a sheepish grin – I had seen his smile many times, but I'd never seen that embarrassed look! I never saw him again. He died in the Royal Derby Hospital on 20 September 2004, aged sixty-nine. His wife Barbara died on 20 July 2013, aged seventy-five.

There was one more involvement with Brian Clough for me. The unveiling of his statue took place just off Nottingham's Old Market Square on 6 November 2008. I was not planning to go, as I was hosting back-to-back TV shows that finished at midnight. Sky had booked me into a nearby hotel. But the night before the unveiling, I had a call from a former member of my Central TV sports team, Keith Daniell, who told me that Barbara Clough was not happy with the person hosting the public address and had told Keith that Brian would have wanted me to do it. So, I got to Nottingham early with a faxed script ready for rehearsal. All set to go. The actual event was going well for me until I interviewed Councillor John Davies, the leader of Nottingham Council. 'So,' I asked, 'what did Brian Clough really mean to the city of Birmingham?'

I didn't even realise what I'd said until 4,000 people started booing. Anyway, I corrected and composed myself and off we went again without another hitch. Afterwards lots of people said 'well done', but I knew the media would pick up on my major error. I have always got on with them and they were kind in their comments! However, two days later Ron Atkinson, who was always doing quizzes and ringing me for answers, was on the phone. 'Hallo, pal, quiz question: what is the capital of Peru?' Quick as a flash, I replied: 'Lima.' Ron then quipped (before putting down the phone): 'How come you know that, but you don't know where Nottingham is?!' Brian Clough would have enjoyed that!

CHAPTER TWO

SIR ALEX FERGUSON
– THE BOSS

The first time I interviewed Sir Alex Ferguson I fell out with him, although I did not realise it at the time! I interviewed him at the end of a match at Old Trafford, and I asked him about getting the sack. He gave me a sort of brush off. There were rumours at the time that he was under early pressure at Manchester United with suggestions that he was facing the sack. It is often said that the goal by Mark Robins that gave United victory in the FA Cup at Nottingham Forest saved Sir Alex, but that has never been proved.

Anyway, a few weeks after my first short interview, ITV's live match was Norwich vs Manchester United. I was, as usual, doing the interviews, so I checked with Sir Alex: 'OK for a quick interview afterwards, please?' 'No,' came the reply.

This had never happened before. I thought I had good relations with everyone, so I asked: 'Why not?' The reply: 'Because, you ask crap questions.' A little stunned, I enquired: 'May I at least talk to the players, then?' To the manager's credit he did not ban me completely, saying: 'You can talk to anyone but me.' So I thought, what do I do now? Was Sir Alex being fair? I normally hate that journalistic justification – 'I was just doing my job.' Realising that I might have pushed him a bit far with my sacking question, I decided that I should have warned Sir Alex beforehand. I could see his point of view. But what was I to do about it? This was not a boxer I was dealing with, an athlete of whom I could ask some pretty direct questions.

Manchester United have always attracted TV's highest ratings over the years, but they were not featuring so much on ITV then – around 1986. There therefore wasn't going to be much opportunity to help him set the record straight, since I would not be in a position to ask him questions if we were not covering a United match. Even so, I wanted to make it up. Trust has always been an important factor in my career. Without realising it, on that first interview I had broken Sir Alex Ferguson's trust. I was not angry with him at Norwich. I was disappointed that I had put myself in that position.

In those days, newspaper journalists often accused TV interviewers of being soft with their questions. But the writers always swapped quotes and stories if one of their kind had been banned, therefore covering one another's backs. With TV you have to get the manager or player in front of a camera. News reporters hardly ever see their subjects again, apart from politicians, who have thick skins and for whom the banter is part of their lives. But sport is different. Emotions run high and people can become riled. I was not dealing with Brian Clough here. As luck would have it, however, an opportunity presented itself a few weeks later. I had covered boxing for the regular series *Fight Night* in Manchester and was staying at the Midland Hotel. When I went for breakfast the next day, I was surprised to see Ferguson sitting on his own. 'May

I join you, please?' I enquired. To my relief, he nodded. I sat down with my buffet breakfast and asked Sir Alex: 'May I start again?' To which he asked: 'How?' I promised that, from now on, if I had what I described as a 'curveball question', he would know about it before any interviews. I tried to assure him that he could really trust me. He agreed and it began what I considered a really good relationship built on trust. I know I must have irritated him at times with my requests, but he always accommodated me, including by doing live half-time interviews in European Cup matches. I have always believed you have to take people as you find them – not as other people would have you believe.

I have heard some journalists' negative opinions about Sir Alex, but they only hold those because they have been banned from interviewing him. They should give him credit that those bans were lifted! Journalists and newspapers, as well as football managers, can be sensitive souls at times – they reserve the right to dish it out, but they are not too good at taking it. Sir Alex had to be very tough and ruthless at times. But he had to be fair with us as well, and with his players, as long as they gave him 100 per cent on both the field and the training ground. He would not tolerate idleness and was a stickler for making sure his players trained like they played. He once told me that if any player challenged his authority as manager, they would have to go – and they did. I realised how important that principle was, and it was an important factor that I took into my twenty-two years as controller of sport at Central TV, which in that time was a major player in both national and regional sport.

He also handled the media with, at times, an iron fist. He fiercely protected his players and the club, particularly against criticism. The big difference between the Clough and Ferguson days in England was the sheer expansion and volume of the media. In Cloughie's early days, there were usually about twelve trusted football reporters. Local and national press, TV and radio and agencies. Broadcasters and reporters had to come back time and again to basically the same football people. Then we had the introduction of the news reporters, the rolling TV news, the overseas media, the online media and eventually social media. Sir Alex, for instance, did not know a lot of them. He wondered what their motives were. What was the agenda? He had to be cautious when packed press/media conferences took place. At times, he would rather they not report on United, as they would often be highly critical. The media were thirsty to dish it out and then puzzled when they did not get what they wanted from the manager. I never asked questions at news conferences. That was not my brief. Some of the questions then and now strike me as overladen with the interviewer's personal opinions and observations. Since the object of the exercise surely is to get your subject's opinions, it seems absurd for interviewers to make it so aggressively about themselves.

Moving on from that, I want to write about the compassionate side to the man. As previously mentioned, on 2 February 2002 I suffered a stroke while in the Lowry Hotel in Manchester on the morning of a United–Sunderland match, for which I was scheduled to do the interviews. I was one month from being fifty-seven years old. But suffice to say I recovered, and Sir Alex was on the phone three times when I got home checking on my recovery. As I write this I have reached seventy-eight and am still going! Then in 2010, while my wife Katie was suffering from a deadly malignant melanoma, she discovered that she also had a large brain tumour. Sir Alex had been told this by our old floor manager Stan

Harding (whom Sir Alex was also fond of) as he was leaving their Birmingham hotel for the match at West Bromwich Albion. Sir Alex rang me from the team coach wanting to know all about it and wishing Katie well. My wife, against the odds, recovered, and although she is not into football, she really appreciated his concern. I am pleased to say that Katie, too, has made a great recovery. We will always appreciate Sir Alex's concern and kindness.

There are other examples too. Joe Melling was a *Daily Express* football reporter who I knew well. Sir Alex and Joe did not get on very well, but when Sir Alex was told that Joe, a heavy smoker, had lung cancer, he rang him and said: 'Joe, you fight this cancer as hard as you fought me!'

Bryan Robson, one of his great players and captains, developed throat cancer and received the usual caring approach from his old manager. Thankfully, at the time of writing Bryan is now eleven years clear and, like Sir Alex, a United ambassador. It is little known that, if at all possible, Sir Alex would go to the funerals of friends and people he had known well both north and south of the border. He always wanted to pay his respects. I attended two of those funerals – Paul Doherty (former head of sport at Granada TV) and Bob Patience, who had been the interviewer when Sir Alex won the European Cup Winners' Cup final for Aberdeen against Real Madrid in Gothenburg. Bob moved to London Weekend Television and produced the *Saint & Greavsie* show. The funeral was in Basingstoke and the reception at the Wentworth Golf Club. The United manager made both venues. Football management is a cut-throat business. There is a relentless need to win matches and never-ending stream of out-of-work hopefuls waiting to take sacked managers' posts. But there is care as well. When a manager lost his job, Sir Alex would often invite that person to spend time at the United training ground – in latter years, at Carrington. Those that went never forgot his kindness. He is loyal to his friends and many others, including his former players.

Then in May 2018 Sir Alex suffered a form of brain haemorrhage, which required emergency surgery. It was such a relief for family, friends, former players, the club, supporters and admirers to see him recover so successfully. Obviously I had nothing to do with his success story, but it was a satisfying experience to be interviewing Sir Alex on such a regular basis. I have a few other memories to share.

His predecessor Ron Atkinson had won two FA Cups but dipped out on winning the holy grail at the time – the Football League title. United as mentioned had been waiting since 1967 when they were last league champions under Sir Matt Busby. Sir Alex had become Manchester United manager in 1986 and after a shaky start began to hunt down the holy grail. They finally won the new Premier League in 1993. But there was immense disappointment the previous 1991–92 season when Leeds just pipped United. United went to Liverpool for their league game on 26 April having led the table for most of the season. They needed to win but lost 2–0 to goals by Ian Rush and Mark Walters. It meant that Leeds, watching at home, had won the title under manager Howard Wilkinson. I was doing the interviews for ITV's live coverage at Anfield. Unlike the future sports channels we were tight for time at the end of the match. I was under pressure to get a reaction from Sir Alex and (as you could in those days) was with my cameraman right outside the away dressing room. After a couple of requests and my knocking on the door in desperation, Alex came out and, choked as he was, gave me the interview. He may or may not recall that, but I will never forget it and will never lose the huge respect I have for him for doing it.

Moving on to United's first European Champions League campaign in 1998/99, ITV thought I should go to Gothenburg for a bonding session. United would play the winners of a qualification match, who turned out to be the home team. After the match, I was invited to join a ceremony in a type of hall on a hill where Sir Alex was honoured by being made a Viking. I bet you did not know that! I offered to take Sir Alex for dinner, and he said we would be joined by Nestor Lauren, a close friend of his who was a leading executive at Volvo and insisted on paying the bill. Sir Alex wanted to catch a redeye flight to Manchester so he would be back in time for training. We were in the same hotel. There was little time for sleep, and I was charged with making sure the manager woke up on time. 'Oh, my God,' I thought. 'If I cock this up, the bonding will be in vain.' I stuck notices on the wall saying 'wake Alex', booked two alarm calls and did not sleep. When I finally rang, I thought on time, I was greeted with: 'You are a minute late!' and then laughter.

Back to the trust element, which has been so important to me in my long career. If nothing else, no one can ever accuse me of breaking their trust. For the European matches, Sir Alex would give a few of the ITV team, including me, a confidential briefing, knowing that we would not use anything before the live transmission. He also trusted that anything really sensitive would not be used at all; it was just being fed to us for context. This was so helpful. The meetings took place at 4 p.m. in the Old Trafford grill room on home matches and 11 a.m. abroad in the United team hotel. There was one amusing incident on a live half-time interview in

Turin in 2003 that gave the wrong impression to the presenter, Des Lynam. United were playing really well and leading Juventus 2–0 at half-time. My cameraman was one of my twin boys Laurence, who is very experienced. One of the difficulties of working with ITV is you have to wait until the commercial break has finished. I was waiting in the tunnel with Sir Alex and making conversation, hoping he and the second-half restart whistle would wait. Laurence was asking me to move into my position and I was not taking it in. 'Dad – please move to your right.' Not happening. Laurence is a big strong lad and, frustrated, he eventually grabbed me and pulled me into position. Sir Alex found this hilarious and was still laughing as we did the interview. Des Lynam picked up on it: 'Sir Alex obviously so happy there and showing it.' Well, I am sure he was happy with that scoreline, which United managed to improve to 3–0, but Des was not to know that that was not what the laughter was about!

There was only one awkward occasion on the 4 p.m. briefing, and that came before the 1998/99 Champions League semi-final against Juventus at Old Trafford, and that was when he told us the news that David Beckham would be on the bench. He explained that David did have a small back problem, but that when performances for United matched his performances for Sven-Göran Eriksson and England, he would start again. This left me with a problem. Sir Alex always gave me a recorded chat before the match. How was I going to ask him properly about this without breaking his trust? It was a hot April evening, and Sir Alex came out of the dressing room in his shirt sleeves and a good mood. I asked him if we could just go down the long tunnel as I needed to ask him something. How would he explain the Beckham situation? 'A back injury,' was his reply. But then I would have to ask why he was still a substitute. Sir

Alex agreed. When we returned to the interview spot, I had made up my mind that if the back injury was the only response I got, I would leave it at that. But I was pleased and relieved when the full explanation was given! I heard Des say: 'Top of the show with that, please.'

And so eventually, after winning the Premier League and the FA Cup in 1999, we were all off to Barcelona as United hunted that memorable treble – the first by a British club. What a climax in added time. ITV's commentator, Clive Tyldesley, gave a famous line as Beckham took a corner: 'Can Manchester United score? They always score.' And they did – twice. So to the interview. Sir Alex in his autobiography writes that '[all] Gary Newbon got for his efforts was gibberish.' No, Alex, I got the most famous football interview of them all. Thank you.

But a sad end to this chapter; I have to note the passing of his wife, Lady Cathy, in October 2023. They were married in 1966, and Sir Alex described her as his bedrock.

CHAPTER THREE

HOW IT ALL BEGAN

My first job as a £5-a-week apprentice journalist came at the age of nineteen. It was in September 1964 with Jeacock's News Agency in my home city of Cambridge. Little did I know that some of my schoolboy heroes would turn out to be big players in my own career. Billy Wright was head of sport at ATV and took me from little Westward Television in Plymouth to the ITV giants in Birmingham. I was one of the people to bring Spurs goalscoring legend Jimmy Greaves into his first pundit role in TV and was his presenter at ATV and then Central for nineteen years. Yet when I was at school, I used to get the train to Northumberland Park to go to White Hart Lane and watch him score! There were obviously many more, including the 1966 England World Cup team, famous Test cricket stars and boxing legends. It is funny how life works out.

My parents (who had done well for themselves financially after starting a successful wool-selling business that expanded into four shops selling ladies fashions, underwear and children's clothing), decided that my brother Ian and I should have the private education they never had. So at the age of nine (quite young really), I became a boarder at Culford School, in the village of Culford near

Bury St Edmunds in Suffolk. Four hundred boys in 400 acres – a beautiful park with woods, lakes and pitches for three different sports, swimming and tennis facilities, as well as a big gym. It was the country seat of the Cadogan family and many years ago the famous Cornwallis family. It is now co-ed with some magnificent new facilities.

Back then the sport was excellent. I loved the matches against other top schools. I was in the football team who won most of their matches. When we were twelve, football was replaced by rugby. I was not looking forward to that, but I misjudged my apprehension. I was very fast, strong and heavy. The centre and wing three-quarters positions suited me and by the age of fourteen I had developed a strong tackling ability. I was in an outstanding year of players at all sports. Little Alfie Long, at the age of thirteen, had beaten the school tennis captain in the school knockout cup final in front of all 400 boys. Alfie went on to later reach the final of Junior Wimbledon, where he lost to Stanley Matthews Jr. Alfie also won his blue in the Cambridge University team.

There was an incredibly hot summer in 1959. The autumn term was the rugby term and, as a result of the heat, only one pitch was playable. The first team (under-eighteens) was the holy grail, but it was decided to give the pitch to the outstanding Colts team (under-fifteens), for whom I played in the centre. We thrashed everyone. We beat deadly rivals Framlingham College 55–0, with fly-half Guy Abel and centre John Lister dropping three goals in the first two minutes. Three of those fifteen-year-olds went straight into the first XV the next season. John Bolden, Lister and I were on the wing. I was to play for four years without missing a match and became captain in my last season. This was when my ruthlessness kicked in.

I had only inherited one player from the previous year's first XV: a talented scrum-half named Deryck Gowland. In fact, only second- and third-team players from previous seasons were available.

I said to the school coach, former Northampton and East Midlands scrum-half Bill Murray, that I would move to the middle of the back row of the scrum – No. 8 – and we would spend hours and hours on my squad's tackling and passing. Since we weren't a particularly talented team, nothing else mattered. It paid off. We beat all our rivals, losing only one match, which was a result of our selection being hampered.

The best result we achieved was when we became the first school to win at Woolverstone Hall. The London County Council had obtained use of this property near Ipswich with its fifty acres. This was in the 1950s, and it was turned into a state grammar boarding school that excelled at rugby, regularly beating the surrounding private schools. I was desperate to win on their soil. We were not good enough on paper, so I decided to use gamesmanship. In those days, a player was allowed to kick the ball directly into touch from anywhere.

These days, apart from penalties, you are only allowed to do that from your own 22-metre area (25-yard area in my day). Perhaps we had something to do with that! I said to Gowland: 'We'll rely on penalties and the backs will line up on our scrums and you will kick into touch even in *their* 25-yard line or up to ten yards from their in-goal line. We ran out 6–3 winners. I kicked a penalty and my back-row forward Tim Mutton scored an unconverted try. The home side had just the one penalty goal.

It was pretty disgusting on my part, in the days when the present tactics of head down and different phases of continual mauls were unheard of. School teams were expected to run with the ball. We were booed by the home spectators and shunned at the end by the opponents. I said to my team: 'Bollocks to them all. You are f******* heroes.'

On the coach back, Bill Murray sent for me to join him at the front where he had been sitting on his own. 'Gary – that was terrible. I was completely shunned by their masters in the tea-room afterwards. You were completely out of order!'

He then sent for Gowland, my vice-captain. Murray said: 'Gary should not have played like that. But I have to admit, I am thrilled we won. The school will be celebrating with news of that result.' I stayed lifelong friends with Bill Murray until he passed away.

Going back a bit, when I was eleven, in 1956, a new boy joined my year who was to become one of the most famous sports broadcasters in BBC history – John Motson, the son of a Methodist minister in the London Docklands. Motty, as he soon became known, and I hit it off immediately through our love of football, and we remained friends for sixty-six years until his death in 2023. He was not a great sportsman, although he could play football. Culford, though, was not a football school. His father, the Rev. William Motson, would write to the headmaster, Dr Christopher Storey, every year requesting football be put on the sporting agenda, but his prayers on this occasion were not answered! However, hidden among the 400 acres of school ground we found a spot to form a football pitch, and our outstanding under-fifteens played the under-eighteens. The games were very close, with results going either way. Motty played on the wing with his thin legs and was a good crosser of the ball. I played centre-half to deal with the big threat, the tall centre-forward 'Dobby' Dobbins, who I kicked at every opportunity. According to Motty, I was 'self-elected captain'. I took the goal kicks, throw-ins, free kicks and penalties. That figures! But I did let Motty take the corners.

When I appeared on Motty's *This Is Your Life* on ITV in October 1996, I told a story of how my grandmother used to send me the *Leicester Mercury* Saturday sports paper – the only boy to receive one at the school. Motty was keen to read it, so I used to make him queue for an hour outside the tuck-shop while I read it. Then I would take his place and hand him the paper!

As I went to sit down with other guests on the stage, Motty said to the TV host, Michael Aspel: 'Did you know, Michael, that Gary was captain of some of the school teams? He never picked me. I used to turn up with my boots and he would say: "You are a weed. You will not be playing in my team!"'

My wife, Katie, was in the audience at the Thames TV studios in Teddington and said it was the only time in our long marriage that she had seen me embarrassed. I had to sweat until the show went out, but, as I had hoped, it was edited out of the transmitted version.

Motty wrote in his book, *Motty*, that I had one boxing match in the school's annual tournament, which I won on points and then 'retired' to manage the best of the others! No change then – still interviewing winners. Motty used to love to recall how my father had an early cinecamera and used to film me winning the races on the school sports days. My favourite sports have always been football, boxing, rugby and cricket.

Another Culford boy, George Zeleny, shared my love of boxing. The tuck-shop was run by the cricket coach Johnny Boughton, who had played football for Charlton Athletic and cricket in the Lancashire League. Mr Boughton and his wife Marjorie, who worked with him, lived just outside the school grounds. George and I used to slip out of school at night to go to the Boughtons' house to watch BBC highlights of Muhammad Ali's fights – Cassius Clay in those days. Little did we know that in years to come I was to interview Ali three times on TV.

When I finally left school at nineteen years old (sport detained me, not lessons!), I just wanted to play sport. I went to Cambridge United at pre-season for trials but was too one (left) footed and heavy, so I reverted to rugby and won a first-team place in the Cambridge City side who went into senior rugby for a season with former England and British Lions scrum-half Dickie Jeeps and Andy Hancock, who was to go on with Northampton and score a memorable last-minute, full-length try for England against Scotland at Twickenham in 1965. He ran seventy yards from well inside his own 25-yard line, beat two opponents down the left wing and raced in to save the match. One of the great tries. Sportingly, the final Scottish player who failed to tackle him reached down to congratulate the exhausted Hancock on the ground. Both were wonderful players and it was a great thrill to play outside them, even if I did not receive the ball much on the left wing! Both Dickie and Andy are now dead, as are many people who feature in this book. But their memories live on with me.

As wonderful as all this was, my wise father sat me down one day and said: 'There is no real money in sport. When you are thirty, do you want to be doing a job that you will hate for the rest of your days – or do you want to be enjoying a lovely career of your choice?' 'I want to be a journalist,' was my reply. My dad had a few friends in journalism, but most of them drank a massive amount of alcohol. He was concerned, but he always said, as I have to my own children: 'You must do what *you* want to do and not what *we* want you to do.' My father then took out Robin Esser (William Hickey gossip column editor at the *Daily Express*) to Simpson's on the Strand for lunch and to ask his advice. Esser told my dad that Mike Jeacock, a top former *Daily Express* reporter, had bought the Cambridge News Agency in our home city and he would have a word with him. The result was a successful interview with Mike and my first job as an apprentice reporter. I was so excited.

I am grateful that I had a chance to thank Robin Esser in public. Many years later I was hosting Variety's charity sports lunch with a host of award winners, including Formula One's Bernie Ecclestone, England manager Sven-Göran Eriksson and a lot of other big names. As I was talking, I suddenly spotted Robin on one of the tables. I explained my debt of gratitude to him. Robin died on 6 November 2017 aged eighty-four. I am sure he followed my fifty years in TV with interest knowing that he had opened the door – always the most difficult step in anyone's career.

Meanwhile, my parents were pleased for me. I did however receive contrasting instructions from my father and mother. Dad said: 'I just want you to be happy.' My mother: 'We have spent a lot of money on your education. You *have* to be a success.' No pressure there then, Mum! Mind you, within exactly four years of that first interview in September 1964, I was a sports presenter at ITV!

I have always loved newspapers. I have four papers delivered at home every day. My early ambitions were to be a famous sportswriter in a national newspaper. I was a man in a hurry. My first day at work was different than anyone else I have since spoken to on the subject. It was September 1964 and I was nineteen years old. Mike had offered me just £5 a week, which was not a problem, because I was living at home and my parents did not want any money off me.

I had been editor of the school magazine, *The Culfordian*, and showed my new boss. He was not impressed. 'That does nothing for me. Our world will be completely different.' He then took me on a long walk into the city centre, where the first stop was Heffer's, a famous stationery and book shop. He bought me a leather-bound, loose-leaf address book with A–Z pages. 'This is known as a contacts book, and you will fill it with the telephone numbers and addresses of everyone you meet because of work. This will be the most important book that you ever own.' He was right. I have filled many contacts books and live off them to this day. Of course I have some on my phone, but many more in my books. There was hardly direct dialling then, let alone the invention of mobile phones or computers. The internet was many years away.

The next visit was not so good. 'Now you have to learn to drink,' said Mike, a member of Fleet Street's old school. I have always loved wine. My mother always had a bottle on the dining table at home. Draught beer was good too. But thank heavens I have always hated spirits of any kind. We visited Miller's Bar on King's Parade – an establishment long gone. He ordered whiskey after whiskey before sending me home drunk in a taxi. I was sick down the curtains in the bathroom. My elderly grandmother, Jesse, heard it all in the adjoining bedroom and was both angry and horrified. She complained to my father, who was a non-drinker. I awoke the next morning as white as a sheet and feeling like death warmed up. 'Right,' said my dad. 'The office will be looking to see how you react. You will tell them you are fine. You feel great.' As usual, sound advice. He was right. Respect came my way.

I was a quick learner, a natural journalist, as indeed many years later my daughter Claire proved to be, as she also followed with a successful career. Soon I was let loose on my own. My first interview was for the *Daily Mirror*. I was to interview Mandy Rice-Davies, who was appearing at a nightclub in the Cambridgeshire village of March. Mandy was five months older than me, but she had made international headlines with her association with Christine Keeler and her role in the Profumo affair. She was so helpful and brilliant for my debut interview. I was very grateful.

The next day I was sent to interview the famous novelist E. M. Forster, who by that stage was eighty-five. He had suffered a fall in April 1961 and had moved for a grace-and-favour (free) room at King's College in Cambridge. I was to ask him questions on behalf of the William Hickey gossip column in the *Daily Express*. I was excited. I had read his novel *A Passage to India* and I was tempted to buy a copy and ask him to sign it. I decided it would not be professional. It turned out to be the right decision! I tracked down his room and knocked on the door. 'Who is it?' barked Mr Forster. I told him. He asked what I wanted. He did not open his door and told me to go away in rather ungentlemanly terms. I returned to the office and explained to Mike what had happened. He put an arm around me and said: 'Get used to it. It won't be the last time you're told to f*** off.'

I have always loved my home city of Cambridge. I miss it and try to spend a day every year at the Hotel du Vin to enjoy that wonderful place. The beauty of working for Jeacock's of Cambridge was that I was reporting on students who were my age, enjoying their social events, like the spectacular May Balls, and not having to study, which I hated at school. I did develop the agency's sports coverage, particularly of the cricket, rugby and rowing teams. The Hawks' Club (for those who had won their Cambridge blue for sport) was a great source of stories.

There were four Cambridge rugby captains who were great sources of stories for me during that time. David Rosser was the first; I was actually to meet him again when I gave the eulogy at the funeral of my great friend David Bucknall, who was hooker for Moseley and the county champions Staffordshire. Rosser went on to be a teacher and rugby coach at the famous Millfield School.

Another Cambridge captain was Mike Gibson, the great Irish player who played sixty-nine times for his country and twelve times for the British Lions. He played in four different positions behind the scrum. Mike was at Queens' College and a real class act, rated as one of the greatest players of all time. I recall telling him while he was at Cambridge that he would one day play for the Lions. He was not so sure and bet me dinner. Gibson went on to tour with the Lions *five* times. I saw him at Rugby School for the launch of the 1991 World Cup. My daughter was a pupil there, and when I went to introduce Mike to my family, his first words were: 'I owe you dinner!' He is a great bloke. I forgive him.

Then there was the hooker Brian Rees, a tough competitor who was the Cambridge University captain in 1966. He won four blues playing in four Varsity matches from 1963 to 1966 while studying at Christ's College. He won three caps for Wales in the 1967 Five Nations Championship. He played for Neath and London Welsh.

Brian went on to be an eminent surgeon. Sadly he died in December 2021 aged seventy-nine.

The final Cambridge captain during my time at the agency was Martin Green, a Moseley player who went on to play for England and became a coach for the national team. He too was at Christ's College, which was quite a rugby college. There was also a future personal connection there. Martin was actually at the time dating my future wife, Katie While, who I was to meet four years later and soon marry in 1973. Then a few years later, one of my twin sons Laurence was a pupil at Warwick School, where Martin was both a master and Head of Rugby. Martin had high hopes for Laurence, who was a tough, strong prop-forward who played for Warwickshire Schools. But before he reached first XV age, Laurence left school of his own accord.

For the first few months with the agency, I was still playing for the Cambridge City rugby team, who actually went first class for one season. This was before the rugby leagues were formed, so they were regular fixtures in which the only ambition was to win – not score points! I was on the left wing. It was all going well until we played an American touring team. I was a crash tackler, but early in the first half I mistimed one and my head hit my opponent's hip. In the home dressing room at half-time at the Grantchester Road ground, I asked a teammate what the score was; I had no recollection of the half after that tackle. An ambulance was called for me and off I went to Addenbrooke's Hospital, where severe concussion was the verdict. I had to stay in a ward overnight while they continued to assess it. I had been due to fly to Jersey for a commissioned magazine article but was told there was no way I would be allowed to fly.

Mike called me into his office on my return later in the week and said, bluntly: 'Are you going to play sport or work for me? Choose!'

It was a no-brainer really, so I ceased playing rugby and football at the age of twenty! I did go on to play cricket for twenty-five years for the Lord's Taverners, but the decision to walk away from rugby especially hurt because Cambridge City were due to play Cambridge University at Grange Road later that year. I finished up reporting on the match for the papers instead of playing!

So, it was back to the grindstone… Regional and national newspapers were so strong in that time with big circulations. I covered the two football teams, Cambridge City and Cambridge United, who were both in the Southern League. In those days the Sunday newspapers carried regional reports. I wrote regularly on the two clubs' home games in the *Sunday Express*. Several players became great friends. City's goalkeeper Bill Heath, a former Bournemouth and Lincoln goalkeeper who joined Cambridge City in 1962, the season they won the Southern League. He is eighty-nine as I write these words.

I was also very friendly with Reg Pearce, who was a wing-half with Luton and Sunderland and had two spells with Cambridge City (1961–63 and 1964–66), with Peterborough United sandwiched between. He is still with us as I write, aged ninety-three. They were great pals at the time and both attended my twenty-first birthday party in 1966. They presented me with an engraved silver tankard, which I still have today.

Word got around that the bright young reporter in Cambridge (me!) had great contacts at both football clubs. Tony Marchi played for Tottenham Hotspur at wing-half from 1950 until 1965. He was mostly an understudy to Danny Blanchflower and Dave Mackay.

He did make 131 league appearances and was one of the players used in the double-winning team of 1960–61. He came to my house for tea to talk to me about landing his first managerial job – Cambridge City in 1965. I put a word in and he got the job. He left after two years to manage Northampton Town. Tony died on 15 March 2022 aged eighty-nine.

I was not so successful with Raich Carter, who was looking to manage Cambridge United. He played football for Sunderland, Derby County and Hull. He played for England thirteen times between 1934–47. He was manager of four clubs – his last being Middlesbrough, who finally sacked him in February 1966. He applied for the Cambridge United job and came to see me at home again for tea, but he did not get the job. In fact, he did not manage a football club again and died in October 1994. Younger readers will probably not know any of these people, but they were household names at the time. Sport has a rich and often overlooked history. Modern television helps preserve the memories of today's stars, but TV pictures were restricted in the days of the superstars from years ago. It makes the memories that bit more special.

By this point, I was gaining a reputation among the sports editors of national newspapers in Fleet Street. One of them, Bob Findlay of the *Daily Sketch*, asked to see me. He loved a bet on horse racing and offered me a job as his racing correspondent reporting on training of flat horses on Newmarket Heath. As much as I liked racing, I was not a gambler and that was not what I wanted to do! Then came my big break through a freelance journalist with the *Sunday Mirror* called Paddy McGarvey. Journalists were frequent visitors to our office, including a young Oxford University graduate called Nicholas Lloyd, who was the universities correspondent for the *Daily Mail*. He later became editor of several national news-papers, including the *News of the World*. Later he was knighted and is married to Eve Pollard, another well-known media personality. We used to sell stories to all these papers.

One day I told Paddy of my ambition to be a sportswriter in Fleet Street. As luck would have it, Paddy was in the *Sunday Mirror* soon afterwards and talking to the legendary sports editor George Casey, who was moaning to Paddy that he had just lost his rugby union writer, Terry Godwin, to the *Sunday People*. Where could he find another? Paddy told him about me – a 21-year-old in Cambridge who had played top rugby and now covered the university team. This was January 1966.

George rang me at our home and explained why he wanted me. He said: 'I will pay you eleven guineas a match, first-class rail fare and your "grub money"'. He was surprised that I said the fee had to be paid to Jeacock's News Agency. I thought it was the proper thing to do, and Mike appreciated my honesty and loyalty. One of the top freelance photographers in Cambridge at that time, and an associate of Mike Jeacock, was Louis Garnade, who was the National Photographer of the Year in the 1950s when he was on the *Daily Mirror*. He won it with a terrific, emotive picture of a fireman climbing down a long ladder after bravely rescuing a small boy from a high building that was engulfed with flames.

I asked Louis for his advice. Should I travel to these rugby matches second class on the train and pocket the difference or go first class? Louis was adamant. 'You travel first class and you will feel and think first class.' And I always did. It was another lesson learned.

My first match was the Barbarians v. Australia at the old Cardiff

Arms Park in January 1966 – the month my wonderful maternal grandfather died aged sixty-six. I was so excited at my first byline in the paper but became very emotional when the Welsh crowd near the end sung 'We'll Keep a Welcome in the Hillsides'. I was ashamed that I was crying until I looked around and saw other reporters in the press box doing the same. Good, long-serving rugby writers who I had previously befriended like Pat Marshall of the *Daily Express*, Terry O'Connor from the *Daily Mail* and Vivian Jenkins, the *Sunday Times* rugby correspondent. Those were lovely days.

The *Sunday Mirror* sold millions of copies in those days. Money was no object. George and his team treated me so well. The sports editor liked how my name looked in print and gave me bold bylines to promote me. He also asked me to do subediting duties in the summer to speed up my learning process.

I was soon on my way to London, but while I was still based in Cambridge there were a few incidents to recall. My dear dad, generous as ever, had bought me a Volkswagen car (a Beetle, as they were then known), and with little traffic I used to drive to the giant *Mirror* building in High Holborn opposite the Gamage's store.

My dad had drilled certain etiquettes into me from an early age: 'You always pay your corner [round]!' Fleet Street was full of heavy-drinking journalists. The *Sunday Mirror* sports team used to drink in the Globe pub (no longer there) across the road from the office. It was nicknamed 'the Stab in the Back'. It was run by a man named Peter and his lovely wife. Every time I tried to pay my way, Peter would say: 'I will come back to you, relax.' What I did not know until I was about to leave those days behind was that the paper's sports columnist, Sam Leitch, would tell Peter to 'put the kid's round on my tab. He cannot afford it!'

I was to catch up with Sam later when he became a Thames Television head of sport.

During my time at the *Sunday Mirror* there was a France v. England rugby international in Paris, and I'd been sent to cover it. I was given a £40 float to cover expenses after my airfare and hotel had been paid for. The top rugby writers were always invited to the post-match banquet for the two teams and their guests; this one was at the Hôtel Lucien in Rue Chénier. As it was my first trip I was not invited, but the press lads said: 'It's a dinner-jacket event, so if you have one, pack it, because one of our lot always forgets to take one and you might get swapped in for them.'

As it happened, one such reporter did just that: Bleddyn Williams, who had played twenty-two times for Wales as a centre – some as captain, as he was for some of the 1950 British Lions team in Australia and New Zealand. He was in Paris for the *Sunday People* and dutifully handed over his dinner ticket. The dinner was fantastic and the wines flowed. I paced myself but was staggered to see several very old members of the England RFU and their equally old French counterparts collapse off their chairs and be picked up by no one! I was also excited because I was included in the England party who were heading to Le Lido de Paris and the cabaret show that I had read so much about.

When I left the dinner, I bumped into the France captain, Christian Carrère, who played flanker. He spoke perfect English and I had a long chat hoping to pick up some follow-up lines. After a while, I went to excuse myself to join the England party for Le Lido. He explained that they had left some time ago and, seeing the disappointment on my face, offered to take me with the Camberabero brothers, Guy and Lilian, to a discotheque in the Pigalle. They were the small French half-backs: scrum-half Lilian was 5ft 5in. and fly-half Guy was 5ft 7in.

Inside, it was packed. I insisted on buying the drinks with the *Sunday Mirror* float. After being jostled down the stairs, I went for my wallet, but I discovered to my horror that it had been stolen! Christian ordered the owner to freeze everyone and had a collection to more than reimburse me. It was so kind. However, it was my turn to freeze on the way back to my hotel. Shaking off the effect of all the drinks, I recalled stuffing my wallet down the side of the hotel bed in case I got drunk and lost it! I was beside myself.

It was heavily on my conscience, so I poured the entire collection out when I rejoined the press lads at Paris Airport. They promptly spent it *all* at the bar to ease my worries, leaving me with the remains of my *Sunday Mirror* float. Another lesson learned, and I even learned another when I was back in the office. I had taken that £40 float. I did my expenses and returned £12 unused. After leaving them on the desk of John Simmons (the assistant sports editor), I noticed that the entire team apart from me was summoned into his office. Then, after a while, I was called for: everyone completely piled into me. Everyone it seemed had huge expenses, genuine or not, in those days, so they were furious at my meagre spendings of £28! 'That's not how it's done around here, son. Mr Clarke, our speedway writer, will rewrite your trip to Paris.' The new total had the paper owing me £5–£10 more than I had taken – and I was sent to the cashier's office with orders to lose the £12 float and not be an idiot again!

A few weeks later George Casey told me I was doing well, and while I would continue to write rugby and soon tennis for the *Sunday Mirror* he had arranged for me to work under a new boss

– Reg Hayter at the highly rated but very tough sports agency Hayters, which was next to the then *Evening Standard* building in Shoe
Lane. So I left my home in Cambridge for the move to London. I
was never to live in the Cambridge area again, but I still love my
home city so much, and I try to make a yearly visit with my wife
Katie to bring back those lovely days.

CHAPTER FOUR

BEFORE TV BECKONED

The week before I joined Hayters Sports Agency and moved to London, Reg Hayter rang me and said he was looking forward to me joining on Monday, but would I cover Charlton v. Millwall for the *Sunday Times* on Saturday? It turned out to be goalless, but I wrote a good report – or so I thought.

I arrived at my new office and Reg immediately called me in to see him. He flung the paper at me. He had put rings around ten words. He said, fiercely: 'Do not use those phrases again and *never* start a report with "it was".' He underlined that the agency had a high reputation that I must live up to. I was shaken and rather crestfallen when I went into the main office. My great friend Chris Lander simply said: 'That's a Hayter welcome. Head down and you'll survive!'

The year there was tough and demanding. I was working almost round the clock. But I would not have missed it for the world; it was a journalist's finishing school that would stand me in fantastic stead. Stories, stories, stories. That was the Hayters name of the game, plus reports of matches at every level.

They owned phones in every press box and would hire them out on a match-by-match basis, plus you would sometimes be the only reporter at a youth team match, covering it for, say, ten local newspapers. With evening deadlines I remember covering a Chelsea Youth Cup game at Stamford Bridge in 1967 for nine local papers and being the only person in the press box with no one else near me. I never wrote a word and at one stage had to run down to ask a linesman who had scored! No mobiles or computers in those days. You were on your own, relying on just what you saw. The phoned rewrites after the final whistle took so long I had to use a box of matches (always had a packet to light ladies' cigarettes!) when all the lights at the ground were switched off. At one game I actually had to climb over a gate to exit Stamford Bridge!

Managers and players, by and large, were always helpful. This was made easier with there being so few football reporters, and all of them trusted; access was easy in those days. But I recall that trying to get stories out of Millwall manager Benny Fenton and Brentford's Jimmy Sirrel was like pulling teeth.

Fenton always treated me well. I recall leaving my flat early one morning for Millwall. Benny was in the dressing room. He gave me a lecture on dressing properly. I was dressed smart in a suit and tie – everyone was dressed for work in those days. But he still talked about keeping your shirt cuffs at the right length. All I wanted were some stories!

One day I only got two. Fearful, I rang the office and the editorial chief Ron Surplice. He was really demanding, but I learned more from him than anyone, apart from Mike back in Cambridge. After I had told Ron my two stories, he asked me for more. He twice said: 'You are saying you have no more? Well, what do you plan to do now?' I explained that I had been on the move since 7 a.m.

and thought I would go and find a bacon sandwich. Ron thought instead I should return to the office and provide more stories! Welcome again to the Hayters of 1967.

Sirrel acted as physiotherapist at Brentford as well as manager. I would stand alongside him in the physio room, but all I got was an 'aye, lad'. I was to come up against him in my ATV days when he was the Notts County manager. I remember a live interview with him in the studio in which he told me that there was no such thing as a 'bad player'. I asked him why he then gave some a free transfer. 'Well laddie,' he replied, 'some of them have to go!'

Bertie Mee, physio-turned-manager at Arsenal, was difficult too. Ironically he had taken over from Billy Wright, who was later to play such a key role in my TV career. But Mee did help me when covering his signing of striker Bobby Gould from his home club Coventry City for £90,000 on 28 February 1968. I had a fallout with Hayters that was never properly healed, because I refused to take a photo of the signing with an office camera. This was before the days of multi-tasking and mobile phone cameras. The signing, though, started a lifelong friendship with Gould.

Meanwhile back at Hayters one day, I was asked to go and interview Gary Player, the great South African golfer, for the *Johannesburg Telegraph*. He won nine major championships on the regular tour and nine majors on the Champions Tour, and he is considered one of the greatest of all time. He had just won the US Open and was about to win the (British) Open Championship in Scotland. Reg Hayter told me that Player was staying at the Savoy Hotel on the Strand. I was to do the interview and must absolutely not mess it up. In those days we all looked smart both at work and at play. Casual gear was years away.

I arrived at reception at the Savoy on time at 9 a.m. I was twenty-three. I explained that I had come to see Mr Player. 'Really?' said the Savoy man, who clearly did not believe me. He asked me again, and then deliberately asked my name three times! He rang Mr Player in his suite and was clearly surprised when asked to send me up!

Gary greeted me at his door with a towel round his waist, ushered me in and explained he was taking a shower. Having seen how slim I was in those days and correctly assuming I had not eaten, Player asked me to order anything I wanted for breakfast. I then ate a really big breakfast!

When he emerged dressed and smiling, he proceeded to give me a brilliant interview. When we finished he explained he was modelling DAK trousers that evening in Simpsons on Regent Street (now Waterstones) and there was a buffet there. I was welcome to come and should bring a friend. I took Chris Lander. That evening in Simpsons he spotted me and Chris and came over to make sure we were looked after.

I thanked him again and have not seen or spoken to him since. But his kindness and helpfulness on the interview left an indelible impression on me. I was an unknown agency reporter and he was a sporting superstar. I vowed that day that if I ever became well-known, I would treat everyone I met like Player treated me. I hope those I have met in my TV days would say I have lived up to my promise, although of course I have never been a sporting superstar!

Meanwhile in my closing weeks at Hayters, I was still covering rugby and, by that point, lawn tennis for the *Sunday Mirror*. At one Twickenham international, I was seated next to Mr Uel Titley, the rugby union correspondent for *The Times*. The rest of the press lads did not talk to Mr Titley, an old-school person who kept himself to himself, but he was always smart and sported a neat pencil moustache that had twisted ends.

However, they set the young Newbon a challenge. If you can ask Mr Titley why he is called 'Uel', then we will each buy you a pint of beer. So just before the start and fired with the fact that Mr Titley had always been polite to me, I plucked up the courage to ask him why he was called 'Uel'. I could feel the rugby writers leaning forward to hear the answer, which eventually came: 'My father never forgave his parents for christening him "Sam" instead of the full "Samuel", so when I came along, he decided he would lumber me with the rest of the name.' After I had phoned in my match report and quotes I went to the press box bar, where seven pints were lined up and I was applauded with great laughter. I had to ask for help with the beer!

Later on, the top sports columnist on the *Sunday Mirror*, Sam Leitch, was off to the USA to cover a Muhammad Ali fight, so I was asked to fill his page with a preview of the Wimbledon Championships. The reigning champion, Billie Jean King, who was to retain her ladies' singles title in the last amateur Wimbledon in this 1968 Championships, was so helpful. But it was not my finest work. I could feel that George Casey was disappointed, but he was OK with it. I went to see Sam on his return and explained that I had let him down, but he was reassuring. Then he asked me what my ambition was. I said it was to be a great sportswriter like him. 'No,' he said. 'You are young and handsome and you need to go to television. It has to be the future.' I left his office determined to follow his advice.

A few weeks prior, my friend Chris Lander had been unavailable to cover an All Blacks match in Wales. I became 'Chris Lang' for the day for the *Daily Sketch*. On the return rail journey I was standing in the bar (those were the days!) with two Wales rugby legends both as players and media men – the BBC's Cliff Morgan and the *Sunday Times* writer Vivian Jenkins. The more we drank, the more adamant they were that I should become a broadcaster. When we got to Paddington, we were all sitting on the floor of a black London taxicab. They dropped me off first and, poking me in the chest, they repeated: 'You *must* be a broadcaster, boyo!' When I did get a job with Westward TV, I rang them both to thank them, and neither Cliff nor Vivian could recall a word they had said to me! Ah well!

So, I wrote to all the TV stations. The BBC sports supremo Bryan Cowgill, another legend, who was responsible for the action replay on football, offered me a job as a studio floor manager. Many years later we were at a party at my Central TV programme controller Andy Allan's house, and I apologised for saying at the time: 'No thanks, I want to be a star!' Arrogance on my part. I went to see Billy Wright, head of sport and outside broadcasts at ATV at his Elstree office. He said he would put me on file. They often say that at interviews, but it never develops. That answer is a 'no'! How ironic that he offered me a job three and half years later and could not remember our first meeting. But it was fortunate that I went to a smaller station first to cut my teeth and build my confidence.

Eventually I was offered two jobs in two days. The first was at Anglia TV through their boss Dick Joice and news chief Jim Wilson, who offered me a job on the spot. No screen test, just the interview. In hindsight, I probably should have taken it. It was a biggish station and close to London and my Cambridge home. Still, it worked out all right in the end!

Instead of accepting Anglia's offer, to their surprise I took a three-month contract with Westward TV in Plymouth. I was impressed with the programme controller, John Oxley. He insisted on a screen test and medical. He was looking to replace his sports presenter (as were Anglia) and I clearly fitted the bill, although I had no broadcasting experience. I felt Westward would be a great place to cut my teeth and gain experience and confidence. I was not getting on too well at Hayters and, after a year, it was time to move on. They were a good operation, and they have a tremendous record of turning out great broadcasters and sportswriters. ITV's commentator Brian Moore and *The Times*'s Martin Samuel are just two examples. Ron Surplice wrote me a lovely letter, and ironically Hayters were soon to claim me as one of their successes. I was very happy to receive both acknowledgements.

CHAPTER FIVE

THE WESTWARD
TELEVISION YEARS

On 6 September 1968, I had my first day at the Westward TV studios in Plymouth. It was the first ITV franchise for the south-west of England. It opened in April 1961 and closed in December 1981 – ten years after I had left for ATV in the Midlands. The broadcast area was Devon, Cornwall, South Somerset, Taunton Deane, West Dorset and West Somerset. A small area; I felt it would be a perfect way for a young man who had never spoken in public to learn the ropes.

Everyone at the television station made me feel so welcome, but presenting was a scary prospect. There was no autocue and it was all live. I was on a three-month contract as one of two sports presenters – the other was the sports editor, a lovely Devonian called Don Arnold. The plus side of it being a black-and-white transmission was that I wouldn't need many changes of clothes! Also, my programme controller John Oxley was understanding and wanted me to succeed. I was so relieved to finish my first live show, *Sports Desk*, that I wished everyone a good weekend! Mr Oxley had me up in his office afterwards for a drink with encouraging words but pointed out that it was Monday and my weekend show was four days away!

I was determined to succeed, but when you first start it can be hard. The red light comes on. You are live with just a script. The TV camera lens gives you nothing back. It is cold, disinterested. It does not laugh. Your attempted funny lines have no reaction from the camera. So what do you do? I found one of the very early little recording machines in an office (which were then not available to households) and taped my programmes. This was long before VHS systems. It was painful. I winced but tried to learn. How to relax and not worry if you made a mistake. The viewers may not even notice it, but it throws the inexperienced presenter when they start. There was a brilliant anchorman to the local news programme *Westward Diary* called Kenneth MacLeod. He had been an actor. He was forty-one when I arrived and was calmly holding the show together whenever there were technical complications, as there sometimes were. Often there was a minute to fill at the end and he would be amazing. I would study him. I remember two fills – once he said: 'A Mrs Kathleen Jones from Redruth [pulling a note out of his inside pocket] has knitted me a lovely pair of socks. I would show them to you, but I realised I am only wearing one of them, as I seem to have odd socks on. Anyway, thanks, Mrs Jones, and with that, goodnight.' All made up of course but pure on the spot genius, as was another: 'Just time to mention that a Mrs Smith from Cawsand wrote to me this week and said: "Kenneth, you waffle too much at times, so why do you not shut up for a few seconds?" So to keep Mrs Smith happy let us enjoy ten seconds of silence. [He then paused for that exact period of time.] I hope that makes you happy, Mrs Smith, but I warn you I will not be doing that tomorrow night, when I hope you will join me again at six o'clock.' Wow!

Well, the end of my three months was quickly closing in, and I was still nervous. I bought Kenneth a Scotch or six in the Westward bar and eventually asked for his help. He said: 'Remind me, dear boy, your *Sports Desk* shows on Mondays and Fridays. How long between mine and yours this Friday?' 'Ten seconds,' I replied. 'I see. Leave it to me.' Ken had always been kind to me and I learnt so much, providing I kept his Scotch flowing in the station bar. A kind lady called Doris Inch treated me like a son and said to me one day: 'Ken never watches your show, you know.' It did not worry me. I just wanted to learn, and he was kind to me.

In the early days he took me with him to open a fete. One of the paid perks for in-vogue celebrities. A total stranger approached: 'Kenneth. Do you remember me? I said hallo fifteen years ago at a fete in Charlestown.' Ken clearly did not, but unperturbed he said: 'Of course I do, old love, it's just the name that escapes me, now remind me.' The man was clearly chuffed that he had been 'remembered', which he had not of course, and was pleased to carry out the request that he 'now be a good love and buy a double Scotch for me and a glass of white wine for my young friend here'. Another lesson for the young lad! Pretend you know the person who greets you, even if you do not. First impressions are always the most important.

So to the Friday *Sports Desk*. We went to pass in the studio and no words! When is it coming, I thought… Then, as we passed, he gave me a tremendous whack in the testicles. I was in agony! I sailed through the show, word perfect with no nerves. I had just one thought: get to a dressing room and put some ice on them. Mr MacLeod saved my career. Shortly afterwards I was given a new longer contract and I became anxious rather than nervous. I realised if I just concentrated on what I was saying and banished thoughts of the live audience, I could do the job. But live TV is like golf. Just when you might feel you have cracked it, you go into the bunker. I am grateful for all those years without autocue. It is great in some ways, but I would like to see some of today's heralded presenters work without it. The original idea – a great one – is to keep the news presenter's eyeline straight at the viewer. Once you look down the viewer often wonders why.

The sport meanwhile was limited in the south-west. There were just three football teams of note: Plymouth Argyle, Torquay United and Exeter City, who were all then in the Football League. After the football there was Somerset cricket, two horse racing courses in Newton Abbot and Devon and Exeter (now known as just Exeter) and some very strong rugby, including Cornwall reaching the county championship final, losing to Lancashire at Redruth in the 1968–69 final. Twenty-three thousand were packed into the ground famous for its sloping 'Hellfire Corner'. I did commentary on the match. Lancashire won 11–9, despite having been 9–0 down at half-time after Cornwall scored two penalties and a drop goal. One of the penalties was from the flanker Ray George. He had injured his knee in the semi-final, and I told the coach Bill Bishop that he could stay in my Plymouth flat and that I would take him for treatment at the Argyle ground. We got him fit for the final! I was always invited to the Cornwall post-match dinners and got on so well with the players. The local folk hero was the legendary prop-forward Bonzo Johns, who was also the local coalman.

Sport was otherwise thin on the ground, so I tried to manufacture some for coverage. Through contacts, I arranged two matches for the Cornwall team in France – one in Lyons against the state team and then a return to France and Clermont-Ferrand to play, incredibly, the French national B-team, led by the legendary Walter Spanghero. He was part of the French side that had won the Five Nations in 1967 (as he did in 1973) and played at No. 8, second row or flanker. He was 6ft 2in., which was tall in those days. But the likes of Ray George and second-row forward John 'Cheyenne' Blackburn of Penryn knew nothing about him. They showed no respect! I recall Cheyenne throwing Spanghero out of a maul. He was so tough. Both Blackburn and the French captain finished up in hospital. Some of the other players finished up in jail for a few hours after a few post-banquet incidents in the town. Nothing too serious but another headache for Bishop and me! The banquet was held in a restaurant above the local bus station and the food was sensational. I can see it now – wild boar and rice with a pink-coloured sauce.

I had a great source for rugby stories in Cornwall: a local rugby club official called Paul Bawden, who fed me the latest news, much of it confidential to the public, and was never discovered doing so. Cornwall was mad on rugby and I know how ratings soared down there as they waited for me to break the latest gossip! Mind you, both *Westward Diary* and my *Sports Desk* shows got huge ratings. There was little competition apart from BBC *Spotlight*. There were really just the two main channels at the time, and everyone watched TV in those days. No mobile phones, computers, internet or streaming. Life was very basic and the black-and-white trans-mission meant I only needed two suits, two ties and a handful of shirts. After three months of regular appearances I became a well-known name in this small region.

I was not alone for long in Plymouth. I lived with a much older woman from the studios called Sheila. Chris Lander had taken me to talk to Derek Ufton, who had been sacked by Plymouth Argyle in February. I was still in London and Derek, who had played for Kent at cricket and Charlton and England at football, set up a meeting for me with Ted Mercer in Plymouth. Ted had retired as the rugby coach and maths master at Plymouth College school. Many years earlier, he had played for the Barbarians rugby team. He and his wife Lilian became my Plymouth guardians, almost becoming my adopted parents (my actual parents were a seven-hour drive away in Cambridge).

Ted was kind, generous, great company and very funny. At my fortieth birthday party in Birmingham, when I was at Central Television, he said to everyone: 'Gary's love of ice cream is such that if Nelson's Column had been made of ice cream, he would have eaten the lot and then complained he only had one arm!' Ted also wrote about rugby for the *Sunday Independent* in Plymouth, producing classic lines like: 'Cornwall's Ray George is so deadly with the boot that he would kick the ash off your cigarette!' and: 'It was a hot sunny afternoon in Paris and with the French rugby team leading by over twenty points every English rugby supporter was praying for fog!'

Rob Baxter is the coach of the rugby team Exeter Chiefs. His father John played for Exeter in the '60s, as did Rob and his brother Richard in their footsteps. When I was at Westward I used to go regularly to film Cornwall for their club matches. On a rare visit to Exeter against Torquay, Baxter Senior berated Ted Mercer about me, saying that I didn't visit Exeter enough and cared more about Cornwall. Ted made up a story: 'You have to understand, Mr

Baxter, that young Gary has a whole lot of girlfriends that he visits in Redruth!' Mr Baxter replied: 'Oh, now I understand. I thought Newbon was biased. Tell the lad, no problem.' Football fans always thought I was biased, both at Westward and then at ATV, because they wanted their teams on TV all the time. You can imagine what it was like with just three teams – Plymouth, Torquay and Exeter. I got rude stick wherever I went. It was hopeless. I could not win.

Thankfully, I found during that time with those tough days on the news agencies, I had sharpened my nose for stories. Several married players at Argyle used to entertain their girlfriends after training in my flat on Plymouth Hoe while I was in the studios. They used to feed me with stories. Club manager Billy Bingham used to tell me he knew where the source was but just needed confirmation. Of course he did! No chance. Their secret is still safe with me!

I used to invite any big names visiting the region. England World Cup winner Geoff Hurst, ITV *World of Sport* wrestler Jackie Pallo, world middleweight boxing champion Terry Downes and football manager Malcolm Allison are just a few that I recall. National Hunt jockey John Buckingham rode a lovely horse at Newton Abbot for the Torquay chairman Tony Boyce called Silver Lily. We all won a few bob on that filly! He didn't have any money, so after appearing on my show he slept on my sofa before riding Silver Lily the next day! John steered the 100–1 shot Foinavon to the most sensational victory in the 1967 Grand National. He was so far behind the field until a loose horse called Popham Down brought down or hampered almost the entire field in chaotic scenes at the twenty-third fence. John therefore missed the melee and when he reached this fence he found a gap for jockey and horse to jump clear and go on to win by fifteen lengths. The fence is now called the Foinavon. John even appeared onstage at the London Palladium the next night.

In those days no one was interested in using the gym or bodybuilding, so I was surprised to get a call from a local gym owner. He explained that he needed my help. He had booked a young Mr Universe bodybuilder who had just won the Mr Olympia competition. He had paid a big fee to get this unknown foreign 23-year-old to Plymouth and had only sold a couple of tickets. 'If you could get him on your *Sports Desk*, it would save me. Everyone watches your show.' I explained that I was not interested and had that night's show schedule filled. He wore me down. So I said: 'Look, the best I can do is record him at 2 p.m., and if I like it, I will do as you ask.' I asked if he spoke English and was told: 'No, just two words – "Hallo" and "Tea"!' Chris Robertson, the Westward press officer, asked if I wanted my photo taken with the late guest. I declined, saying that I did not know if he would even be on the show, and anyway: 'We will *never* hear of him again!'

I imagine you can see where this is going. In came the pair of them: the gym owner and this enormous man who asked for 'tea'. He then oiled up for posing in the studio, and he did look fantastic, with, as the gym owner had promised, 'muscles coming out of his ears'. I decided to run it.

Afterwards as I was leaving the building the switchboard ladies who really liked me said: 'We are cursing you, Gary Newbon. Our switchboard was jammed with viewers saying: "Get that man off the telly; he is putting my kids off their pasties!"' That young man who I predicted we would never hear of again, who I would not have my photograph with, was, of course, Arnold Schwarzenegger.

The Austrian became a huge movie star, businessman and politician, even going on to become the Governor of California. *TIME* magazine named Arnie one of the 100 most influential people in the world a few years ago. At least I did put him on the TV in the end!

I had great fun throughout my career, but one night I thought it was all going to end in tears. There were several of us from the studio having a fun night out at the Pussycat Club in Plymouth. Somebody suggested that we all went skinny-dipping in the Plymouth lido on the Hoe. I recall a very attractive Rosemary Wight, the wife of the Pussycat Club owner, swimming around with just her knickers on her head to keep them dry. There was, I assure you, no actual hanky-panky. Maybe because, soon after we got in, the surrounding residents began reporting the noise we were making to the police. We were soon aware of a ring of officers round the pool. We were ordered to get out, keep quiet and get dressed.

My girlfriend at the time, Sheila, defused the situation by inviting the police and guests back to our flat for drinks and food. I had flat five, Chichester House on the ground floor in a nearby tower block on the Hoe. We had a great time, but sadly it was not a great ending for the police. There was quite a noise coming out of our flat and, unknown to us, higher up was a flat belonging to a lady chief superintendent, who spotted some of Plymouth's finest leaving the premises! I am not sure how the boys in blue talked their way out of it, but they did and our careers were saved.

I really enjoyed the social life and the company of the Westward team both sides of the camera. Devon and Cornwall have always been great places to live, although even with the motorway (it used to start near Taunton!) it is a long way from London and the Midlands. I realised there was no future there. My mind, however, was made up when I discovered that the next programme controller, Terry Fleet, had refused a request from ITV for me to be a reporter at the 1970 World Cup in Mexico. John Bromley at London Weekend Television was surprised that I had not been released. The thinking by Fleet was that I would not want to come back to Plymouth afterwards, where I was highly thought of inside and outside the television station. Well, flattering as that might have been, Terry got it wrong. I realised I had to leave. Soon, ironically the *On the Ball* pre-season cocktail party at London Weekend Television in August 1971 presented me with the perfect opportunity for a big move. I met Billy Wright again, who had put me on file when I'd enquired about TV work before I went to Westward. On 2 December 1971 I arrived in Birmingham to become the new sports presenter at ATV.

CHAPTER SIX

ATV

Often in life it pays to go that extra mile, or several. Plymouth and Westward Television seemed a long way from most places – particularly in 1971. The train out of the West Country, then as now, was the easiest route. So, when ITV's legendary head of sport John Bromley (a great personality and social man) invited me to his pre-season *On the Ball* cocktail party at his London Weekend Television studio, I jumped at the chance.

Brommers was known and loved by all. He pulled off many rights contracts. When ITV started *World of Sport*, he wanted to call it *Wide World of Sports*, after the USA show, until his sports team pointed out that he had to drop 'Wide' because all they had at that time was cliff diving from Acapulco, horse racing and wrestling. Brommers spent so much time travelling to expand the rights, both in London restaurants and in far-flung countries. One day there was an unpleasant report that Brommers's team did not want him to see. They asked his No. 2, Stuart McConachie, where they should put it so Brommers would not see it. McConachie replied: 'Put it on his desk!'

As chance would have it, the great former England and Wolves captain Billy Wright, now head of sport and outside broadcasts at ATV, was at the *On the Ball* cocktail party. He had forgotten that I went to see him in my closing Hayters years for a job. This time was different. Billy was on the lookout for a new presenter. I should come up and meet him and Tony Flanagan (who was the executive producer on *ATV Today*, the local news programme) in Birmingham, he said. I did not take much persuading! I gave it a week and then I rang Billy. 'Can you come up on Tuesday?' I said yes and duly spent seven hours on the train, only to arrive at ATV to be told that Billy was at his home in London, taking his daughters to the dentist. Great! So I insisted on seeing this Tony Flanagan.

He chatted for a while and asked if I was prepared to come back on the next Tuesday. Would Billy *definitely* be in the Birmingham studio? I was assured he would! So back I came. Billy was his usual charming self – a man with the best memory for names and faces that I have ever met.

I was asked if I would not mind interviewing Billy in the studio so they could see me in action. I had taken a show-reel, but they understandably wanted more. I came from a hard school of journalism, as was to become evident in my later boxing interviews and the disastrous start I had with Sir Alex Ferguson.

'Billy Wright – you won 105 caps, but were you good enough towards the end?' Wow, that was the first and *only* time I saw and heard Billy really angry. After two minutes of a touchy reply, Tony and the news editor, Bob Gillman, were frustrated! They stopped the interview and replaced Billy with the news hospitality room hostess, Denise Feeney. Denise was cast as a Wimbledon tennis player and I have to say I tried really hard, knowing what was at stake for me. Our chat went really well as Denise gave very good answers, as if she was great at tennis.

After the studio chat Billy, Tony and Bob offered me a one-year contract. Gillman told me everyone was on the same money in the ATV News and Sports team. I suspected that was not true, but I wanted the job, so I accepted it.

Westward said they were sorry to lose me but understood that their recruit had gone from a 23-year-old rookie to a very amb-itious 26-year-old developer. They gave me a great send-off, except for my then girlfriend Sheila, who was a production assistant at the TV station. Although Sheila was thirteen years older than me, we had got on from the start, and she soon moved into the flat I was renting on the Hoe. When I broke the news that I was leaving for Birmingham and ATV and *not* taking her with me, Sheila was deeply hurt and an intense argument ensued. There was a lot of persistent tension in the weeks to come, but it eventually settled down. Sadly she died quite a few years later, by which time I had been married for some time.

I duly arrived at the ATV studios on 2 December 1971 vowing not to go out with anyone I worked with again. That lasted all of a week! Tony Flanagan had asked the attractive blonde personal assistant to Bob Gillman if she had fancied any of the presenters. She was Katie While, aged twenty-five. I had noticed her wearing hotpants!

Katie told him that she liked the look of the new sports pre-senter (me!) but he looked a hard case! I was blissfully unaware of this when Tony came to see me and said: 'You don't know anyone here, luv, do you? Why not take Katie out for dinner? I sign your expenses, so take her out to the Westgate Arms in Warwick [long gone but excellent in its time] and put her down as Freddie Goodwin, manager of Birmingham City!'

I did and fell in love with her. That was just before Christmas 1971 and we married in October 1973. Fifty years later we celebrated. If it was not for Katie I am sure I would not still be alive to tell this tale. I am blessed with a wonderful family.

The Midlands football teams were enjoying good Football League status in these times. I followed Trevor Francis to Birmingham – strictly by coincidence of course. He remained a close and valued friend until his shock death from a heart attack in July 2023 aged sixty-nine. I miss him greatly. Freddie Goodwin was a classy person. I really liked and admired him. I saw him play in the post-Munich crash year when he played wing-half for Manchester United in their shock FA Cup defeat at Third-Division Norwich. I was a young schoolboy and one of my parents' fashion shop garment representatives had taken me.

I was the first person ever to interview Trevor Francis. He was the standout fourteen-year-old playing for Plymouth Schoolboys at Home Park with scouts from all over the country watching him. I invited Trevor into the Plymouth TV studios for a live interview. It was early on in my TV career. I do not know who was more nervous, but luckily for both of us the chat was never recorded!

Birmingham was a very good team in my early days in the Midlands with the Latchford brothers: striker Bob and his goalkeeper brother Peter. Goal scorer Bob Hatton, Trevor Francis (who scored four goals in a home game when he was sixteen years old), winger Gordon Taylor, full-backs Garry Pendrey and Malcolm Page, and Roger Hynd, Alan Campbell and so on. Soon after they secured promotion back to the top division they celebrated at their St Andrew's ground; I gave Goodwin a lift back to his Tanworth-in-Arden home. The next time I picked him up some time later was to bring him to the ATV studios when he had been sacked. He bravely gave a brilliant interview.

Francis eventually made his England debut under manager Don Revie. My big friends restaurateur Lorenzo Ferrari and comedian Jasper Carrott and I travelled to see his debut. Lorenzo and Jasper are huge Birmingham City fans. Lorenzo is godfather to my children. A top guy who has been back in Italy for many years, but in his time Lorenzo's Italian restaurant in Birmingham's Park Street was *the* celebrity haunt and always packed. He and I formed the Midlands Soccer Writers and, aided by three late football journalists, Alan Williams and Jeff Farmer of the *Daily Express* and *The Sun*'s Hugh Jamieson, we had regular luncheons at Lorenzo's with special guests Brian Clough, Johan Cruyff, Don Revie, Trevor Francis, Bill Shankly and many other big football names. That was in the mid-'70s. Not one brick of the restaurant has survived because of the Bull Ring area development.

I hosted the televised Midlands Player and Young Player of the Year dinners in the ATV studios. The company backed me with a big budget to turn the biggest studio that staged the likes of *Crossroads* and *The Golden Shot* into the MSW dinner, which was to be a dinner-jacket event with all the top football writers and broadcasters, club managers and players.

I recall Derby County's Charlie George (with his shoulder in a sling) as the first winner with West Bromwich Albion's Bryan Robson as the Young Player. The following year, Trevor Francis was the Young Player, and he received the aforementioned quip about his pockets from Brian Clough, who was the guest of honour and making the presentation.

Jasper Carrott in his early days did a very funny comedy turn. He is still very funny today. Another year we enjoyed the wit of the accomplished after-dinner speaker Bob 'The Cat' Bevan. He was called the Cat because he played in goal for the Old Wilsonians tenth team and gave his defence kittens (an old phrase for being very worried), plus the fact that he claimed he was 'once rogered by a bloke called Tom'. Fellow goalkeeper Gordon Banks, England's World Cup hero, was the guest of honour that year. We showed his fabulous close-range save from Pelé's header, only for the Cat to say to Banks and the assembled diners: 'Actually, Banksie, as a keeper myself I thought Pelé's header was going wide!' A great line!

As soon as I established myself on ATV, I was invited into various boardrooms, including that of Birmingham City. The directors' box was in the old stand at St Andrew's in those days. There were steps up to it. There was one person who always stopped me for a chat and who became a close friend over the years.

He was Ron Atkinson, in those days player-manager of Kettering Town. He had spent his first-team playing career with Oxford United, where he had been captain. When sixteen-year-old Trevor Francis made his home debut, he was marked by big Ron, who told me recently that Trevor did not get a kick! When I put that to Francis he protested, saying: 'I scored our goal in the 1–1 draw,' to which Ron responded: 'Well, it was the only kick he got!' Ron is quick and with Tommy Docherty king of the one-liners. When he was manager at Manchester United, the Aston Villa chairman Doug Ellis asked my No. 2 Jeff Farmer at Central TV to ask Ron if he would switch to Villa. Ron's reply? 'Tell Doug I'll fit it in on Tuesdays and Thursdays!'

After Kettering Town Ron went to Cambridge United where he got them promoted. One day the West Bromwich Albion director Brian Boundy rang me at ATV with a problem and needed my help. Albion wanted to change their manager, but their chairman, Sir Bert Millichip, was also chairman of the Football Association and could not risk tapping anyone up. Boundy said: 'Everyone trusts you, Gary, so who would you recommend?'

I told him John Bond, who was boss at Norwich City. I told Boundy that he was good, had done very well for Norwich and had a big personality, which would suit the Baggies. So I rang Bond, who said he wanted the West Brom job. However, all he actually did was persuade his Norwich chairman Arthur South to double his salary. Oh dear! A day later, my private phone went in my ATV office (reminder that there were no mobiles or computers in those days) and it was Ron Atkinson. 'Hallo, it's your friend Ron here. Bondy has rung me. I cannot believe you put Bond before me!' I replied: 'Ron, I never even thought of you!' Ron, feigning shock, said: 'Do not make it worse. Now be a good lad and get on the phone back to your other friend Brian Boundy and get me that job.'

And that, believe it or not, is what happened. Ron, loyal as ever and is always so to this present day, rang me two days later, saying: 'I have met the chairman in Oxford, got the job and I am on my way to the studios to give you the first interview.'

Ron went on to do a brilliant job at West Brom with such an exciting team. Three of his fantastic players were Laurie Cunningham, Cyrille Regis and Brendon Batson – at a time when football was even more riddled with disgusting racial abuse than it is today, these three really made a trail for black players in the English game.

The 5–3 win at Old Trafford on 30 December 1978 is still among the best English league matches I have ever seen. At the time it was described as 'the Game of the Century'. The weather was cold with some snow. Albion were top of the old First Division at the time. The Albion goal scorers: two from the prolific Mr Tony 'Bomber' Brown, plus Len Cantello, Laurie Cunningham and Cyrille Regis. Atkinson loved attractive football, as did his successor at Old Trafford – Sir Alex Ferguson. Ron was close to winning the league but fell away at both clubs – West Bromwich and United. He did win two FA Cups with Manchester United, and League Cups with both Sheffield Wednesday and Aston Villa.

Ron loves a quiz. His favourite question: Who is the only English manager to win a major domestic cup competition with three different clubs? Answer, of course: Ron Atkinson. When Sheffield Wednesday, then in the Second Division, beat Ferguson's Manchester United on 21 April 1991 Ron allowed me with a film crew on the Wednesday team coach to Wembley – the last time coaches and cars were given access up Wembley Way.

It was a great experience with comedian Stan Boardman telling the players jokes all the way to relax them. Ron as ever being a great mate. After his management days he became a great co-commentator for ITV, Sky and then ITV again until that infamous racist remark in Monaco in 2004, which I will return to later in this chapter.

I love spending time with Ron. So many laughs and so much fun. I only once lost my cool with him. For domestic live matches we used to arrive at the venue three hours before kick-off – the exception was Ron, who used to cut it fine. The worst time was the Birmingham City–Leeds United League Cup semi-final on 11 February 1996 at St Andrews. It was live on ITV. I was the interviewer. It was getting close to kick-off. The pundit was Jack Charlton, who was not the best at remembering names to say the least. No sign of co-commentator Ron who lives just outside Birmingham in Barnt Green. I rang from the production scanner. It was open talk back on the phone. I asked him: 'Where are you Ron?' 'Longbridge.' 'What? Why are you so late?' 'Held up by a demonstration.' Do not ask me why but I found myself enquiring: 'What demonstration?' Reply: 'I think it's an animal rights demo.' Again, stupidly I asked: 'How do you know?' Ron's reply: 'Well the men are carrying huge banners that state "Save Rover".' We just fell about laughing, and I said: 'Well, get here as soon as you can.'

Ron hated hospitals, but his humour was always present. When I had my stroke, I finished up in the private Priory Hospital in Birmingham. I had lost everything, including my speech. It was scary, but I was so tired that all I wanted to do was sleep, which I did, for hours. All I remember was the specialist I was under, Professor Adrian Williams, telling my wife on that Saturday that I would probably need a major operation – which I did not in the end – and that she must be the *only* visitor. Not even our children. No exceptions.

This was 2 February 2002. So I was amazed when, the following early afternoon, I saw my big friend Ron Atkinson at the end of my bed. 'Sorry I'm late, but I had to walk round the hospital three times before anyone recognised me,' he began. 'Anyway, how are you?' Now up on my haunches and feeling like death warmed up, I could not talk properly and produced nothing but gurgled nonsense. 'You sound better than you do on the telly!'

He continued: 'Have you got anything to eat?' At which point a nurse entered my room and gave Ron a right telling off. He told her that he had not come to see me; his TV was not working at home and he heard, correctly, that there was Sky in the hospital. 'Before I go,' Ron continued, 'may I have a plate of prawns with a lemon and a pot of Rosie Lee [tea] on his bill?' The nurse said firmly: 'No, and you must leave in three minutes.'

Ron switched on Sky and we started watching the worst Premier League match of the season – Middlesbrough o Charlton o. Ron looked at me and commented: 'Move over Gary, this match is making me feel ill!' I tried to laugh but collapsed back into a long sleep.

My phone went on Wednesday as a nurse was testing my blood pressure. She answered: 'He is improving, but he still cannot talk. Oh, you have a message for him to listen to?' The nurse handed me the phone: 'Good news. I have all the pall bearers organised. I will take you in the middle!'

When Katie visited me and heard about Ron, she was furious. But when I recovered, I told her that actually Ron had stopped me feeling sorry for myself, and I appreciated his visit. He never stopped. For instance, he told the press later that I had taken up golf and he was giving me a stroke on every hole! And when I had a hip operation, he rang me shortly after I came round from it to ask if he could have the bones for his dog!

I did get my own back in a way. For a while we were lucky enough in Birmingham to have a Ronnie Scott's jazz club on Broad Street, owned by our good friends Barry Sherwin and the late Allan Sartori. Most of the world's top jazz names played there.

One day the owners asked me to do a charity concert there. So

I rang Earl Spencer (after I had attended a private dinner at Althorp as the guest of my great pal Nicholas Parsons) to say that if he would attend, I would donate the funds to his chosen charity Deafblind. He said he would love to be there and brought top chef Raymond Blanc.

I asked two close pals to help me. They were Big Ron and Jasper Carrott. Jasper said he would open the show. Ron, who fancies himself as a singer after his lifelong hero Frank Sinatra, agreed to do a number. A few days later, Ron was showing his Manchester-based daughter Susan around Birmingham in his car. As he was passing Ronnie Scott's, Ron screeched to a halt as they spotted a big poster: 'Ron Atkinson Sings Sinatra.' He said to Susan: 'Newbon has stitched me up!'

In the event, Ron recruited music expert Cedric Whitehouse and the City of Birmingham Symphony Orchestra strings to help him rehearse and prepare for the big night.

With Ron still in his pomp on TV, it became the hottest ticket in town and sold out in twenty hours, with hundreds on the waiting list. The media were clamouring to attend too, but there was no room for them apart from Central TV, the *Birmingham Mail* and BRMB's sports radio reporter Tom Ross.

Ron came out in top hat, suit and silk scarf and sung four songs brilliantly, although he had to be rescued on 'My Way' by Ruby Turner and Steve Gibbons. There were cries for more! So I asked Cedric, but he panicked, saying: 'No more, we have not prepared any others.'

That did not stop Ron going from table to table, soaking up the plaudits and explaining that I wouldn't let him do any more songs! Thousands of pounds were raised, and local businessman

Tony Ryan doubled the sum. Even more was raised when Earl Spencer asked me to invite millionaires for a private dinner party at his Althorp home with one of my favourites Ruby Turner singing…

The Bayern Munich–Manchester United European Champions League final in Barcelona ('Football, bloody hell!') brought another quick Ron quip. UEFA were inviting ITV to a pre-match dinner. ITV's controller of sport, Brian Barwick, was worried that Ron and I would get bored and possibly misbehave, so I was called in and told: 'You and Ron should go to any restaurant for dinner and put it on the firm.'

We picked a packed outdoor fish restaurant in the city's Port Olympic. We were reading the menu when a young waiter suddenly recognised Ron, who had been manager of Atlético Madrid. This waiter spoke very quickly to Ron and, much to my amazement, Ron replied in what appeared to be pretty good Spanish. When the waiter left I said: 'Blow me, Ron! You were only at the club for three months; how much did you pick up?' I was referring to Spanish, but quick as a flash Ron replied: 'Half a million quid tax-free.'

I have seen Ron's sharpness too. When he was Coventry City manager, he wanted to make a serious complaint to me about something said on the telly. He was halfway through it after a match at Coventry when some supporter rudely broke into the conversation, edged me to one side and said: 'Great to meet you, Ron,' to which he replied: 'I suppose it must be!' as he edged him away and continued talking to me.

I talk to Ron most weeks, and he still makes me laugh. Recently I was writing a column about how average players often make great managers and more often great players do not. I said to Ron: 'Take you, you were a very good manager with lots of cup triumphs, but you were not a great player.' He protested indignantly: 'What do you mean? I was a great player!' To which I retorted: 'No you were not – you spent your whole first-team career with Oxford United!'

Ron, Jim Smith and I were going to a football dinner in London one year and staying at the Royal Garden Hotel in Kensington. West Bromwich Abion were second in the league; Smith's Birmingham were bottom. Ron and I were waiting for the lift to come down, when the doors opened with just Jim inside. With his usual quickness, Ron quipped: 'Going down?'

Around this time, Ron, Jim and their wives went to see the Scottish comedian Billy Connolly at the New Street Odeon. They were taken backstage after the show to meet Billy, but no one really knew what to say. Smith broke the ice with: 'Did you like playing Birmingham, Billy?' Before Connolly could reply, Ron jumped in with: 'Billy, everyone likes playing Birmingham!'

His TV co-commentaries were brilliant; he made use of phrases like: 'Hollywood ball' (wonder pass), 'lollipop' (step-over trick), 'eyebrows' (flick on at near post), 'a reducer' (an aggressive, early tackle on a key player) and, if a player tried a spectacular shot with no chance of scoring, Ron would say: 'He must have been reading comics.' We miss him on air. Sadly, his TV commentating career came to an abrupt end over a racist remark after the Monaco–Chelsea European Champions League game in 2004. We were off air, but you are never alone with a microphone.

A Middle-Eastern TV station had been pirating our commentary, and Ron was talking to Clive Tyldesley with the microphones still 'live' when he made a racist remark about the Chelsea defender Marcel Desailly. An ex-pat heard the muffled sound in Dubai and rang *The Sun*. Barwick urged Atkinson to resign the next morning.

There is no defence for what Ron said, and there would be none even if it had stayed private. You cannot use the 'n' word or make racist remarks. However, after almost twenty years, it is my view that it is about time Ron was forgiven. Racism is a terrible thing, but some form of fairness and balance is needed in these times. Ron Atkinson is a valued friend of mine and will always be.

CHAPTER SEVEN

THE MUNICH OLYMPICS

The England and Wolves legend Billy Wright was my boss for twenty years. The footballer was a lovely man with a great gift for remembering the name of *everyone* he ever met. He had 105 caps for England – ninety of them as captain. He was a record holder for many years. Billy played twenty-one years for his only peacetime club Wolverhampton Wanderers and was never booked.

He was the forerunner of Posh and Becks when he married Joy Beverley, the eldest of The Beverley Sisters, a famous chart-topping singing group.

Billy Wright was a famous man who never chose to remind you. Everyone loved him. He never refused an autograph and would have been the same with selfies if they had been invented before he died in 1994, aged seventy.

When my twin boys were born on 13 August 1977, he gave me two of his England caps for them on the condition that I handed them over when they understood what they had meant to Billy. He also sadly became an alcoholic in his later years, but with typical determination and bravery he overcame that illness and drank not a single drop of alcohol for his last five years, before dying from pancreatic cancer – a fate that was sadly suffered this year by his beautiful oldest daughter Vicky at the age of sixty-three.

Management however was not Billy's strength, and neither was presenting on TV. But his image, fame, charm and contacts made him worth his weight in gold to ATV and the owner Lord Lew Grade.

Billy was simply too nice for management and not able to take tough decisions. He developed players at Arsenal like Charlie George and signed the likes of Frank McLintock but could not break bad news when he needed to drop players. There were stories that he would hide away after posting the team sheets.

In TV, administration was not his strong point either, and I was always retrieving unpaid invoices. One other thing that frustrated me was that if someone rang him wanting their sports item to be filmed, he would agree even if the subject was naff!

I persuaded Billy to let me be the judge of what should and shouldn't get onto the agenda, and he accepted that. But those were just my criticisms. The rest were all plus factors. Billy was support-ive, loyal and loved by all 1,000 people working at the ATV Centre in Birmingham. He knew all their names.

As we expanded the regional sports coverage, Tony Flanagan, Billy and I agreed that I needed help. I would like to think that he made a good signing in taking me to ATV. His next one proved to be a real winner – a 22-year-old from Raymond's News Agency in Derby called Trevor East. He was to go on to be one of the first presenters of *Tiswas*, the hit Saturday morning show with Chris Tarrant, before a stellar career as a TV executive in the UK. More on that later. Trevor joined Billy and I a year after I arrived and we took regional sport to another level.

One of the biggest problems at that time was actually the power of the trade unions: there were many restrictions and a lot of overmanning. The electricians were on overtime as soon as they arrived. You had to take a whole team of union people with you to do a simple interview, and they would insist on their lunch breaks. It could be a nightmare, and they would block an item if it was not properly crewed.

On one occasion, the ATV news reporter Bob Warman was filming a building project and pulled out a compass. His film item had to be dropped because a props man had not driven the compass from the studios! Honestly, would you believe it? The problem with life is that you cannot get a happy balance. It's either management making people redundant while paying themselves big bonuses *or* the unions making unreasonable demands and calling chaotic strikes. Or, in these modern times, both!

These days, if Central TV want to film an interview with me at my home, the reporter arrives alone to do the job. Camera, sound, lights and questions. In the ATV days, an entire crew had to accompany them. Since at that time we had a monopoly on advertising, it was a case of measuring how much revenue we would lose if the crew walked out, for whatever reason, against how much it would cost us to settle the dispute. Since there are now so many TV channels available, those days are over; the unions' leverage is severely weakened, allowing modern reporters the freedom to get on with their jobs with far less restriction. They don't realise how lucky they are...

In my first season in the Midlands, Derby County won the Football League title and Stoke City won their only major trophy – the Football League Cup in 1972. Because of union restrictions our budget did not stretch to sending a full crew to the Stoke pre-match hotel, the Selsdon Park in Croydon.

ITV were due to cover the final so Billy, having confirmed that the outside broadcast was available to cover the match the next day, was able to use it the night before. We booked a link from the Wembley studio live into *ATV Today*. He rang Tony Waddington, the Stoke manager, and asked if I could drive to the hotel and take one of his first-team players to Wembley for the interview.

Tony nominated George Eastham. Can you imagine that today? So far so good, but now the story gets worse. I had a soft-top (convertible) MGB sports car that had only two seats. At the last moment, the Stoke trainer and former player Frank Mountford decided he wanted to come and look at the Wembley pitch to decide what studs his team should wear! He was stockily built to say the least.

I was horrified, but I did not want to upset Stoke, so we bundled George into a narrow space behind the seats where he had to crouch at an angle. It was Friday night and the North Circular Road was packed. The journey took an hour and a half each way. I was really worried for George, but I need not have been as it turned out the next day.

Stoke beat Chelsea 2–1 with George scoring the winner. I might have been the most relieved person in the stadium, besides his club and their supporters!

Billy and I were invited to the Stoke after-match banquet at the Hotel Russell (as it was known then) in London's Russell Square. What a night! We sat with songwriter Tony Hatch and singer Jackie Trent, his wife at the time, who was from the Potteries. When you ordered a drink, the waiters were instructed to bring a *bottle*! Our table of four had a bottle of Scotch, a bottle of wine and two bottles of champagne. The Stoke chairman, Albert Henshall, a man of few words, got up to make the speech but within seconds he said: 'My drink has arrived, so I will sit down. No speech!'

What a club. The chairman went to bed clutching the cup; the top floor, where he was sleeping, had to be evacuated because someone had fallen asleep with a lit cigarette. It was actually unproven who did it, so no names no pack drill! Those were the days!

By this point I was starting to establish myself. I was thrilled to be picked for the ITV team to cover the 1972 Olympics in Munich. For reasons best known to themselves, ITV decided to let the news operation Independent Television News (ITN) run the coverage. In the end it paid off.

I started off as a sports news editor, but I was soon turned into a roving reporter by the man in charge, David Phillips. He and ace reporter Gerald Seymour (these days a bestselling novelist) had been responsible for the coverage of terrorism in the Middle East. Their experience was to pay off in the tragic events that followed.

My ATV 'boss' Tony Flanagan was directing, my tape editor and good friend Graham Thompson (later to be sadly killed in a road accident) and production assistant Jane Alexander were also out there.

With our accreditation as media personnel for the Games, it was easy to walk in and out of the Olympic Village, which housed all the competitors and their officials. That was all to change for ever more.

The German organisers had showered us with lots of goodwill gifts, watches, chocolate bars, clothing and so on. I had been given two free air tickets from Munich to Berlin and day return. I asked Graham Thompson to join me.

On 4 September there was a rest day at the Games. That night Graham and I went out for dinner and had quite a few beers. We got to bed around 1 a.m. with intentions to get up about 8 a.m. and head for the airport. I was woken a lot earlier by Gerald. It was, I think, 5.30 a.m. 'Come, now,' he barked. 'Just a moment; I need to brush my teeth and shave,' I responded. I was told no chance. I slipped on a pair of trousers, red shirt and shoes. Nothing else. I was bundled into a people carrier with Phillips explaining to me and the crew that there had been a terrorist attack an hour earlier and we had an early tip-off from one of the security guards.

We arrived at a wire fence outside the village, which by now had been sealed off. We therefore had to climb over. Seymour, the aging ITN film crew, London Weekend Television's Stuart McConachie and I scrambled over the fence. Phillips failed but was still yelling instructions as we ran towards the Israeli quarters in Connolly-straße, where they were housed at No. 31.

We managed to get onto the terrace of the Puerto Rican house opposite to observe and film. It was a group of eight terrorists, who we later discovered were called 'Black September'. Luttif Afif, also known as Issa, was their leader and was wearing his much-photographed white hat.

It turned out that he and two others had been working as gardeners in the village while the other five arrived by train and plane just before the Games opened on 26 August.

At one stage we were between the German police and the terrorists. I foolishly tried to get closer and finished up at the nearby South Korean quarters talking to their boxing coach Terry Spinks. He had been an Olympic gold medallist in the 1956 Olympics. Terry had seen the terrorists arrive at the Israeli quarters and raised the alarm. We thought we were in the village early, but while I was not surprised to see the Israeli TV crew I was shocked to see the USA's legendary ABC presenter Howard Cosell broadcasting live nearby.

My vivid memory of the following hours is Issa and one of the hostages, the fencing coach Andre Spitzer, who spoke fluent German, leaning out of the window. They soon talked with the German negotiating team, which consisted of the Head of Munich Police, Manfred Schreiber, and the Interior Minister, Bruno Merk.

They offered Issa huge amounts of money to release the hostages but were told money and their own lives meant nothing to them. They demanded instead the release of 234 Palestinians and non-Arabs held in Israeli prisons, the freeing of the two founders of the Red Army faction from a German prison and a plane to fly both the terrorists and their hostages to an Arab destination. Issa and his gang had already killed two hostages who had resisted in the initial attack – cutting the testicles off one as a warning to the other nine.

Eventually an 'agreement' was reached, and the hostages were led bound and blindfolded by their captors to buses and then helicoptered fifteen miles to Fürstenfeldbruck Airport.

This was a disaster for the Germans, who had seen these Olympics as a way of cleaning up their image after the propaganda of the 1936 Olympics. However, worse was to come. I was exhausted and cold. ITN stood me down, sent me to the Adidas shop in the village to buy some warm clothing and go to bed. At least, I thought, the nine hostages are still alive. How wrong I was; the next morning, when Seymour woke me again, I discovered that the hostages had all been killed.

There were so many cock-ups by the German authorities and

police. The German assault team had earlier made an attempt to break into the Israeli quarters until they realised that the whole world and the terrorists themselves were watching them prepare their rescue attempt live on television.

Then to their airport, where there had been a dispute between the German Army and the police. The result was that armed but untrained police were waiting to fire on the terrorists when they landed with the hostages in two helicopters. Several armoured cars on the way to the airport were stuck in traffic. A plane was waiting for them at the airport, but the 'crew' were German police in disguise. One of the terrorists inspected the plane and worked out what was happening. The other police opened fire, killing some terrorists, but the remaining terrorists opened fire on the hostages in the two helicopters and threw grenades into one of them, incinerating the shackled Israelis inside.

It was so terrible, so amateurish and so tragic. I went to Munich as a 27-year-old television reporter and became a war correspondent.

I had been shocked when running film tapes to throw over the fence to *World of Sport* presenter Dickie Davies that any British competitors I saw en route seemed uninterested in my progress reports of the assault. This was a matter of life or death in the village – never mind your medals.

I was sickened by the tragedy once it was over. I could not believe that the Games would go on. ITN sent out another top reporter called Robert Southgate, who mopped up brilliantly for twenty-four hours non-stop. I really admired those guys.

Before these Games, Seymour had obtained exclusive film of Middle Eastern terrorism that consisted of planes being blown up in the desert, while Southgate had covered the Vietnam War, reporting on drug-fuelled helicopter pilots diving down on the Vietcong and taking obscenely dangerous risks. Southgate was later to become my boss at Central Television.

At the end of the Games, Phillips told me that ITN were so impressed with my work that they wanted to offer me a job as a sports reporter. Flattered as I was, that wasn't what I wanted. Presenting and interviewing on actual coverage was my choice.

However, my major boss at that time, Tony Flanagan, overheard the conversation and was furious. I told him not to worry as I did not want to accept their offer. I was, like most presenters at ATV, on a one-year contract. Tony told me he would put me on the ATV staff with a final salary pension. He was aware that the previous month I had successfully proposed to the editor's secretary Katie While and said I would be grateful for the pension in years to come. He was right and I still am!

We had arrived in Munich the week before the opening, and this meant that I was in Munich on Katie's twenty-fifth birthday, but I knew she was taking her lovely mother Janet and some girlfriends to our favourite Birmingham restaurant, Lorenzo's.

I had asked a jeweller friend of mine, Brian Buxton, to make a diamond engagement ring for me and made a booking for him and his partner next to Katie's table. I asked Lorenzo, still one of my closest friends to this day, to hand it over during the meal.

The restaurant was packed as ever. The lights went out, the flowers and cake were presented to Katie with all the diners clapping and singing happy birthday. Lorenzo then said to Katie: 'This box has arrived from Munich.' Katie was stunned and asked her mother if it was a signet ring before my future mother-in-law assured her daughter it was an engagement ring! I rang from Munich within the hour to receive the acceptance. I knew Katie was the one for me.

We married in October the following year and are so lucky to have three great children – 48-year-old Claire and 46-year-old twins Laurence and Neil – with three wonderful grandchildren and three potential step grandchildren. Just before this book was published we will have celebrated fifty years of marriage. I was lucky enough to receive the MBE in 2019. My friends insist it should have been awarded to Katie instead! They are probably right. I could not have achieved what I did in my career without her.

CHAPTER EIGHT

THE 1974 WORLD CUP

After the disappointment of Westward TV stopping me going to the 1970 World Cup, I was pleased when ITV picked me for the 1974 tournament in West Germany. I was given the role of roving reporter with two special duties as well. England had failed to reach the finals after being held 1–1 in the final qualifier at Wembley against Poland, which I covered in the first chapter of this book.

The England manager Sir Alf Ramsey was sacked and ITV moved quickly to sign up the 1966 World Cup-winning manager as a pundit. I was asked to act as pitch-side interviewer with Sir Alf, as well as be his minder and travel companion.

I sat right behind our commentary team of Hugh Johns and Sir Alf for the actual final in the Munich Olympic stadium. The whole thing was an interesting experience. Sir Alf was a man of few words. On reflection we spoke more on the interviews than in the long car trips when we were chauffeured around Germany. I had only met and interviewed Sir Alf once: in Plymouth, when he brought the England under-23s to Home Park and selected the Argyle star Norman Piper. I found him reserved and quite difficult, but I got the job done. This was different and he was much easier. This time, I enjoyed the interviews.

Several memories stick out. He liked to have his wife Lady Vicky with him in the back of the car. Occasionally I would turn round in my seat and say: 'Alf, we are approaching an autobahn service station; would you like to stop?' He would always politely say: 'No, thank you.' My bladder was also much stronger then than it is today!

Once, when we were entering a stadium on match day, we spotted his England successor Don Revie approaching. Sir Alf said: 'Gary, let us walk another way please. I do not wish to speak to that man.'

Another night we were dining at a Düsseldorf restaurant on the night of the Greyhound Derby final at London's White City. The favourite, Jimsun, was trained by Geoffrey De Mulder in Meriden, and the owners saw me as a lucky charm placing the regular winning bets.

They asked me to fly back for the final, but ITV understandably said no! So they went to see my new wife, Katie, in the ATV newsroom and gave her the money to fly out to join me. Strange logic, but they thought that would maintain the lucky charm.

I was so nervous before the race. No mobile phones in those days. So in the end, I used the restaurant's phone to ring a national newspaper switchboard, where a clearly fed-up switchboard operator immediately said: 'And if you are calling for the dog final result, it was Jimsun.' I yelled my delight, kissed Katie, jumped into the air and ordered champagne. All Sir Alf simply said was: 'I take it the dog won and you had a big bet on it!'

Another day Sir Alf and I went out to lunch at the famous Haxnbauer restaurant, where the speciality is pork. Our waiter brought us a tray of pork joints and I explained to Sir Alf that he had to pick one. 'What, a *whole* one?!' he asked. I explained: 'Afraid so...' Sir Alf was staggered.

The night after the final, the ITV outside broadcast lads asked Sir Alf, Lady Vicky and I to join them on a night out at a rowdy, large and packed beer garden marquee in Munich with an oompah band playing. To my amazement, Sir Alf agreed. There were bottles flying everywhere, and I was worried, although Sir Alf amazingly was not recognised. He was relaxed, telling me: 'It's a bit different, ain't it? Vicky and I are quite enjoying it.'

As we drew to the end of the trip, Sir Alf put a good word in with my bosses, for which I was grateful. Then he thanked me and said that he had no idea how difficult my job was and in the extreme unlikelihood that he was ever a manager again he would be different towards the media. But you know football people often revert to type when they are working again.

Remarkably, three years later Sir Alf became manager of Birmingham City after a spell as director. He lasted less than a year.

In what proved to be his last match, Birmingham lost 4–0 at Coventry. In those days, access was very easy. I was presenting the match for ATV's *Star Soccer*. I went straight up to the Birmingham dressing room and knocked on the door. Sir Alf answered: 'Hallo, Gary, nice to see you again. What can I do for you?' I asked to interview him, to which he said simply: 'No, thank you!' And shut the door.

No one in our production team could understand my laughter! I never interviewed Sir Alf again, but it was a great experience working for a short while with a national hero who was, and still is, the only England manager to win a World Cup.

Back to the 1974 World Cup. The runners-up were the

Netherlands, who lost the final 2–1 to the hosts, West Germany. It was wonderful to watch this Dutch team playing their total football. They were captained by one of the sport's great players, Johan Cruyff, whose agent was the Englishman Dennis Roach, who also advised the likes of Trevor Francis and Ron Atkinson.

Dennis did a deal on Cruyff's behalf with John Bromley, ITV's head of sport, for regular and exclusive access for interviews with the great player. I was chosen to do those interviews. Cruyff spoke perfect English and was easy to talk to. Access again was much easier in those days. I was surprised to see Johan eating a massive bowl of ice cream before one match, while I also recall Kevin Keegan eating a big Mars bar in the Hamburg tunnel shortly before a tie with Real Madrid. Kevin explained that it was for the energy! Sadly neither work for me. I love both but have to watch my weight!

The night before the 1974 final, I was told that FIFA had picked Jack Taylor, the English referee from Wolverhampton. I was to track him down and make an interview. He was surprised when I found him and was at first reluctant to give me an interview, fearing he would upset FIFA.

However, after explaining that we were from the same area, Jack from Wolverhampton and me with the Birmingham TV station, he decided that he trusted me, and I was able to go ahead and interview him with a few restrictions. Jack passed away on 27 July 2012 aged eighty-two from pneumonia. As a referee, as in life, he was a big, strong and honest person. Those qualities were certainly tested in the final.

Previously there had never been a penalty kick awarded in a World Cup final. Jack gave two within twenty-six minutes – and the first was against the host country in the *first minute*! The date: 7 July.

Jack was certainly alert. There was a delay at the start. Jack had noticed that the corner flags had not been replaced on the pitch after the tournament's closing ceremony, which had taken place before the match. Then when the Dutch side kicked off in the first minute, before the West German team had even touched the ball, Uli Hoeneß felled Cruyff in the German penalty area. Taylor said afterward it was 100 per cent a penalty. Johan Neeskens scored from the spot for the Netherlands. One–nil. Franz Beckenbauer, the West German captain, told Taylor: 'You are an Englishman…'

Then, in the twenty-sixth minute, the Dutch midfielder Wim Jansen tripped Bernd Hölzenbein in the penalty area and Taylor awarded a penalty. Paul Breitner equalised. While both penalties were considered by some to be controversial, there was never ever any doubt in Taylor's mind. He explained the second: 'It was a trip or an attempted trip and the laws of the game are that's a penalty.'

Cruyff continued his protests as the teams left the field and became the last of four cautions issued in the first half. By then the Germans had taken the lead with what proved to be the winning goal in the forty-third minute by Gerd Müller in his last international match. West Germany now added the World Cup to the European Championship they had won two years earlier. Taylor was hailed by the Football League as the greatest English referee up to that time.

At that time, ITV comprised fifteen companies, and there were some real politics among the big ones. There were a lot of frustrations in sport, where the two London companies (Thames and London Weekend) had far more control over coverage than the smaller regional ones. World Cups and Olympics involved many more staff because of the sheer numbers required for the coverage, but on domestic sport like football and boxing it was a different story.

I did break through with speedway and greyhound racing and eventually I was part of the big sports scene. The traps were there, but I overcame them. In fairness, it made me a better TV operator and by the mid-'90s I was on top of my game, until the Granada–Carlton TV merger, when it was all taken away from me. But do not worry for me. On a personal level it forced a move to Sky Sports, where instead of having to retire at sixty-five I stayed in the studios in front of camera until I was past seventy-three. However, the problems with ITV started really during the coverage of the 1974 World Cup.

For one thing, post-match interview studio time was booked so late that I had the stressful experience of hanging on to players like Breitner (who spoke very good English, as did the other West Germans) outside the studio, knowing there would probably be another twenty minutes before my slot. I would tell fibs, saying: 'Any moment now; please wait!' Suffice to say I did eventually get all my interviews. I will give London Weekend the benefit of the doubt and say it was not deliberate.

There were to be other examples, including asking my good friend Barry Hearn in years to come to request that I did not do the interviews at his promotions. Barry refused and even told me about it.

There were a couple of other things that really disappointed me. On my return Grahame Turner, head of sport and news at Thames Television, gave me a real dressing down, telling me I was untalented and he would never use me again. I did not reply. I knew I had delivered everything required – Cruyff, Sir Alf (who had praised

me to the other ITV company bosses) and many interviews against
the odds.

The other blow was that for the 1978 World Cup in Argentina,
John Bromley, normally a fine operator, made a wrong call, deciding to not take *any* reporters. Instead, he took another production
director, Tony Parker, who worked with me at ATV and made it
clear he did not really want to go!

Towards the end of that 1978 tournament, my old great friend
at the *Sunday Mirror*, Sam Leitch, called me to London. He was
now head of sport at Thames Television, replacing Turner, and in
charge of the London end. Sam took me to dinner at the Tower
Hotel, which was used to house those working on the World Cup.
Sam told me: 'You should have been out in Argentina. That was a
stupid decision. You will be my first name on the list for the 1980
Olympics in Moscow.' So it proved, and I was to be in the form of
my life, particularly with Sebastian Coe. Sadly, Sam did not live to
see the Games open on 19 July. He died earlier that year in London,
aged just fifty-three.

CHAPTER NINE

THE MOSCOW OLYMPICS

The year 1980 brought the Moscow Olympics and the second Games for me with ITV. The British Prime Minister Margaret Thatcher supported the USA's boycott of the Games because the Soviet Union had invaded Afghanistan. The US President Jimmy Carter had unsuccessfully given the Soviet Union a month to withdraw their troops. Mrs Thatcher pleaded with the British Olympic Association not to send their competitors but only the British equestrian, hockey, shooting, fencing and yachting teams did not attend. In all 6,000 competitors took part instead of the 10,000 that had been expected. Eighty nations took part – the smallest number since 1956. Sixty-five countries and nations failed to participate. That certainly made it easier for competitors, and it also made for easier conditions in which the media could move around and work – especially without the USA.

This was the backdrop that led to the Soviet Union winning a record eighty gold medals (a record that has since been broken by the USA) and their overall medal haul of 195 is still the second largest in history. There is no doubt that the presence of drugs was affecting results, but testing back then was more rudimentary, and doping could be more easily concealed. I covered Sharron Davies swimming to a silver medal and we found out years later that drugs had cheated her out of gold.

For the Games, ITV decided to pair up the successful reporting team of ITN's Gerald Seymour and myself. On paper, I drew the short straw by starting being based in the Olympic Village. Gerald was selected to be the interviewer at the track, swimming and other top events. Gerald and I always got on very well. He was a top professional, but he did not have any relationships with the competitors, a problem that was clearly illustrated by events concerning javelin thrower Tessa Sanderson.

I thought that Tessa, from Wolverhampton, would win the gold medal, which in fact she went on to achieve in Los Angeles four years later. I had worked hard on our relationship for two years before the Games, and she promised to give me the first interview.

However, I was not in the stadium. But there was a big shock. Tessa failed to qualify for the final and left the stadium in tears, refusing to talk to Gerald or anyone else. My ATV colleague Trevor East rang me: 'Tessa has flopped and stormed out. She blanked Gerald. Its down to you, mate. I have told everyone in our office here in Moscow that you will get the interview. Brommers said if Gerald failed, so will you. I know different.' Trevor was always supportive of me as a presenter/reporter.

I waited at the Olympic Village gate with a crew. In came Tessa, who looked at me in floods of tears and said: 'Gary, I cannot talk.' I guided her to a seat next to my camera crew saying: 'Come on, Tessa, you promised me the first interview. Please. We can do it. The camera is rolling.' And with all due credit to Tessa we did the interview. It was dramatic television and she sobbed all the way through the nine minutes. It changed my Games and although the village was my main job, I was now being used at events.

Earlier I never protested and soon began to really get satisfaction over interview upon interview, which guaranteed me the same role at the 1988 Seoul Olympics after ITV had pulled out of the 1984 Games through a trade union dispute. John Bromley in fairness was a great leader, although he was political at times, reserving the majority of sporting coverage for the two London ITV companies – an arrangement I was to break in time.

He certainly was a great personality, and everyone loved him. He had one idea for which I was deeply grateful. He decided that I should be the ITV reporter who worked with Sebastian Coe. His logic was that I was based in the Midlands with ITV and Sebastian was a student at Loughborough University and would watch my sports shows.

It worked and I will always be grateful to Sebastian as well for his help and friendship. Our regular interviews went very well, apart from one awkward incident. His fiercest competitor was another top Brit called Steve Ovett. Unlike Coe, Ovett was being very difficult and not talking to the media. Coe was the world record holder for 800 metres and favourite to win that event, while Ovett was the hot favourite for the 1500 metres, where he was the world record holder and unbeaten in forty-five straight races since May 1977.

Unknown to me, Bromley and ITV's former Olympian Adrian Metcalfe courted Ovett successfully with a big fee for an exclusive interview. The BBC's David Coleman discovered what had happened and wound up Seb. I walked onto a left hook and was very unhappy that I had not been told. We did not pay Coe a penny and throughout our relationship he has never ever asked for money. I assured him I had no part in the Ovett payment and had been shut out of it. 'However,' I said, 'if you do not want to talk to me again, I will fully understand.' Thankfully, however, Coe is a class act. He explained that he was unhappy with ITV over the payment, but it would not spoil our relationship and he would carry on doing interviews with me.

So we came to the 800 metres final, and inexplicably Coe got his tactics wrong and was beaten by Ovett into second place. The silver meant little to Coe and even less to his father and coach, Peter. Allan Wells, who was with Coe in the same room, had just won the 100 metres gold medal – the first Brit to take gold in this event since 1924. Peter picked up Allan's medal and said: 'We should have won this colour.' Earlier that morning the great character and Olympic hero Daley Thompson had visited Coe, who, as he awoke, asked Daley what the weather was like. As Daley pulled open the curtains, he announced: 'Sort of silvery!'

Four days later, Sebastian Coe was to show what makes real champions. Obviously you need skill and fitness, but attitude and temperament are vital. The rivalry between Coe and Ovett was stirred up by the media. Coe explained to me: 'We do not *hate* each other – we do not *know* each other!'

Ovett had declared he was 90 per cent certain he would also win his event, but Coe turned the acute disappointment of his 800 metres run into relief and glory by winning the 1500 metres – the Ovett event. Steve was third. Having spent so much time with Coe, I was so pleased for him.

I was at the ITV commentary area when the phone rang. The request – another 'impossible-looking' task for me to overcome – was to test our relationship yet again. Like several that I pulled off over the years, this feat would actually be impossible today with there being so much security and media and an unbelievable number of jobsworths (as I call some stewards).

The ITV office in Moscow – the other side of the city – said: 'We need you to use your driver and car and get Seb into our office studio to link up with Dickie Davies, John Walker (the previous 1500 metre Olympic medallist), who is in London, and Seb's mother, who is on her way to the Yorkshire TV studios. Do not hang about. We have booked it live within the hour!' Thanks, lads!

I quickly found Seb after his media duties and put it to him. He then asked his father, Peter, who said 'no'. I pleaded with Seb, saying my neck was on the line and his mother was on her way to the Yorkshire TV studios. Seb went to bat for me by working on his dad, who finally agreed. Then, to my horror, I realised that my car was parked 600 metres away. Time was now of the essence, so I had to ask the Coes to run as fast as we could. There was a touch of the farcical George Eastham pre-League Cup final journey. We were joined by Chris Brasher, part of the historic Roger Bannister first sub-four-minute-mile team and by now an athletics writer for a Sunday newspaper. Brasher talked to the Coes all through the race to the studios. I was a bit miffed because I wanted to brief Seb, but I thought Brasher was with them. It later turned out that Seb thought Brasher was with me! Brasher was very clever with that one!

We got to the studios just in time for the linked-up interview, which, against all the odds, did work like a dream, thanks to Roger Phillcox, our brilliant technical chief.

I later used my village security contacts to get into the Wells–Coe room, with their gold medals laid out on a table in front of them, and conduct a further interview. Norman Giller, veteran and respected sportswriter, had a media column in the now defunct *London Evening News*, and I was proud that he gave a 'Giller Gold' to 'ITV's Gary Newbon for a stunning series of interviews capped by the Allan Wells/Seb Coe interview in their village room.'

CHAPTER TEN

JIMMY GREAVES

I had first come across Michael Grade, now Lord Grade, and John Bromley in my early days as an apprentice agency journalist in Cambridge. Grade had contacted me about the *Sportlight* column he did with Brommers in the *Daily Mirror*. It was a sports gossip column.

Grade wanted me to pick up a schoolboy called Willie Carr, who was at St Bede's School, and take him to a match he was playing in at the Cambridge United ground on Newmarket Road. Lots of club scouts would be there to try and sign him, including the Coventry City manager Jimmy Hill, who proved to be the successful one. The accompanying photographer took a snap of Carr in his classroom with his fellow pupils before we set off. Carr was so small he could not see over the dashboard of my Volkswagen 'Beetle' car.

The young Scot went on to have a stellar professional career for the Sky Blues, Wolves and Scotland.

Grade went on to have a fine career too, holding major executive roles in showbusiness and TV.

Then Brommers and Grade made an attempt to get *Match of the Day* away from the BBC, in what came to be known as 'Snatch of the Day'. The Football League agreed to sell the rights for television coverage for what was then a huge £5 million, three-year deal to ITV. League football was only recorded highlights in those days.

It was a major coup that caught out the BBC, who protested to the Monopolies and Mergers Commission, who in turn blocked the deal. The solution was that ITV and the BBC would both have the rights but would alternate between which of them got Saturday-night coverage.

So with this decision I went into the 1980–81 season with a live studio in Birmingham for the *Star Soccer* regional highlights show for the Midlands. The football was recorded highlights from that afternoon's matches. Who would be my pundit?

Four of us had a meeting to decide who would get that role. Billy Wright, Tony Flanagan, who was overall executive producer and made the big calls, Trevor East, the series producer, and me. We discussed several names, including the Wolves striker Derek Dougan, a great but verbose talker who was chairman of the Pro-fessional Footballers' Association. I really liked Doog, but I had severe reservations about his on-screen discipline.

As it turned out, Yorkshire TV appointed him as a presenter. He rang me and took me to my favourite restaurant, Lorenzo's, to pick my brains. I said to him: 'Keep everything simple and short until you get used to this 'new world'. Presenting is different from being interviewed. Also, you should get a moulded earpiece with a tube to take instructions from the control box. It needs to fit your ear so it doesn't keep flopping out.' Derek took the latter advice, but his opening link was so long that he messed it up. I am not aware of what followed in further programmes, but suffice to say it did not work out in the long run. I was sorry, but my consolation was that I was right about Doog and *Star Soccer*.

Back to the week of the first live show in early August. We had another meeting that week, with no decision having yet been made about the pundit. During the meeting, Tony Flanagan was reading *The Sun* sports pages and said: 'What about Jimmy Greaves? He was a great player, and he has a column in this paper.'

That was a good suggestion, but the thing was that Jimmy was an alcoholic. He had given up the booze and not had another drop from February 1978, but it was obviously a worry.

I said: 'I've just seen a documentary, *Just for Today*, featuring Jimmy and his drinking problems. He spoke well. I think I can work with him and teach him the ropes.'

Trevor said he would ring Jimmy and offer him the job. We discussed money and Trevor went back to the sports office. Soon he came back saying that Jimmy lived in deepest Essex and did not fancy it.

On the Thursday – two days before the opening show – we still had not settled on the right choice when Trevor took a call from Jimmy. He said: 'My missus, Irene, says I *have* to take the job. Am I too late?'

Trevor told him that he was just in time, but he would have to arrive the next day to appear on the Friday news show *ATV Today* with Gary (me!) to promote his arrival. We would put him up in the Holiday Inn hotel next to the studio.

So that is how close Jimmy came to losing a fantastic second career in television.

As a footballer Jimmy scored on his debut for every team at every level and had a fine England career, although he started the 1966 World Cup but failed to make the final after losing his place to Geoff Hurst after being injured in the group stage. He never really recovered from the disappointment of missing out from the quarter-final stage. He played fifty-seven times for England, scoring forty-four goals. His first-class career was from 1957 to 1971 playing for Chelsea, AC Milan, Spurs and West Ham. He played in 526 games, scoring 366 goals. His TV debut, however, was not as good as any of his football debuts. He was understandably nervous.

Viewers and local press were critical to start with. The local newspaper wrote an editorial asking why we had to have a Londoner in the pundit's chair and not a Midlander. Jimmy was immune to it all as he would take the long drive home after the show, which he said helped him unwind. Having been there myself, I was confident Jimmy would crack it. And sure enough, he did. I recall the particular show.

Two of the matches were Birmingham City against Blackpool and Manchester City against Coventry City. His cheeky humour arrived. Blackpool's Alan Ainscow won a dodgy penalty. On the replay Jimmy said: 'That is a deeper dive than Jacques Cousteau!' Cousteau was a famous Frenchman known for his underseas exploring.

In the next match, Coventry's winger Tommy Hutchison beat the Manchester full-back Willie Donachie back and forth at least three times before crossing the ball. Jimmy commented: 'They had to unravel Donachie in the dressing room at half-time and tell him where he had been!' I started laughing. I had never heard pundits cracking lines like that before.

In another memorable moment, the Oxford United chairman

Robert Maxwell was looking for a new manager, so I asked Jimmy who he might go for. Jimmy explained: 'Mr Maxwell says, Gal, that he wants a big name, so he will probably appoint himself!'

Week after week the funny lines came out. The viewers suddenly loved him. Jimmy was in demand. The viewing figures went up and it was not just for the football. Later when the station became Central TV, the new editor, Jeff Farmer, put Jimmy and me together on Fridays. Jimmy used to take the mickey knowing that I was never upset. It was great telly and Jeff used his golf club friends as a barometer of public reaction to the show. They always talked about Jimmy taking the p*** out of Newbon!

Back to *Star Soccer*, and Bev Bevan, a good friend and drummer for ELO, told me that when the band went to Munich for recording sessions, they would always take a recording of the latest *Star Soccer* on their VCR machine and roll around with laughter watching Jimmy.

I have already written about the politics between the ITV companies in London and the regions. As we approached the 1982 World Cup, Jimmy and Jeff Farmer were not in their plans for coverage.

Trevor East and I decided to go and see John Bromley and convince him that Jimmy and Jeff had to be involved. Jimmy was in top form and was well-loved in our region. Jeff was a top-class journalist who had been the Midlands football writer on both the *Daily Sketch* and the *Daily Mail*. Brommers, in fairness, listened and took them both on.

Jimmy was an instant hit, with lines like Italy's hard man Marco Tardelli being responsible for more scar tissue than the surgeons at Harefield Hospital!

Both did brilliantly in Spain. Bob Patience, another LWT

producer, had the wonderful idea of pairing Ian St John (their pundit and a former great for Liverpool and Scotland) with Jimmy. *Saint & Greavsie* was born. An outstanding show that, in my opinion, deserved to survive the chop when ITV lost the new Premier League rights to Sky Sports.

Jimmy's famous saying 'football is a funny old game' became legendary. At least I can claim it was made in Birmingham. He was with me from 1980 to 1998 except for an absence of one year.

There were plenty of funny moments off screen as well. Jimmy had this strange thought that if the big bosses did not know he existed, he would keep his job with Billy, Trevor and me. He was horrified when I made him speak at the hierarchy's Christmas lunch.

By the time Jimmy had finished speaking, I wished I had not forced him to do so. He said: 'I see all these bottles of wine and think that you must wonder whether I still drink. Well, I do not, but having worked with Newbon now for four months I have only just realised I am the only member of the ATV sports department *without* a drink problem!'

I never asked Jimmy again.

When Central TV continued with Saturday night's *Star Soccer*, each night I used to ask my secretary, Olivia Fondyga, to draw £100 from petty cash (doesn't sound like much, but this *was* 1980!). She and Jimmy would then pick the takeaways from a Chinese restaurant in the city centre called Chung Ying. The team was working late, and I have always appreciated production crews. Jimmy would then take a taxi and collect the food. We were on the fourth floor and the sports office had massive long tables. The food was laid out and everyone would help themselves.

It is worth remembering that this was before computers and

mobile phones. The internal exchange was always in memo form. Senior management sent a memo instructing us to stop the food deliveries. Jimmy and Olivia decided that, although it was addressed to me, they would not let me see it. Instead, Jimmy decided to answer it.

Basically, the memo stated that because we pushed all the leftovers and food containers into the large bins, the mice and rats had crawled up from the adjacent canal after we had gone home and were eating it all!

Jimmy's reply memo, signed on behalf of the mice and rats(!), went: 'What is your game? While you are at home on a Saturday night, no doubt with your feet up and drinking a bottle of wine after a lovely dinner, Greavsie, Gary and the boys and girls are working hard to make you plenty of money. So Gal kindly lays on a nosh for the gang, which they deserve. It's our Saturday treat too, so please stop sending these silly instructions. We like the Chinese bits, which we never get down on the canal!'

I was blissfully unaware of these memos until the end of the season. We carried on with the Chung Ying deliveries and never heard another word from upstairs. I often wondered what they made of it all!

I soon came up with the idea of *The Greaves Report*, which was a series of lovely little cameos that could be included in our *Central Sport* bulletins on Friday evenings. Jimmy ran with Sebastian Coe, got knocked out by Frank Bruno, had Test pace bowler Bob Willis bowling flat out in the Edgbaston nets and played tennis with Tracy Austin, who patted his stomach, telling him that he ate too many pasties. He went pillion on the back of a motorbike with world champion Barry Sheene at Donington, and when Barry went flat out Jimmy said over the intercom: 'You ain't half going well, are you? Do you reckon you'll make a good go of this, one of these days?'

On a serious note, we nearly got Jimmy killed on a hang-gliding stunt (accidently of course!) with Rory McCarthy, a world record holder, over Dunstable Downs. Their glider went out of control. Luckily, both survived, but it was a terrifying moment.

I also wanted to do a sports quiz to rival the BBC's *Question of Sport*. I was annoyed when the deputy managing director Bob Southgate felt the sports department could not be trusted with it. Unknown to me, my mate Don Maclean brought in some people who had this concept called *Sporting Triangles*.

I did not like the fact that we could not be trusted or, for that matter, the actual idea. But being a good company man, and re-membering that Bob was normally very supportive of me, I went ahead. Jeff Farmer and I played it in a village hall and made some adjustments, but I thought the idea of three teams was naff... And so it proved. The show was networked from 1987 to 1990 and then dropped.

We had two hosts – first Nick Owen and then Andy Craig. I had no more than a casting role. I used my extensive contacts book to contract the biggest British sports names to appear as guests and upped the fee they had been paid by *A Question of Sport*. I appoint-ed Jimmy Greaves, Andy Gray and Tessa Sanderson as my three captains. Jimmy was really unhappy as he wanted to be the host. I told him that I did not think he was up to that role. He sulked for a while before settling down.

I didn't think that Nick Owen was the right fit either. So I brought in Andy Craig, who was stronger on this particular show.

Nick is a great professional and is still going strong. A great friend and I admire him, but in my role business was business.

Southgate gave me a bollocking for announcing the swap at a press conference. I could not understand why he was angry; I was trying to save what ultimately proved to be a sinking ship.

I then replaced Tessa by poaching Emlyn Hughes to become our third captain. *The Sun* did an 'exclusive', claiming I was paying him £100,000. Actually it was £20,000, but there was a hitch. His agent, Bev Walker, explained that he had to wear Pierre Sangan sweaters. I said fine, but there could be no logos and they would have to supply all the captains and guests with them at no cost to Central TV.

It was soon agreed. I put it to Jimmy, who readily agreed. But by the time he had got home someone had wound him up – I could guess who but not prove it – and he said he had changed his mind and would not wear them.

I had signed Hughes on contract. I was furious with Jimmy. Normally I keep my cool, but I lost it and didn't handle this well.

In the end Jimmy agreed, but he told a national newspaper of our row and that really upset me. He was being disloyal by doing that. And it was not the first time he had gone public. Jimmy was often concerned that others were earning more than him in my team. Dressing room mentality. Actually, I was paying Jimmy five times my salary, which he deserved, holding his Central contract on *Saint & Greavsie*, network football, Central TV productions, *Sporting Triangles* and his own chat show, which turned out to be poor, although that was not necessarily Jimmy's fault.

Emlyn, Jimmy and Andy were great, but the show was axed in the network schedules. It is one of my lasting disappointments that

I was not allowed to come up with a quiz format and control it. Jeff Farmer and I would have done better.

During this time, Andy Gray's agent, the late Dave Ismay, said Andy was retiring as a player and would like to join my team. I had used Andy when he was at Everton as deputy for Jimmy on *Central Sport*. He was a natural from day one. But I believe in loyalty and wanted to keep Jimmy.

I told Dave that I would come back for Andy when I was ready, but I did not have the budget for another pundit. Famous last words, as Andy went on to be a million-pounds-a-year presenter with Sky Sports. He was outstanding.

There was another incident with Jimmy and *Sporting Triangles* that contributed to the deterioration of our relationship. It was Jimmy's birthday on one recording date. There was an audience for every show. We had a big birthday cake made for Jimmy and were going to present it to him beforehand in the studio. His response when he found out: 'Gal, if you bring that cake out, I will walk off set and go home!'

I accepted that he did not want the cake to be presented to him. I sent it to the local children's hospital. But the threat was the final straw for me. I was controller of sport and I would not tolerate it any longer. When his contract came up, I did not renew it.

Not long after, we were both playing for Norma Major's XI against the Bunburys for charity at Alconbury. The Prime Minister John Major – a close friend of my parents – was present, so ITN sent their reporter and former Central TV journalist Terry Lloyd.

I sat with Jimmy and my wife Katie at tea. It was civilised. I said to Jimmy: 'Would you like to come back to work with me in Birmingham? I will pay you the same for Central shows.' After we left the marquee Katie asked me: 'Do you think he'll go for it?' I said: 'I really do not know.'

Jimmy always wore his heart on his sleeve. Minutes later I was fielding deep, and Terry Lloyd came up to me and told me that I had made Jimmy very happy. I knew he was coming back.

I never had a moment's trouble with Jimmy again. I started using him in both the studio and on co-commentary. He was funny again and in good form.

Jimmy did not like going to grounds, because he said that he had to meet the people he might criticise, but I wanted to make full use of him. Jimmy could bring different non-football topics in, like when an old boy called Ron, who was in charge of a car park we used, had a dog who bit Jimmy on the hand... Or saying: 'I will be here next week, Gal, if you agree my new contract!'

We covered Aston Villa several times, and the chairman Doug Ellis and Jimmy Greaves were good friends. Earlier Jimmy had dubbed Ellis 'Deadly Doug' after he sacked a manager. I was wondering if it was OK from a legal perspective, but Doug seemed to like it. Ellis was a good friend to me too, but sometimes he had a selective memory or even just made things up. He claimed 'Deadly' came from his having killed a fish on a stone when he was fishing on film with Jimmy. But I know it was in the studio that day when Jimmy called him Deadly Doug for the first time. Not that it mattered.

When Ron Atkinson was Villa's manager, Jimmy was funny about the chairman's room, which he called 'Doug's Disco', and the manager's office, which he dubbed 'Ron's Bistro'.

He would tell our viewers: 'Gal and I went into Doug's Disco after the match, but there was no one there. Food of course. But instead we switched to Ron's Bistro. It was heaving with people, and the table was groaning with food. Lobsters and large prawns, pies, sandwiches, cakes. What a feast! Gal and I got stuck in.'

After two more shows and more reports from our new food correspondent Greavsie, Ron's assistant manager, then Andy Gray, rang us to say: 'Ron says can Jimmy please lay off talking about "Ron's Bistro". The chairman has pulled us in and is not happy with it at all!'

I tried to freshen up the show a bit and tried using Greaves with his old Chelsea pal John Sillett. It simply did not work. Together they looked like Statler and Waldorf from the Muppets. My error. I had given Sillett a season's contract. I decided to drive to his house to tell him the bad news.

He was furious, telling me he had turned down football offers. I said it was my fault, and we would pay him off for the rest of the season. He said at least I had the decency to front him in his lounge. His Coventry chairman, he said, had sacked him on the phone when he had flu!

John, or 'Snoz' as Greavsie had dubbed him when they were youngsters, because of his nose, then asked if he could be given a co-commentary role, as I was now doing live Midlands football matches. I agreed and he did a good job.

I remember one amusing moment at Roots Hall Football Stadium in Southend, which had a vertical ladder to the commentary position. John was precariously holding onto his briefcase as he came up to the box, when the studio presenter Tony Francis asked Jimmy, live: 'What do you think he's carrying in that case?' Jimmy's instant reply: 'That will be full of Snoz's sandwiches.'

John Sillett and I had always been great friends, and I was

honoured when his family asked me to host a packed memorial service for John at Coventry Cathedral after he died aged eighty-five in November 2021. John had played for and managed Coventry City. He was an incredibly popular person.

Francis, by the way, was a good presenter who I thought was harshly dropped by the ITV network. He was an oddball at times. One Sunday when he was due to present *Star Soccer* in the studio, he rang Jeff Farmer and said he did not feel like working that day. Jeff rang me and I then contacted Tony, saying: 'Feel like it, or you will not be doing another show for me.' The point is that no one is indispensable. We are all replaceable on TV, including me!

When my contract was up at Sky Sports, the managing director Barney Francis (son of Tony Francis) asked me to explain why he should give me a new contract. I told him that was a strange question, as he had axed all my shows with a forthcoming takeover. He told me that nothing lasts for ever. I agreed with him: twenty-three to seventy-three years old was a great run in front of camera, and I duly departed. As it happened, Barney was soon gone as well!

Back to Jimmy. Before too long he was losing his contracts and his Central connection was the only one left. When he had kicked up about not hosting *Sporting Triangles*, I asked Central to try and get him his own chat show, which they did, but it was not well-produced in my opinion, and as previously mentioned it was not a success.

But at least Jimmy got it out of his system. By that point, the only work he was doing was commentating, and I felt, towards the end of his contract, that he was not delivering.

In his book, Jimmy wrote that he was allowed to leave Central TV without any explanation. This must have been a lapse in memory on his part. As in the Sillett case, I drove halfway between the studios and Jimmy's Essex home to the Bridge Hotel in Huntingdon to explain why I was letting him go. Over a pleasant lunch outdoors in the sunshine, Jimmy told me: 'You should have done it a year ago.' I agreed, but I told him it was the hardest thing I had ever had to do in my TV career.

When I returned to the studios, Olivia asked me how it went. I said I thought it had gone very well, given the circumstances. Sadly that appraisal proved not to be true, as a journalist doing his newspaper column told me at a European match. It turned out that Jimmy was bitter, which was disappointing, given he had just had his longest stint in TV. He must have felt that our partnership would last for ever, but, as mentioned above, nothing ever does in TV. He did eventually get over it, and I was pleased about that. Jimmy meant a lot to me as a person. My days working with him had been great and fun, but the bottom line was that I was also a company manager, and with that came responsibility.

But we made it up at the funeral of his *Saint & Greavsie* producer Bob Patience at Basingstoke. The wake was twenty-two miles away at Sunningdale Golf Club, where Sir Alex Ferguson and Jimmy did the speeches. Greavsie gave me a lift and we had a wonderful chat.

Underneath it all we were very fond of each other. The few ups and downs were outweighed by the hours spent together on and off the screen. He was a very important part of my career. Those eighteen years were memorable.

Jimmy's second stroke left him wheelchair-bound and almost speechless. I had one last lunch with him and with his caring son Danny near his home in deepest Essex. When I arrived that day it was so good to see his wife Irene again after many years. I realised Jimmy was pleased I came as well, as he gave me a kiss on the cheek.

I made him laugh over lunch. It was a long car journey from the West Midlands but worth every mile to have one final meeting with him.

Jimmy was five years older than me. As I recalled earlier, I used to catch the train in my school holidays from Cambridge to Northumberland Avenue in London and walk to White Hart Lane to watch the great Jimmy Greaves scoring goals. Now you can understand how strange it feels that I went on to spend eighteen years working with him in television and helping shape his new career.

Jimmy Greaves MBE passed away at his home in Little Baddow on 19 September 2021, aged eighty-one. Jimmy was always in love with Irene, who he married in 1958 when they were both very young. They divorced during the height of his alcoholism, but they were only apart for three months. They had five children, but sadly Jimmy Jr died before his first birthday.

The family invited me to Jimmy Sr's funeral on 22 October at Chelmsford Crematorium. Jimmy had picked the last song: Lonnie Donegan's 'Have a Drink on Me'. A funny, talented man until the end.

CHAPTER ELEVEN

FASTEST NEIGHBOUR ON
FOUR WHEELS

I moved into my present home in Solihull in 1976. About two years later I was about to drive into my house after presenting the *ATV Today* news programme when I stopped to let a young man past. I had noticed he had been running up and down the road before so I wound my window down and said: 'Would you like to come in for a cup of tea? You can tell me why you're doing this.'

He replied: 'I will. I need your help.'

He sat in our TV room and told me and Katie his story. He was a motor racing driver, as yet unknown to the general public. He had been successful at kart racing and he had, using his own money, moved into Formula Ford. He won his first race and six of his first nine races. He then won thirty-three out of forty-two races entered the following year to become 1977 British Formula Ford champion. He broke his neck in a bad crash during a qualifying session at Brands Hatch. Doctors told him that he was confined for six months, may not walk again and would never drive again. He discharged himself from hospital and drove again. It would prove to be typical of him, although he is still in pain to this day.

He was now sacrificing everything to be in racing. His wife Rosanne was working as a cookery demonstrator in Solihull town centre and he was keeping fit. He convinced us that he would be Formula One world champion one day, as indeed he became. He needed my help at this point to attract sponsors and play him at squash whenever possible.

This literally driven man, if you will excuse the pun, was Nigel Mansell.

He and his wife Rosanne lived in a rented flat round the corner from our house.

I was to learn that Nigel was a fearless, obsessed man who would put up with incredible pain and put his life on the line many times in his quest to be the best. He was to achieve his goal with a broken foot in 1992. He would be unlucky not to have been Formula One world champion more than once, with two heartbreaking runner-up season finishes.

His long-lasting marriage is so important to his success story. Rosanne backed him every step of the way, despite Nigel's willingness to put his life at risk. They have been married since 1975 after meeting as students at the Hall Green College in Birmingham. They have two sons, Leo and Greg, and a daughter, Chloe.

The pain from his injuries and exertion leaves a terrible legacy today: he cannot even tie his shoelaces up. The couple spend most of the year in the warmth of Florida, where Nigel talks to me on the phone from time to time. He has a reputation for being a tough businessman, which does not surprise me, considering where he came from before he entered Formula One.

Back to those very early days. I played squash with him many times and never won once. I cheated, hit him with a racket, claimed points I knew were his. All to no avail. I even drew blood, and all he did was laugh and carry on winning!

We played at the then named Albany Hotel in Birmingham city centre, where Jonah Barrington, one of the world's top players, trained. He used to watch us play and also laughed at my antics, saying I was the dirtiest player he had ever seen. I am a bad loser. We played once at the posh Edgbaston Priory Club, but I was soon banned for consistently using bad language in my frustration.

Nigel used to come into the studios to meet me for squash and would wait until Trevor East and I had finished getting ready for that night's show. We would give him money to buy rolls from the canteen for the three of us. When he did a commentary for us years later as world champion, we both joked that he probably would not fetch the rolls now.

I asked Mike Burley of P. J. Evans, who sponsored my cars, to help Nigel, but he chose a female driver instead. He was to regret that as he told me many times, as Nigel made Formula One. Similarly, I took Nigel in to see ATV's head of documentaries to try and set something up that followed Nigel's career as he was breaking through. The boss turned it down. I wonder what he thought years later.

One day Nigel asked me to send cameras down to Silverstone because he was having a test drive for Lotus and wanted to impress them with my presence and plenty of cameras. I duly did so.

Shortly afterwards we were changing at the Albany after he had beaten me yet again and he said: 'I am off to the Isle of Man tomorrow, so no more squash here.' Colin Chapman had signed him for Lotus and he needed to move. Big money overnight.

We have stayed in touch over the years and he always does interviews for me – there were plenty in my Sky Sports days, and more recently, for instance when I was hosting an online *Daily Mail* TV show. He has proved to be a great and valued friend. Motor racing is not my game, although my wife is a petrol head!

But Nigel has never forgotten the early days. When we stayed with them on the Isle of Man, he picked us up at the airport in his helicopter and wave hopped for a few minutes. Thanks, Nigel!

We went out for dinner in his top-of-the-range BMW. On the way back, he mounted a wall at speed on two wheels! I was scared until Rosanne said that she was getting bored with that trick. She added that he did it every time they had visitors!

He plays golf regularly. There is a golf club in our road. Rosanne bought him one golf lesson as a present in those very early years. Within a year he was a scratch golfer and later in life he went on to own a golf course and hotel near Exeter.

Woodbury Park Hotel in Exeter was Nigel's for a few years before he sold it. He had a special birthday party there once, inviting all his old friends, including singer Leo Sayer and Katie and me.

I cannot recall any motor racing people being there. If there were any, it would have been just a handful. Nigel and Rosanne have their feet firmly on the ground and value all their friends, old and new. We were all given bedrooms there as well after dinner and cabaret.

He was once stopped for speeding on the Isle of Man, and the policeman said: 'Who do you think you are driving at that speed, Nigel Mansell?'

He is still emotional at times. I asked him back to Birmingham to receive a lifetime achievement award and he had just lost a dear friend and dedicated the award to him through near tears.

His Formula One career was amazing. He won both the Formula One title in 1992 and the CART IndyCar World Series in 1993 for actor Paul Newman. He became the first person to win the CART title in the USA in his debut season.

The night he quit Formula One after a public disagreement with Frank Williams, I met him in secret at the Chewton Glen Hotel. I was contacting him to endorse a charity leaflet for Central TV and his PA, Nikki, said Nigel would meet me for dinner, but I must not tell anyone he was there.

Over dinner he explained there were contractual problems and he had quit. He was tired and retired to bed early, but he said it was good to spend the time together. Nigel was to make a brief return to Formula One.

In 1989 having driven for Lotus and then Williams he became the last Ferrari driver to be chosen by Enzo Ferrari before the great man's death. In Italy Nigel became known as 'Il Leone' because of his fearless driving style. That sums Nigel up: brave enough to walk again, brave enough to drive. There was an instance in which he drove with first-degree burns on his bottom in the Australian Grand Prix, after petrol had spilled into his driving seat. He was fearless in coming from humble beginnings and using his own money to get started. Nigel knew his value and the value of money. He always struck a hard bargain once he got going in Formula One.

His Formula One record as a British driver is second only to Lewis Hamilton. He finished with 187 starts, 31 wins, 59 podiums (first, second or third position), 32 pole positions, 32 fastest laps and 480 career points. First race, Austrian Grand Prix 1980; first win, European Grand Prix 1985; last win, Australian Grand Prix 1994.

Mansell won the British Grand Prix three times – 1987, 1991 and his championship-winning 1992. He was associated with the racing number 'red five' for many years. He drove in Formula One for Lotus, Williams, Ferrari and McLaren.

He received many awards, including being named OBE for services to motor racing. He was later given the CBE in the 2012 New Year Honours list for services to young people and children as president of UK Youth. Nigel was twice BBC Sports Personality of the Year in 1986 and then in 1992.

I am proud of being involved in his early days, pleased that he still considers me a good friend and hopeful that with his bad back I can at last beat him at squash, even if, as I write, I am seventy-eight and he is seventy!

Nigel Mansell is the most remarkable sports person I have ever met.

CHAPTER TWELVE

A TERRIBLE TAKE

My style, at times, was controversial and outspoken. I have since mellowed a bit. But in the late '70s and '80s, several football crowds in the Midlands had a regular chorus of 'Gary Newbon is a wanker, wanker, wanker'. It started at Stoke City, after I gave their striker Garth Crooks a grilling in a live interview. Then it quickly spread to Birmingham City, where there was a regular chant. Even now some of them think I am an Aston Villa fan. I like all the Midlands clubs, but I have been a Leicester City supporter since I first went with my grandad, who lived near Filbert Street. That was 1951, when I was six years old!

But the worst chanting was at Wembley by Wolves fans at the 1980 League Cup final. I had written them off as the worst team to go to Wembley and gave them no chance against the European champions Nottingham Forest, who were also League Cup holders. The match played on my birthday, 15 March, was decided by a scruffy Andy Gray goal in the sixty-seventh minute. Forest's goalkeeper, Peter Shilton, coming out for a ball, had collided with his centre-half David Needham and the ball fell loose to Gray, who put it into the empty net. Immediately the Wolves section of the 96,527-strong crowd started chanting 'Newbon is a wanker'.

The then *Daily Mail* Midlands writer Jeff Farmer had to explain to his colleagues in the press box why that was happening. I probably deserved it. But Trevor East, my sports editor and a fine journalist, had wound me up. My usual studio guest Brian Clough was at Wembley, and the next Jimmy Greaves was yet to be discovered, which meant that I was on my own. The problem Trevor and I had with our Friday night preview show was that, since it was a Midlands regional show, we had exhausted everything we had to say about the two teams. So before we went on air one night, Trevor asked me who I thought would win. I told him it would no doubt be Forest.

I said that Wolves, in my opinion, were one of the poorest teams to reach a Wembley final. 'Well, get out there and tell it like it is, mate. You can do it!' he responded. And when we went on air, I did. I went well over the top! 'They have no chance. In fact, if they fluke a win,' I told the viewers, 'I personally will buy a crate of champagne and present it [to the team] on the Town Hall steps in front of the Wolves fans. No chance.'

You have to remember that in those days before the internet, hundreds of channels, digital platforms and catch-up, the only sports channels in town were the BBC and ITV. People watched TV, including regional TV, in vast numbers. I could not believe the reaction to my comments. I am told that, overnight, T-shirts were made with 'I hate Gary Newbon' printed on them. Naturally, these were being worn by Wolves supporters arriving at Wembley. The Wolves striker John Richards said that their manager John Barnwell (a good mate of mine normally!) used my comments in his pre-match motivation speech. John told me it had a real effect, as I discovered the next day when the Wolves captain Emlyn Hughes told me what an idiot I had been.

Forest had plenty of the game, but the Wolves defence were heroes, and they even hit the woodwork and had another goal disallowed.

The next day was painful. I had to buy a dozen bottles of champagne and present it to the team on the council steps before their victory-tour, open-top bus left. They made me go on it. The crowd continued to abuse me, which I again deserved. Mind you, I got plenty of publicity and it has never been forgotten (or I suspect forgiven) by the Wolves fans.

I was a bit worried next time we covered Wolves, but Trevor East, such a good friend as well as colleague over the years, told me to look on the bright side. 'They know who you are, mate. It's great.' I replied: 'Yes,' and apparently stuck out my chest in pride. Criticism has never bothered me since. These days I just ask that critics spell my name right and use an old picture!

The press used to give me plenty of stick – some deserved; most of it not. Anyway, all is well that ends well. I have stayed great friends with John Richards, Kenny Hibbitt, George Berry, Andy Gray and the manager John Barnwell.

As I've mentioned previously, the late Emlyn Hughes worked for me at Central TV and Ansells Brewery booked me most weeks for the next year to appear in Wolverhampton on stage, in clubs and at working men's and social clubs to be told by the customers what an idiot I was. I just kept thinking of the money.

CHAPTER THIRTEEN

HEROES AND VILLAINS

By now UEFA have got their act together and host broadcasters' match-day interviews, but that wasn't the case at the 1982 Aston Villa–Bayern Munich European Cup final in Rotterdam. ITV's line-up in Rotterdam was Brian Moore and Brian Clough on commentary. I was the reporter/interviewer.

What ITV wanted of us in those days was short build-up, a quick interview and then off as quickly as possible. Adverts were always the priority.

I have had to pull some strokes in my time, but the one I am about to describe is among the biggest.

Everything on this night was going well until just before kick-off. Rudi Rothenbühler was UEFA's press officer and informed me quite suddenly that I could not do any interviews until *one hour* after the final whistle. I argued with him; we had paid the rights fee, and if we were to wait as long as he wanted, we would be even past the *News at Ten*, which followed our transmission. But he was adamant and would not budge.

Ron Saunders, the former Aston Villa manager, had resigned in February. I am sure he would not have helped me out. He is the best manager the club have ever had in my opinion, but I always had an up-and-down relationship with him, which I will explain shortly.

Desperate for an interview, I managed to get a message to Tony Barton, who had been the assistant until Saunders resigned. Now he was the manager of the Villa team in the final.

He emerged from the tunnel and I explained my problem. 'What can I do for you, then?' he responded.

'May I please sit on the subs' bench with a hidden microphone for the end of the match?' I asked.

He agreed. My camera team were accredited with a field position. I sat between reserve goalkeeper Nigel Spink and midfielder Pat Heard.

After a few minutes, the Villa goalkeeper Jimmy Rimmer had a serious shoulder injury and had to come off. Spink turned to me and asked: 'What happens now, Gary?' I told him he was on!

I remember Nigel, whose only first-team game had been a League Cup tie, saying: 'I hope my mum has the telly on!'

He then played a blinder making lots of saves, and Villa won 1–0 against the mighty Bayern Munich with a goal from striker Peter Withe after very good build-up play on the left.

As the final whistle went I got my interview! There was a bonus too. I thought: 'I'll be in trouble no matter what, so I might as well take my camera crew down the tunnel and into the Villa dressing room.' Winners are much easier to talk to and so it proved! I got a range of exclusive, up-close and personal interviews with the jubilant players as they got changed.

When I finally left the dressing room, I found Rothenbühler in tears, as no one had ever done this to him before. It was his own fault. He should have been more reasonable. I was expecting a backlash but it never came. I assumed he did not want to focus on his failure to have stopped me.

The date 26 May 1982 was the greatest day in Villa's history, and I can claim I suppose to be the only unregistered sub in European Finals history!

Ron Saunders did very well at Aston Villa. He joined from Manchester City in 1974 and was with Villa until he suddenly resigned in February 1982 with the club on its way to winning the European Cup. He won two Football League Cups – 1975 and 1977 – as he put together an outstanding team that won the Football League title in 1980–81.

It had the likes of Gary Shaw, the speedy Tony Morley, striker Peter Withe, big central defenders in Ken McNaught and Allan Evans and goalkeeper Jimmy Rimmer. The captain Dennis Mortimer was a skilled midfielder together with the outstanding Gordon Cowans.

The team were loyal to Saunders. Tony Barton deserves the credit he receives as manager of the European Cup winning team – he would have taken stick if they had not won or even qualified for the final – but it was really a Saunders team who won it.

Saunders was born in Birkenhead and started with a few games as striker for Everton before joining Tonbridge, Gillingham, Portsmouth, Watford and Charlton. He was more successful as a manager with Manchester City and Villa after Yeovil, Oxford and Norwich. He was less successful at Birmingham and West Bromwich Albion.

I had my ups and downs with Saunders. Sometimes he was good to be with. I lived fairly near his impressive home, which is now a private health clinic in Knowle, and he would sometimes drive me to Villa's home matches. Those journeys were really good and I warmed to him.

Other times I really thought he was unpleasant, but I would never undervalue his worth to the club.

In his early days he had signed Andy Gray aged nineteen for around £110,000 from Dundee United. He was a great signing, but Saunders didn't like Gray's personality and was clearly unhappy when he opened a nightclub called 'Holy City Zoo'.

He did not like big characters. He certainly disliked Ron Atkinson. When Big Ron was the Manchester United manager and Saunders was in charge of Birmingham City, Atkinson was holding court with the media after winning when Saunders passed by, and he said to Big Ron: 'Giving them the usual bull, Ron?'

Big mistake, because quick as a flash Atkinson replied: 'Yes Ron, as a matter of fact I was telling them what a good manager you are!' Pick that out.

Gray's arrival in October 1975 after Saunders had got Villa promoted back to the top division saw him soon become joint-top scorer with Arsenal's Malcom Macdonald; they scored twenty-nine goals apiece to share the Golden Boot. Villa finished fourth in the table and they won the Football League Cup. A fine season for club and player. The Professional Football Association members voted Gray both their Player of the Year and Young Player of the Year awards.

At that time he was the youngest player to win the main award and the first to win more than one award in the same season.

ITV were due to televise the league awards dinner in London. But next thing I knew Saunders had banned Gray from attending, and I was asked by ITV to put an outside broadcast into his Sutton Coldfield home to link him straight into the dinner. I sat with Gray, who was clearly disappointed. I thought it was petty by Saunders.

When Villa won the Football League title, I was pleased for Saunders and his team. *Star Soccer* was live the next day with the lunchtime show hosted by me and Jimmy Greaves. I asked Saunders to be our guest, coming on with the trophy. He said he wanted £300 or he would not come in. This was 1981 and that would have been a massive fee for a local programme. I declined.

I thought there would be a time when he would want something from me. People always cross each other's paths when you least expect it. Sure enough, five years after he had retired Ron rang me at home. He told me that he had been watching my shows and thought he could do better than the pundits I was using.

I would never have picked Ron for that role because I thought he was dull, but he deserved my respect and so I simply told a fib: 'Ron, I am using people who are present players or managers or, with the exception of course of Jimmy, those who have only just retired.'

He accepted that and we left the call on civil terms.

There was an incident a few years earlier that I imagine did not help our relationship. It took place on a televised Midlands Sports Awards show that I hosted on ATV. Saunders finished second to Paddy McMahon and his show-jumper Pennwood Forge Mill, who had won a major event.

Saunders had won the League Cup and on stage twiddled his award around his finger, obviously fed up with the decision. Mortimer recently reminded me of the 'crass' decision, but it was a subjective view of their various achievements.

Matters reached rock bottom after a disciplinary event for which Blues supporters took years to forgive me. Sadly they did not know the whole story.

In those days there were disciplinary hearings for sending-offs and so on. There were no automatic suspensions. Today's system is far better.

Clubs with players having to appear before these commissions in those times often asked me for filmed evidence of the incidents involving the player. I was always happy to help. I recall Liverpool's Bill Shankly taking over our video room with his centre-half Larry Lloyd moving bemused video editors into different positions to illustrate what Lloyd should say.

Something different happened after a feisty local derby between Villa and Birmingham. Noel Blake headbutted Villa's Steve McMahon and the FA discovered my camera crew had captured the moment. Ron Saunders was tipped off that they had asked me to send the clips to them.

He rang me up saying he forbade me from giving them and said if I did he would have me banned from all the Midlands clubs – something he failed to do when he tried. I saw red. If he had not threatened me, I would reluctantly have considered it, although since the FA were rights holders I did not want to upset them. So I supplied the evidence and Ron slagged me off in the local and national press. I replied and the media war continued until my Central TV bosses told me to stop it.

Meanwhile two Midlands MPs Peter Snape (now Lord Snape) and the late Bruce George read Saunders's quotes in the House of Commons reading room. They decided to table an early day motion condemning Saunders's attempted censorship of Central

TV and described his actions as one of the reasons this great game is in decline.

Saunders and his lawyer Neville Bosworth threatened to sue Snape and George until Snape pointed out that if they heard one more peep out of either of them they would have them charged with contempt of the parliamentary privilege.

Saunders's attempts to have me banned failed at every turn, apart from his own club of course. Ron Wylie, who was the West Brom boss from 1982 to 1984, told Saunders it was not his problem, and that anyway, I was a friend. Indeed it seemed I was far more popular with the clubs than Saunders was.

I realised that Saunders did not go for big names. A long-standing close friend Jon Holmes was agent to Peter Shilton and the likes of Gary Lineker. Jon asked me if Saunders, while at Villa, would like to sign Shilton. I passed his message on to Saunders, who said yes but did nothing about it. The same happened on behalf of Trevor Francis but again nothing happened. That was Saunders's prerogative as manager of course. That is not a criticism but just an observation.

So Saunders and I never spoke again after the FA problem until that phone call five years after he retired.

Despite these ups and downs, I was genuinely sorry when I heard he had dementia and sad at his passing. There is no doubt that he helped give Aston Villa some of their finest moments to date. For that, he deserves our respect. He was quite a loner and a hard man who really did not care what people thought of him.

But even though that's who he was, it didn't necessarily make for the best working relationships. The boxing promoter/manager Mickey Duff once said to a boxer: 'Nowhere in our contract does it say we have to like each other.' No, Mickey, but it does help.

CHAPTER FOURTEEN

WIND-UPS AND WORLD CUPS

Although football and boxing were the most high-profile sports I covered, I have in fact covered most sports over my sixty years in journalism.

In 1980 I found myself presenting the ITV network coverage of the Volvo Show Jumping World Cup at the National Exhibition Centre, a few miles from my home in Solihull.

I went to the French show to get to know some of the riders like David Broome and Harvey Smith and struck up good relationships – particularly with Harvey Smith, who was a great help.

Harvey came to my house in his riding boots to talk me through the entries and classes before I took him out to dinner in a Birmingham casino. He promptly sang some Roger Whittaker songs to the bemusement of the mostly Chinese gamblers on the gaming tables at the time!

I used to host the Midlands Sports Awards in those days at what was then called the Albany Hotel in the city centre. I asked Harvey to be the guest of honour and to speak before handing out the awards. It was before the start of the 1980 Moscow Olympics and, as previously mentioned, the British Prime Minister Margaret

Thatcher was calling for a British boycott of the Games because of the Russian invasion of Afghanistan. Another top-table guest was Thatcher's Minister of Sport, Hector Monro. Harvey launched into an attack on both Thatcher and Monro, pointing out that Harvey's son Robert was being denied a chance of an Olympic medal by the boycott.

It was pretty savage stuff from the blunt Yorkshireman. Somehow we steered the awards back to a place of calm.

Harvey was a great help during my four days of live presenting, although I was faced with one tricky moment with Nick Skelton, another rider and good friend. We were coming up to the Puissance event, where horse and rider are required to clear a huge and beautiful brick wall. I needed a comfort break during the TV commercials.

When I rushed back, I was told by the floor manager that we were coming out of the break in ten seconds and that I was interviewing Nick about why his top horse for the event was not competing.

He was not about to use Lastic, who at the time held the world record with a clear jump of 2.32 metres, which they had set two years earlier when Nick was twenty-one years old.

This is how the live interview started:

Gary: 'Why are you not riding your world record holder Lastic in this Puissance event?'

Nick: 'What the f****** hell has it got to do with you?'

I was stunned. We were live and he said that!

Suddenly in my ear there was laughter in the control room; Nick was doubled-up. It was a wind-up! I then heard twenty seconds left on the break. Stand by everyone! I felt a right idiot for not handling it better, but it was funny!

Nick still dines out on it all these years later. He and his family took me out for dinner recently at the Malt Shovel gastro pub in Barston near Solihull. We still have a good laugh about it.

While we're on the subject of wind-ups, there are others to recall.

In the 1996 European Championships I was ITV's reporter/interviewer with England. I went on their pre-season warm-up tour of China and Hong Kong. I was only asked to do one interview and that was in Beijing with Paul Gascoigne. After we finished it, Paul said he knew I liked horse racing and that a waiter in the team hotel had given him a tip in the big race there that day.

He handed me a screwed-up piece of paper and ran off. He was out of sight by the time I read it – just a lot of Chinese calligraphy! Another wind-up.

I was the only media man allowed on the Cathay Pacific plane bringing the players home. In the business lounge I gave everyone a wide berth, but Gascoigne saw me and wandered over to make sure I was OK. It was his birthday. I had been unaware of the notorious 'dentist chair' drinking episode, but Gazza was clearly still recovering. A lovely Hong Kong hostess brought over a tray of champagne, and after I had taken a glass Gazza stubbed his half-smoked cigar into another full glass. I found myself having to apologise, but the lady was fine with it.

On the plane the players were in the upstairs sets. I stayed downstairs with the England head coach Terry Venables, his assistant Ted Buxton and physio Dave Butler. We had a good time chatting and pacing ourselves drinking.

A few days after our return, the media had a field day after a story was leaked about Gazza on the plane, allegedly breaking a TV set at his seat and other things. Apparently it came from an aircraft cleaner at Heathrow. I had no idea, as I had again kept away from the players.

At the first pre-Euro news conference, Terry invited the media to talk to me as I was on the plane. No one did come to talk to me, but I was not sure what help I would have been if they had.

Gazza refused to then speak to anyone, including me. I was miffed because I had not mentioned anything, including the cigar incident. I was in a position of trust and as ever I kept that trust. Why wouldn't Gascoigne talk to me? Unfortunately, I never found out.

As host broadcasters, the BBC and ITV had cabins as TV studios at the end of the long garden at the England team hotel for the tournament – Burnham Beeches Hotel.

ITV's producer was my Central TV colleague John Dickinson, the son-in-law of Peter Taylor (Brian Clough's assistant manager). Ray Stubbs was my opposite number at the BBC. I was late arriving one morning to be greeted by 'Dicko' and Stubbs: 'We have good news and bad news for you,' said Dicko. 'The good news is that Gazza will give an interview. The bad news is that he will only do one, and Ray and I tossed for it; Ray won.'

I was furious. How could I make it so that I did the interview? Stubbs, a good mate normally, said that he would ask any question I wanted, but I promptly told him to f*** off! I insisted we tossed for it again as I was not present. Dickinson said that we were gentlemen and must honour the outcome. In desperation, I said: 'No, no, don't you guys realise that I am the *official ITV tosser!*'

I did not realise what I was saying! Dicko and Ray collapsed with laughter. This had been a complete wind-up by Dicko and Stubbs on me, and the outcome was far better than they could have hoped for. They were soon on the phones.

Sports columnist Charles Sale, then with the *Daily Express*, made a big thing of it. Venables, normally an ITV pundit, loved it and told the players the story on the coach en route to Wembley for the match against Spain.

Later, during the 1998 World Cup, the England players came up with a game – they had to work the titles of well-known songs into the live TV and radio interviews while in La Boule, the golf club where they were based. The BBC and ITV certainly fell for it.

Alan Shearer, who really can keep a straight face, kicked it off. He had to work in a Phil Collins song while he was being interviewed by me at half-time in the Norway–Morocco match.

My first question to Alan was: 'What do you think of Scotland's performance against Brazil?' He replied: 'They played well today, but now they have it all to do "Against All Odds".'

Phil Collins and I know each other, but I never spotted that one. Nor did anyone else outside the England camp. They were enjoying this, so on they went on other channels. Graeme Le Saux even worked a Wurzels song into a BBC Radio 5 interview, mentioning that he had just bought a combine harvester. How on earth did he get away with that one?!

I finally rumbled the game, but I made a right idiot of myself revealing it to Mr Shearer! I told Alan in another live interview that we had sussed it.

He said: 'Yes, Gary, "It's All Over Now"!'... And I didn't spot it! My colleagues watching groaned. Shearer later suggested I was not a Rolling Stones fan. Not true as it happens, but a poor reaction on my part. A fair cop!

My second World Cup was Spain 1982. I love Britain, Spain, Italy and France – all great venues for World Cups during my career.

I was based in Madrid and had a general reporting/interviewing role, which meant that I did a lot of travelling.

I was helped by a Spanish restaurateur from Leicester called Ramon Fernandes, who ran the Costa Brava in Leicester. It was a popular venue and he was always telling everybody about his friends Ron Atkinson, John Bond and Gary Newbon.

He turned up to find me at our Madrid HQ. I was wondering about hiring a car as well as using the train, and thankfully Ramon offered to drive me around in his Jaguar. Problem solved.

ITV had left buying the plane tickets and hotel booking too late for my producer Jeff Farmer and I to make the opening match, which was Argentina against Belgium in Barcelona. So we were put on the Talgo train, which linked the two main Spanish cities. In those days it was a luxury train that would not exceed fifty-five miles per hour. Not that Jeff and I were bothered. We found ourselves sharing a space near a bar with an attractive lady who claimed to be a film actress and a Russian who was adamant that he was a spy. It was a long journey and we were all rather drunk when we arrived.

We were given rooms in the Ritz Hotel in Barcelona now known as El Palace. It is the oldest luxury hotel in the city.

As we went inside we passed Xavier Cugat, a Spanish musician and bandleader. He was eighty-two then and accompanied by two young ladies wearing tight leather catsuits and walking two miniature dogs. Jeff and I were staggered to see this then-famous Cugat with two such attractive women. But he stopped and called us two dirty men! I said: 'Who is the dirty one?' before Jeff sensibly pulled me away!

That opening match produced a surprise result with Belgium

beating the defending champions Argentina 1–0. But I was to be present with the biggest shock for years when Algeria beat one of the favourites West Germany 2–1 in Oviedo.

Before I got there, there were two incidents with Ramon in his Jaguar saloon car. First of all, I was set a difficult task by the London producers. No change there, and I came up yet again with the goods. I did like a challenge.

Bobby Robson was staying somewhere in the area we were travelling, but they did not know where. After a long day, we tracked him down. I went to the bar with him. I did not have a camera crew, but I had to ask him about a rumour that he was going to take the England job.

I always liked Bobby; a smashing person with time for most people. At that time he was the Ipswich manager and had had considerable success following in the footsteps of Sir Alf Ramsey, Jackie Milburn and Bill McGarry. Indeed Ramsey joined in 1955 and Robson was there until 1982. They did not sack people at Ipswich in those days under the Cobbold family: twenty-seven years covering the four managers. For me that was key to our conversation in the bar.

Bobby asked me: 'What would you do: take the England job or stay at Ipswich?'

Having seen what it did to Sir Alf in the end after winning the World Cup, Don Revie and Ron Greenwood and knowing the wonderful way Ipswich treated their managers, I said I personally would stay at Portman Road.

I was surprised he asked me and even more surprised when he agreed.

I left Bobby and told the office: 'He won't take the England job.'

But, naturally, soon the news came that Bobby was the new England manager.

Meanwhile the normally efficient ITV Sport travel department were unable to find me and Ramon a room each at such short notice. There was nothing available. So we had to sleep in Ramon's car on the beach.

I find it difficult to sleep in cars, so I had a wine-fuelled dinner to assist.

Ramon woke me late the next day. I had vaguely heard some shouting but he was unable to wake me earlier.

Ramon explained what had happened: we had been attacked by a gang, and he had somehow fought them off. There was broken glass and wine all over his car bonnet.

I rang the office and someone gave it to the press. The *Daily Star* painted me as a hero and there was not mention of brave Ramon, who was not best pleased, given I had been sleeping and the heroics had been his!

So on the match, and Franz Beckenbauer was there to see the huge underdogs Algeria beat his West Germany 2–1 – a massive shock. Der Kaiser, who had captained Germany and was to be their manager at the next World Cup in Mexico, spoke very good English and, like Pelé, was to give me an interview at each of the seven World Cups I was to cover. I did not have a crew, but I was desperate to get his view for our ITV show.

I asked a contact who was at the German station ARD and he said he would help me with a cameraman. I explained that I had no way to get the interview back to Madrid. He said if I booked a line I could use his play-out machine. I was not to know, but actually my contact was being very crafty.

Beckenbauer gave me the interview and my colleagues at ITV were very pleased. But before too long all hell broke out.

Beckenbauer was under an exclusive German media contract for their big tabloid newspaper *Bild*. ARD TV recorded my play-out and they presented it on their channel, saying: 'This is what Der Kaiser told our ITV colleague from London, Gary Newbon.' They played it to their viewers with German subtitles. Oh dear! We were quickly on our way back to Madrid.

CHAPTER FIFTEEN

THE HAND OF GOD

The 1986 Mexico World Cup was the most challenging of the seven football World Cups that I covered for ITV because I had no camera crew to work with! It was like a pub with no beer!

My previous record meant that I was 'hoisted by my own petard', which basically means hurt by one's own scheme. I had pulled off too many almost-impossible challenges in the past set by London television producers.

I was to rise to with this one with a big bit of luck. When we arrived at the TV headquarters in Mexico City, I was assigned a wonderful interpreter, a student called Rudolfo Alcocer, and given a driver. Rudi, as I called him, was to be a massive help and in years to come I introduced him to Nigel Mansell, who called on Rudi whenever he competed in Mexico. Rudi was car mad and went on to run a motor business. We are still in touch.

I was given a roving-reporter role. I had Rudi, a car and TV videotapes for recording but no camera. To start with, when trying to do an interview, I would have to explain to crews from other countries that 'my crew had been delayed' and then ask if they could 'help me out by recording my interview'! I was telling fibs in desperation, but somehow it worked.

We then had a big break, thanks to Rudi and his kind willingness to help everyone he meets. In their office at the television centre in Mexico City, ITV had built a video library of all the footage shot during the World Cup, ranging from interviews, match action, ITV shoots on the streets, stadium, training and match action. Plus all the general shots of Mexico.

Rudi introduced me to a cameraman from Costa Rica called Mario, who was in tears. His TV station had sent him without a reporter, accreditation or a car! He had not been able to achieve anything, and his bosses were asking him to return home.

He did not speak English, so I said to Rudi: 'Take him into our library and let him copy all he wants without the English commentaries or interviews. He should give his station the impression he shot it all! They'll let him stay, and he'll then work for us. Two tapes each time. I'll go first with my interview, then you'll do his in Spanish.'

It all happened too. Mario was told to stay as his station gave him herograms (I'm not sure how he went from zero to hero so quickly in their mind, but no questions were asked by them!), and he worked for us for the rest of the tournament.

I was well aware of potential union problems that could arise from using Mario as a cameraman. I had my fill of them at ATV and then Central TV. One of the biggest disappointments of my career was when ITV pulled out of the 1984 Los Angeles Olympic Games very late because of an impasse with the unions over one production assistant. Neither side would give way, and we were all angry when the trip was pulled.

So this time in Mexico I told Thames Television's head of sport Bob Burrows, who was in charge of my plans. Bob was always very supportive and he said we had to be very careful with the unions. No one must know about it outside our editorial team.

The first thing to decide was what we should call him. I told Bob: 'His name is Mario, but he is very big and *very* heavy, so from now on we'll dub him "the Big Package". And so we began.

We travelled to different locations and the arrangement worked like a dream, although there was one scary incident after the Scotland–Denmark game in Nezahualcóyotl, which Denmark won 1-0. Scotland were managed by Sir Alex Ferguson, although I did not know him at that time.

On the way back to Mexico City, our driver got lost in what turned out to be a very poor area. The residents were resentful of the ticket prices for the World Cup. The fact that they had been priced out of a tournament in their home city illustrated the fact that football is followed by the rich and poor alike. Our driver's car had World Cup accreditation posters on its sides. These posters granted us entry to training grounds and stadium car parks, but in this moment they acted as something of a red rag to the angry masses.

A swarm of human bodies jumped all over the car, trying to open the doors and attack us. It was absolutely terrifying; strong, sunny daylight turned to pitch darkness. I told Rudi to tell the driver: 'Foot on the pedal and just go,' which he nervously did.

When we got back to the ITV office in Mexico City and said what had happened, no one believed us! Sometimes you can't win, although escaping from that lynching was probably our best result of the tournament.

One day I was asked to produce an unusual look at these poorer Mexicans who could only watch the games on the massive screens that had been erected in the city's parks.

I met one family and asked if I could take their young son to the Azteca Stadium, which was the biggest of the eleven stadiums used by the hosts. It staged nine games, including the final, and held 114,600 spectators.

These days the request might not have been granted. But back in 1986 it was viewed as the innocent request it was, and the family agreed.

Pulling a few security strokes, Rudi and I (with the Big Package having taken shots of the family with the boy in a local park) got down to outside the Mexican dressing room an hour before kick-off. We managed to get the Mexico captain, national hero and attacking midfielder Tomás Boy to come to the dressing room door and talk to the boy with us filming.

We then took the youngster to the ITV viewing box (called the Palco), which we had hired for the World Cup, and filmed him talking to Peter Chapman's son, who was a similar age and spoke Spanish. Peter was a freelance journalist who worked with us.

After the match finished I took the boy to a bus stop and gave him a load of Mexican pesos to get home and have plenty left over!

I was also pitch-side for the notorious Argentina–England quarter-final tie at the Azteca Stadium on 22 June.

I was behind the goal where Diego Maradona, the 25-year-old Argentine captain, scored 'the Hand of God' and then 'the Goal of the Century'. The first was a blatant, cheating handball, and the second was a fantastic dribbling run where he beat four England players and then Peter Shilton.

That first goal from Maradona: the England goalkeeper Shilton went to punch the ball with his right hand – he was eight inches taller than his opponent – only for Maradona to use his left to punch the ball into the England net.

I saw Shilton going potty, but a post blocked my view. A few seconds later I found myself asking Peter what had happened. Although he has been a good friend over many years, he stared at me for a couple of seconds as if I was completely mad!

The Tunisian referee Ali Bin Nasser and I must have been the only two people in the ground who did not see Maradona handle the ball.

The second goal by Maradona was astonishing. On his run he beat Peter Beardsley, Peter Reid, Terry Butcher (twice) and Terry Fenwick before feinting Shilton to put Argentina 2–0 up.

Gary Lineker scored for England, but it proved too late. Argentina won 2–1 and they saw it as revenge for the Falklands War!

Argentina went on to beat Germany 3–2 in the final at the Azteca on 29 June. This time Maradona was heavily marked by Lothar Matthaus throughout the game, but he still managed the pass to set up Jorge Burruchaga to regain the lead at 3–2. So Argentina achieved their second World Cup final victory in three tournaments, having won the 1978 tournament on their own soil.

Maradona was no doubt a wonderfully gifted player. He got five goals and five assists at the Mexico World Cup. He went on to help Napoli win two Serie A titles, the UEFA and the Italian Super Cup. They have named their stadium after him. He died in November 2020 aged sixty.

Before the final there were two more tasks for me to do. I had to go to Cuernavaca, the capital of Mexico's Morelos State about

100 miles south of Mexico. My task was an interview with the German manager Franz Beckenbauer. I set off at 7 a.m., arriving at the team's pre-final hotel to be told by Beckenbauer that he would not do anything until the planned 6 p.m. press conference, but he would give me an interview then.

So I had to spend a long time waiting and wondering whether he would remember the Oviedo incident when he was working exclusively for *Bild* at the 1982 World Cup and ARD TV turned me over after I had interviewed him!

Obviously he had not, as he kept his word and gave me a good interview.

When I returned to our hotel, the Maria Isabel Sheraton in the centre of Mexico City, my Central TV editor Jeff Farmer and Bob Burrows were waiting for me. 'We have one more job for you. Go and see your contact at FIFA [he was an Englishman whose name I had better protect] and steal three photographers' on-field bibs so that Jim Rosenthal and a crew can get pitch-side.'

I caught my contact working late in the FIFA office surrounded by bibs. I explained my request. He knew he could trust me: 'I will turn my back for ten seconds. You had better be done after that.'

Thanking him I grabbed the bibs and ran off. Another near impossible job done.

I would like to stress at this stage that I have only ever stolen and lied in the course of television duty.

At the end of the tournament, Burrows made a presentation to the Big Package in front of our editorial team. We gave him a signed England shirt and an ITV football we had used in the studio, signed by all of the talent.

Mario broke down in tears again. He started saying he had

learned so much and had made a big impact with his bosses, for which he would always be grateful.

'And I will always be grateful', I told everyone, 'for Rudi and the Big Package.' With so many technicians union members in the big ITV team in Mexico, I am sure they got wind of what we were up to with the Big Package, but in the spirit of 'what happens on tour stays on tour', our secret never got back to London.

CHAPTER SIXTEEN

ROYAL CHAMPION

Terry Biddlecombe, a top jump jockey, and Sir Martin Gilliat, a Colditz Castle prisoner of war, were key to carrying out my idea of making a documentary on the Queen Mother and Her Majesty's interest in National Hunt racing.

I eventually produced the film, which was shown on ITV and attracted an audience of 7.5 million viewers. But it was not without its problems.

Biddlecombe was a fine and, in his time, famous jockey, who was champion jockey and won the Cheltenham Gold Cup and Champion Hurdle before retiring after riding 905 winners. I then employed him as ATV and then Central TV's racing pundit.

With his third wife, Henrietta Knight, he trained the horse Best Mate, who won the Cheltenham Gold Cup three times. Sadly Terry died in January 2014 at the age of seventy-two.

Terry often talked to me about riding winners for the Queen Mother, and it planted a seed in my mind: why not make a documentary on Her Majesty's interest in the sport? There were several angles besides the public's love of the Royal Family and interest in the great lady. For instance, her ownership of Devon Loch, a horse which fell on the final straight while leading the 1956 Grand National with the race seemingly won. The jockey was the bestselling crime novelist Dick Francis, and the horse's fall on the flat on the run-in to the finishing line remains one of sport's great unsolved mysteries.

Biddlecombe recommended I speak to Sir Martin Gilliat, who was the Queen Mother's private secretary. This was early 1987 and Sir Martin was seventy-four years old, but he was not to be underestimated.

I went over the details at a meeting between Terry, Sir Martin and myself. I got the go-ahead but with certain restrictions. They included that the Queen Mother would not give an interview and would not talk about Devon Loch. The latter was not so much of a problem because I would be able to talk to the jockey who rode the horse, Dick Francis. But the former was a massive one. I was aware that the Queen Mother did not trust microphones and had only ever granted one interview, and that had been a long time ago to ITN's Alastair Burnet. I decided to keep quiet about the no-interview point to my boss Andy Allan, gambling dangerously that I would obtain one before we finished filming. The attraction to ITV was obvious, and Andy, my director of programmes, was always supportive.

We were on! The budget was fixed and Robert Southgate, my immediate boss, selected a director: Gerry Harrison (not the football commentator), who he believed would be suitable for the Queen Mother.

Sir Martin then asked me to go and talk to Sir Michael Oswald, who was the National Hunt racing advisor to the Queen Mother and had played a key role in the royal family's racing interests for many years. He proved to be very helpful and joined us for some of the filming, including the shoots at Sandringham.

The Queen Mother was a delight to work with and called the film crew 'the gang'. I met Sir Martin several times to keep him updated and took him to his favourite fish bar, Wheeler's on St James's Street, which was quite close to his office in Clarence House. The '30s-style oyster bar and grill is no longer open.

I remember, too, being Sir Martin's guest at his London club, White's, also on St James's Street. I started to learn more about the royals and Sir Martin's own phrases. He referred to the Queen Mother as 'the Boss' and the Queen as 'the eldest daughter'. When I asked Sir Martin which school he attended, he answered: 'The school on the banks of the Thames.' In other words: Eton.

We were filming over several weeks, and it was all going well, until two incidents. First, Andy Allan called me to his office in Birmingham. Always interested, he asked for an update on the project, which was to be called *Royal Champion*. He asked if I had an interview, knowing about Her Majesty's fear of microphones. I told him not yet, but I was working on it! Andy's response? 'Do not come back to this office until you have that interview in the can!'

Terry Biddlecombe was very hard up, so I offered him an extra £1,000 if he could persuade the Queen Mother to give us that interview. Remember, this was 1987, and that price was a big incentive for Terry.

At a cocktail party, which I will expand on later, Terry was asked by the Queen Mother how filming was going from our point of view. Terry assured her it was good, but he said that he needed a chat on film with Her Majesty. Agreement was reached with her for an interview at the Royal Windsor Racecourse, where we would be filming the following week.

Terry then sauntered over to me and said, smugly: 'You owe me a grand!' Never have I been happier to spend £1,000 of my company's money! The documentary and my job were safe. Or so I thought.

A few weeks later, I took an angry call from Sir Martin. 'Why have you given the transcript of the Queen Mother's chat with Terry to the *Sunday Express* magazine?'

I was shocked. I knew nothing about this. I told Sir Martin as much, although for the first time I did not think he believed me. I asked to come back to him in ten minutes.

Peter Rushton was one of Central's press officers, and I angrily asked him what he had done and why he had not told me. It was, I told him, a disaster. We had not even finished filming.

I rang Sir Martin back. He told me if I did not get the article dropped, the film would be cancelled.

The next day on the way to the *Sunday Express*, I took Rushton to Clarence House, where Sir Martin was still adamant I had to get the article dropped. I explained that Peter had done it purely for publicity reasons and not for money; he did not realise that the Queen Mother never gave interviews and that this was a chat for the film only. I said we would now go to the newspaper and sort it!

In a taxi to the *Express*, Peter briefed me about the magazine editor Dee Nolan, a tough Australian, and that I faced a real challenge. Dee, naturally, was angry at this request to drop her scoop. I pointed out that the Beaverbrook family, who then owned the *Express*, were big royalists, and this was a request from the Queen Mother and her office. I told Nolan that they did not give interviews and they were classing this as a 'chat' for the purposes of the film, which was true. They did not want to make exceptions outside of this.

After several hours, Rushton, the director Gerry Harrison, Dee

Nolan and I reached an agreement to drop it. Nolan, smoking and still very annoyed, agreed to my suggestion of a piece with Harrison on the making of the film. She did however make sure to explain that it would cost the *Express* £10,000 for a reprint of the magazine. And I have to say, what they ended up with was rather a tame piece after the original, but I was so relieved.

I stayed in London overnight to approve the new article and then rang Sir Martin to confirm the events. The filming was back on!

My only outstanding problem before that shock was to work out how to interview all the jockeys and trainers who had served the Queen Mother in the limited time I had available.

I thought the cocktail party would be the best way to film them all in one day. So I rang Her Majesty's trainers Fulke and Cath Walwyn and asked if we could host this gathering at their home in Lambourn. Central TV would pay all the costs of food and drink. Saxon House Stables had been their home since 1944 and they had been a pair of the sport's most successful trainers.

They agreed and so did the jockeys, trainers and most important of all the Queen Mother. The only person I had to pay was Brian Fletcher, the jockey of the famous Grand National winner Red Rum, who had no money and lived in Ireland.

I rather cheekily asked Sir Martin if the Boss would pose for a team photo with me and my crew. The answer was yes, and I am so proud of that photo.

As previously mentioned, that is also where Terry obtained the 'chat' with the Queen Mother, which was filmed the following week at Windsor Racecourse. Often you need continuity with clothes in filming. Thankfully, the Queen Mother always wore the same blue hat – even for the chat, which was indoors.

Sir Martin had always insisted that the team did not gamble. However, we were filming the royal horses running that day, and Jeff Farmer, who liked a regular punt, and I sneakily followed Sir Martin down to the bookies and watched him place bets himself! We followed when he left and, to use the phrase, lumped on. Both runners were beaten!

The transmission of *Royal Champion* was for peak time on ITV of the Friday night (3 April) before the 1987 Grand National, which we attended to celebrate the completion of the documentary (as you did in those days of decent budgets!).

But beforehand we were concerned that the 87-year-old Queen Mother would be nervous about how the documentary would look in front of a television audience of millions.

So I rang Sir Martin and put it to him that we could hire BAFTA, a private industry cinema in London's Piccadilly. He soon came back with acceptance and a date.

I suggested the Queen Mother invited 150 of her friends. I would take my crew and my bosses. Sir Martin also sorted out his own guestlist, including Sir Michael Oswald and his wife, so let us say the final attendance was around 180. Sir Martin pointed out this was an unofficial event, so there could be no pre-publicity. I asked about food and drink. Sir Martin explained they had to attend an official dinner that evening, so we could maybe provide an urn of tea and a few sandwiches but nothing else.

The day before the screening, I had a nervous moment when Olivia told me that Sir Martin urgently needed to speak to me. 'Oh no!' I thought. 'Don't tell me this event is off!' But, I needn't have worried.

Sir Martin's call went like this: 'Hallo, Gary. The Boss [the Queen

Mother] is really looking forward to tomorrow. Just a couple of things. The eldest daughter [the Queen] has an elderly visitor on a sort of state visit and was hoping to encourage him to have a rest so that Her Majesty could join us, if that is all right.'

I could hardly conceal my excitement, and indeed the Queen did attend the screening.

Sir Martin added: 'As I have told you, this is an unofficial engagement. We have agreed the little catering, but I wondered if you thought a bottle of Bolly would be a good idea?'

I told him to leave that to me. He thanked me and was gone.

I asked Olivia to order 120 bottles of Bollinger on sale or return. She asked me if I had been drinking (I had been out for a long lunch at Lorenzo's), but I assured her that I was sober and knew what I was doing. It was all part of the royal speak. For the record, around sixty-five bottles were consumed. Not bad going!

I sat behind the two royals, who thoroughly enjoyed the film. Afterwards, Sir Martin asked me if I had ever met the Queen. I told him no.

Sir Martin guided me to the Queen and said: 'Ma'am, this is Gary Newbon, whose idea this whole thing was. He also produced the film.'

I had three minutes with Her Majesty and when I got home I told my wife Katie how excited I was to have had that conversation. Katie asked me: 'What did you talk about?'

I said I could not remember. You cannot ask the royals questions and must just answer theirs, which I did, but I was on automatic mode! I just kept thinking: 'Her Majesty is smaller than I had always imagined. This is one of the most famous people in the world. I was eight years old when I watched the Coronation in 1953 on the TV. I am talking to the Queen and nobody else is involved. Wow!'

Silly really, but that meeting with the Queen and having dinner with opera singer Luciano Pavarotti are the only occasions when I have really been in awe of anyone.

I was to meet the Queen Mother just twice more.

At the end of the BAFTA event, Sir Martin said they would like to invite fifteen of us who had been involved with the production to come to tea with the Queen Mother at Clarence House the next week.

When we arrived there, I was surprised to see the great BBC commentator Sir Peter O'Sullevan. I was the only one in our party that he knew. Obviously the Queen Mother thought it would be a good idea to include Peter.

We brought a video of the documentary and some framed still pictures taken at the various filming locations. We had a really enjoyable tea and when they said goodbye and we were walking down the drive the penny dropped in my mind. They were really saying, with some style: 'Thank you, but we will not be seeing you again. It is over.' Classy, but as it turned out I was to see Her Majesty one more time.

Central TV brought out the VHS, as it was in those days, of *Royal Champion* and decided to give all the profits to the Injured Jockeys Fund, of which the Queen Mother was a big supporter. I handed over the cheque with my Central managing director Leslie Hill to Her Majesty at Newbury Races.

I was so sad when the Queen Mother passed away on 30 March 2002 aged 101 years. I have covered many sports events and been responsible for or involved in many TV shows. But *Royal Champion* was a special experience. I am so proud to have made it.

CHAPTER SEVENTEEN

1994–98

Jack Charlton was the eldest of the famous Charlton brothers, who were in the England team that won the 1966 World Cup final at Wembley.

Jack, the taller of the two, played centre-half and spent his club career with Leeds. Bobby was the goalscoring centre-forward who was with Manchester United for nearly all his career. I knew both very well, although as I write Bobby has dementia.

Jack did well as a manager after playing for Leeds from 1952–73. He was a real star turn as the Republic of Ireland manager and became a folk hero as an Englishman in the Emerald Isle. He was in charge from 1986 to 1996, qualifying for two World Cups and a European Championship.

Some of the Irish were not so impressed when he took the job, but they soon came to love him. He took them to the quarter-finals of the 1990 World Cup in Italy. They lost to the hosts in Rome 1–0. Salvatore Schillaci scored the only goal after an Irish lapse in concentration.

Jack, noting that many of his squad played their club football in England, had changed the tactics from the continental style of a deep-lying midfield to a 4-4-2 formation. He had his team pressing the opposition to such an extent that the ball-playing opponents made mistakes. It paid off. Two years earlier, he had taken the Irish to the final stages of Euro 1988.

He became a popular man. He also had a bit of a reputation of being careful with money in those days. The Irish captain, Andy Townsend, told me how one day, back in Dublin, he shamed Charlton into taking the squad into a pub after training and buying them all a drink. He did, but he insisted on paying by cheque. That cheque and many more he wrote in pubs across Ireland are all uncashed, framed and hung in the bars. There was method in Jack's madness.

I worked with Jack quite regularly when he was an ITV pundit, but when the Republic of Ireland qualified for the 1994 World Cup in the USA, I was selected as ITV's reporter to work with him on a daily basis.

In the old days, we (the in vision/commentators' talent) were all allowed first-class travel on the railways and business class in the air. However, if you travelled with Jack and wanted to visit him, you had to move back into the other seats. 'We travel with the people,' Jack used to say, and indeed he was a man of the people, even if he was a millionaire!

England had failed to qualify for the USA tournament under Graham Taylor, as had the rest of the UK teams, so I was given Ireland.

I was looking forward to working with John Cherry, my Central TV cameraman, and we were paired together. The union restrictions had been broken up years before so John, with twenty pieces of equipment, picked me up from home at 8 a.m. a few days before the tournament began. John lived in the Black Country area of the West Midlands; I lived in Solihull (as I still do).

American Airlines were the travel sponsors of the World Cup and we flew from Manchester Airport to Chicago after a three-hour delay taking off due to an engine problem. We therefore missed our connection to Orlando in Florida, where the Irish were housed in a Hilton in the north of the city.

We eventually arrived at the hotel after midnight local time and I was totally exhausted, so I pulled rank and said to Cherry: 'Sorry mate, I cannot help you unload the stuff; I'm going to bed!' Or so I thought.

As I handed my passport and credit card over to the bell captain at the reception desk to check me in, I heard a crash behind me. There were two massive automatic sliding doors and two people, rather worse for wear, were trying to negotiate them. They were the Irish manager Jack Charlton and his press officer John Givens, the brother of the former Irish international, QPR and Birmingham City player Don Givens. 'Gerry,' said Jack when they finally came up to me. 'You are coming with us.' And the two of them dragged me into the lift, leaving my passport and credit card with a complete stranger!

The Irish were on the top floor, and as we came out of the lift I was confronted by a guard with an automatic gun. 'Gerry is with us,' said Jack, and I was led into his suite, where there was a (free) barrel of Guinness that had been given to him by the brewers' American arm.

I should explain that for all the years I knew Jack, he called me Gerry. Even though he worked for ITV, he would not change. Indeed, the head of sport and head of football asked Jack to call me Gary on air when I interviewed him, not Gerry. Jack refused, saying: 'He is bloody Gerry, and he is staying Gerry.'

At least Jack was consistent. He often could not remember players' names when he was commentating or even in his own teams that he managed. I must confess I used to love it, because in match coverage our commentator Brian Moore used to have to say: 'Actually, Jack was talking to Gary Newbon there. It is just that he calls him "Gerry".' I used to relish all those extra name checks on air.

Anyway, back to Jack's suite in the early hours of my arrival. Tired as I was, I drank the Guinness with Jack and John, who had already been on a heavy night of drinking in downtown Orlando. I kept up with the pace, even though I had been up for well over twenty-four hours, as I thought it would be a good bonding session. I need not have bothered, as it turned out.

At 5 a.m., Jack asked us to leave. I slept through to 3 p.m. in the afternoon. After a shave and a shower, I went down to the hotel's outdoor swimming pool to join Jack and his staff and players.

Jack greeted me with: 'Hallo, Gerry – when did you arrive?'

He had no recollection of the night before! I had wasted my time, although Jack and his players ultimately were a dream to work with. The tournament was such great fun.

Jack – the man of the people – dismissed the security in the bar, allowing all the fans to join the whole Irish party. It was a little chaotic, but there was never a problem.

The opening match for Ireland was in New Jersey in the Giants Stadium. They would be playing against Italy, and therefore had a chance to avenge the 1990 quarter-final defeat. It was 1–0 again but this time to the Irish, with Ray Houghton scoring in the eleventh minute.

The Irish had been given attendance money of 1 million US dollars to cover their expenses for the group stage. I do not want to be too uncharitable, as I was treated so well, but it must have been a cheap Hilton, because the roof leaked in some places when the heavy rain fell. The plane was the oldest I have travelled on in these modern times. It could not even transport all the luggage! But we all got through it fine.

The day of the match, I was joined over breakfast by two freelance radio producers from London. They were Patrick Campbell and Clare Davison, who ran Campbell Davison. I had never done radio before, so they felt I was a fresh talent for the soon-to-be-launched TalkRadio.

I must admit I struck a hard financial deal because I really was not fussed. I had a packed TV career as I was also head of sport at Central TV, but they still met my price. I loved working with them, and before long TalkRadio morphed into talkSPORT. More on that later.

Back in Orlando, I was looking for feature pieces to film. I spent a lot of time talking to the wives, who were staying in another hotel. I asked them if I could interview them about it all around the swimming pool while they were either swimming or sunbathing. It was certainly a glamorous report, although I am not sure some of the players were keen on the idea. The wives and girlfriends all spoke very well and seemed to enjoy it.

The players had a darts tournament, which was quite competitive, but the mood was always relaxed. One day I was coming down in the hotel lift with the Irish captain Andy Townsend and his wife Jackie, and the conversation turned to his future. He told me he wanted to work in TV, and the result was he joined me on his return while he was still captain of Aston Villa. He is still enjoying an excellent second career. I interviewed him briefly in a Birmingham restaurant and gave him a role immediately.

The Orlando heat was getting to the full-back Steve Staunton and Jack Charlton. They lost 2–1 to Mexico at the Citrus Bowl. During the game, Charlton had a big argument with an official who was stopping substitute John Aldridge from going on the pitch for some time after Tommy Coyne had been replaced and sat on the Irish bench. As a result, Charlton was suspended by FIFA for the final match against Norway. Charlton had to watch the match from the commentary position, but the result was 0–0, which meant they qualified for the round of sixteen against the Netherlands.

With my blessing, Jack used to pop into my room for one of the cigars I used to foolishly smoke in those days. I also took him shopping in my hired Lincoln Town Car. After the Norway game, I told Jack I felt they could go a long way again in the competition. Jack groaned and confided in me: 'If not, I just want to be unlucky losers.'

I think the heat was getting to him.

They went out of the 1994 World Cup in the next stage losing 2–0 to the Netherlands with goals by Dennis Bergkamp and Wim Jonk.

Jack Charlton was awarded the OBE in 1974 and in 1996 was granted honorary Irish citizenship. He was a giant in both the English and Irish game and left me with great memories. Like his brother Bobby, he was a top man. I was sad at Jack's passing in July 2020 from dementia and lymphoma at the age of eighty-five.

My World Cup continued. I was booked on a plane from Orlando to Boston, where Italy were to play Spain in the quarter-finals at the Foxborough Stadium. They wanted a piece for *Dallas Breakfast*, the ITV show that Tony Francis fronted in London. It was a programme that contained off-beat items. My brief was nothing to do with the match or players, and I was to do no interviews with the respective supporters. They just wanted something fun.

I was reading the *USA Today* newspaper on the plane and noticed that the Boston Red Sox baseball team were playing the California Angels in a series of matches at Fenway Park that night and for the next few days. That was it. Talk to the superstar baseball players and listen to what they think of the World Cup and so on.

As soon as I checked in to the Marriott Hotel in Copley Plaza, using my trusty contacts book I tracked down the Red Sox communications manager Dick Blayney. He said he was busy, but he promised he would leave a ticket at willcall and said I should have dinner with the media guests in the press box, where I could talk to him about what I wanted after he had finished his work.

Wow! A great start. Would a top English football team have done that for an unknown American TV reporter who was not a rights holder? I do not think so; mind you, with the mass of modern media, including online, I am not sure the Red Sox would today either.

The conversation with Dick, after everyone was going home, was quite amazing. I explained what I wanted. He said he was not sure most of the players even knew the 'soccer' World Cup was taking place. He did think centre-fielder Lee Tinsley was a 'soccer' lover.

Dick then said he would line up the players before batting practice for me to interview. I had to be set up well before 5.30 p.m. I asked who owned the rights to the match and was told that the Red Sox did and that my cameraman should film it for ITV at the pit near the third base. Wow! I could not believe my luck.

John Cherry arrived the next day. Lee Tinsley was brilliant. Only one player would not co-operate. The others did not know anything about the 'soccer', but they just asked what I wanted them to say! The team's superstar Mo Vaughn and the coach Butch Hobson were brilliant and nailed my script on the first take!

Boston won the match and I discovered afterwards that our commentator Brian Moore loved baseball and had paid to see the game! I have supported the Red Sox ever since and sometimes catch their games on one of our satellite channels.

The World Cup final took place in the Rose Bowl, Pasadena, on 17 July. It was a dull 0–0 after extra time before Brazil beat Italy 3–2 in a penalty shoot-out decider. It was the first World Cup final to be decided on penalties and Brazil became the first nation to win four World Cups.

Three more stories spring to mind. In the World Cup final build-up, my colleague Trevor East invited me down to Santa Monica for dinner. On the way back to Pasadena on a very busy highway, a tyre burst on my hired car. I pulled over in a scary situation. I opened the boot and there was a spare tyre but no tools. I waved furiously at all the passing cars, including an LAPD police patrol car. None stopped, but I got lucky. The police car came back.

'What's the problem, buddy?' I explained what had happened. He asked me where I was from and why I was here, and when he realised I was British, he asked a bizarre question: 'Do you know Eric Bristow?'

I said he had actually been a good mate for many years; I had covered him playing darts and even made a documentary on him for ATV in his very early days.

I asked them if they had been to the UK. They had never been out of the USA, but they were keen darts players and had a team at the LAPD. They had seen Bristow on one of their TV channels showing darts.

By this time the breakdown van they had radioed for had arrived. I told the darts-playing policeman that if he gave me his name and the police station address, I would get Eric to sign a photo and send an autographed message. He then told the breakdown mechanic not to charge me and the police were then on their way.

I always keep my word, so I got Eric to do that for me. He signed it: 'To the LAPD darts team. Thanks for saving my friend's arse! Eric Bristow.' My thanks to his manager Dick Allix for arranging it and sending it to the police guys. I often wondered if that photo still hangs in their darts room.

The night before the final, two mutual friends, Norman and Carol Gidney from Stratford-upon-Avon, rang to invite me and Ron Atkinson to a Three Tenors concert in the nearby Los Angeles Dodgers Stadium. They had VIP seats to see José Carreras, Plácido Domingo and Luciano Pavarotti.

We were standing at the bar after we arrived, and I was buying some drinks with my back to Big Ron. He suddenly kicked me. I ignored him as he often winds me up. He kicked harder. I turned round and his mouth was wide open in shock. His all-time hero Frank Sinatra was walking past with his wife Barbara.

Ron then recovered and said he had to go back to the hotel, even though the concert had not yet begun. I asked why, and he said he had to ring everyone back home to tell them that he had just seen Sinatra walk past!

We did not let him. Instead, we took our seats in front of the

Hollywood actor David Hasselhoff (*Baywatch* and all that) and a bit behind Sinatra and Gene Kelly.

On the day of the final, Atkinson was the co-commentor to Brian Moore. He was dressed in a white Texan hat, blue flowered shirt and shorts. Ron was a big fan of J. R. in the soap opera *Dallas*. Ron pretended to be all sorts of stars and famous footballers at times.

Anyway, we were standing outside the Rose Bowl and it was hot, very hot. Sir Bert and Lady Barbara Millichip (chairman of the FA and Ron's boss at West Bromwich Albion) walked past without recognising Ron, who greeted them with a Texan accent: 'G'day. How y'all doin'?' 'Very well,' they answered and walked on. Ron has a quick, good sense of humour, and it was probably funnier than it reads. But Ron certainly enjoyed that greeting.

The next World Cup was four years later in France. I was ITV's interviewer/reporter with England. We were based at La Baule, a fashionable seaside resort in the Loire region on the Atlantic Coast in western France. The media were housed in the five-star Hôtel L'Hermitage, which features 200 rooms and suites with access to a wonderful beach.

The England party were based four miles away, also in La Baule. The BBC and ITV had studios made up in the team's quarters to do live interviews with the players and manager.

England's opening match was in Marseilles. The nearby airport was at Saint-Nazaire. It was so small that two planes were needed for the flight south – one for the England team and staff, the other for the media.

I had visited the Saint-Nazaire docks when I was very small. My father Jack had cheekily driven his Jaguar past the security there when we were on a French holiday in the 1960s. Hitler had built concrete-covered pens to house his submarines. My father's Handley Page Hampden (he was a bomb loader/wireless operator in the plane in the war) was one of the planes ordered to smash the concrete and destroy the subs on a bombing raid. They failed to break the pens and he wanted to discover why from the ground. I can't remember if he did, but I doubt it!

During the build-up to the opening match, Sir Alex Ferguson wrote in his column in the *Sunday Times* that the England manager Glenn Hoddle should be picking a young David Beckham. The press made quite a thing of this and other selection decisions he had made, so the night before the match, I put it to Hoddle that he might be fed up with the distraction.

I should point out that during the 1998 World Cup, ITV and the BBC had decided to broadcast all our TV shows and sport into both the media and team camps – the players could watch their favourite shows and the media could monitor what we were reporting rather than waiting to hear it from their sports editors in London. I was very supportive of this move. Unfortunately, it led to a bit of trouble for me when the media heard what I'd said about their giving Hoddle a hard time. The press can dish it out, but, like some football managers, they're not always very good at taking it.

As we were going through the X-ray machines at the Saint-Nazaire airport, I became aware of something stirring among the press. I was sitting on my own as Martin Samuel, who then wrote for the *Daily Express*, waited until most of the other reporters were around him and approached me. He then said that he and his colleagues weren't happy that I'd critiqued them in the questions I'd put to Hoddle.

I told him that I could help him with that in future. I would have our programmes switched off in the media hotel and they would have to rely on London telling them what was said.

I actually like the press and Martin, but I was not going to take that after supporting the move to give them the coverage. I had no intention of switching it off, but they were not to know. To his credit, Martin apologised and has been very respectful since. In return I have watched his writing and reputation blossom. He was a big signing for the *Daily Mail* and then *The Times*, winning plenty of awards in the process.

Hostility to broadcasters has been a challenge over the years. I have had experienced players who would not do interviews and were in fact quite obstructive at times. I would like to think that I have never been obstructive to the media. Like I said, I just ask that they spell my name right and use an old photo.

I can only think of two occasions when I have asked for a correction. Mike Walters in the defunct *Today* newspaper wrote that I had embarrassed a manager at the Walsall–Chelsea cup tie to back up his criticism of my interviewing Leicester City's manager, Brian Little, on the whistle at a play-off final (that is what we do!). I was not even at the Walsall–Chelsea match, so he had to correct that one. Also, there was the aforementioned instance of the *Observer* quoting Jimmy Greaves as being let go from Central TV without any explanation. I pointed out that I had driven halfway from my Birmingham studios to Jimmy's home to buy him lunch at the Old Bridge in Huntingdon to explain my decision.

Otherwise, if you're critiqued and it stands up, you should take it on the chin. If you are in the public eye, you will benefit from the exposure (providing you haven't done anything truly harmful), so when the flak comes just console yourself that few people will remember it.

Back to the World Cup. England won their opening match against Tunisia 2–0, with goals from Alan Shearer and Paul Scholes. We had a chance with this England team.

Next up was Romania, to whom England lost 2–1 after Michael Owen equalised in the eighty-third minute. Dan Petrescu scored the winner in the ninetieth in Toulouse. That was on 22 June.

The afternoon before the match, I had tea with the great French hero Just Fontaine. He was the record goal scorer in a World Cup, with thirteen for France in 1958. I once bought a record he made as a singer. Apple Music have his top songs and records.

Also at this stage, Brian Barwick and my colleague Jeff Farmer decided to visit us from the World Cup TV headquarters in Paris.

I learnt a long time ago that when on location you should never tell head office that you are staying in a lovely place and having a great time, because it's probably a much better time and facilities than them!

So when I was talking down the quality of our accommodation, I laid it on obviously too thick. And all of a sudden, Brian and Jeff were on their way! Oh dear.

When they arrived they were shocked to see how great L'Hermitage in fact was. Brian then booked the hotel's fish restaurant in front on the beach, which is described as 'a romantic gourmet dining by the water's edge'. Oh dear, Gary, this is getting worse.

I pleaded with Barwick to book elsewhere, as I told him I had heard that the Eden was too expensive (we had been using it every night, and my dad had always taught me to be a big tipper, especially to the maître d).

It was all to no avail. What happened next is still told by my cameraman Ian O'Donoghue, known as O'D. He is a fine operator and wonderful, funny as well. He was with Brian, Jeff, our producer Simon Moore (son of Brian) and me as we entered the Eden.

The maître d: 'Ah! Monsieur Newbon. Lovely to see you again. Your usual table next to the window by the beach?'

Barwick kept muttering: 'Your usual table!' Luckily we had been producing the goods and Barwick took it all in good spirit, but it was not my finest moment.

Back to the football. Next, England played Colombia in Lens, the final match of the group stage. England recorded the win they needed: 2–0 again, with first-half goals by Darren Anderton and David Beckham. At the end of the match, I was on the touchline and asked goalkeeper David Seaman if I could have his gloves. 'Safe Hands' then peels them off and signs them. I still have them today!

David paid me a great compliment recently by saying the players respected me. It meant a lot to be told that and to know that they always felt they could trust me.

Next we were off to Saint-Étienne for the round of sixteen on 30 June between Argentina and England, which was to finish in great disappointment. England lost 4–3 on penalties after drawing 2–2 having been down to ten players.

The turning point was in the forty-seventh minute, when David Beckham was given a red card by the Danish referee Kim Milton Nielsen. The Argentine captain Diego Simeone fouled Beckham by pushing him in the back and the England youngster foolishly kicked out with a mild kick at Simeone while on the floor. Simeone rolled around as if he had been shot, but it was enough for the referee to deem it violent conduct and show the red. Simeone received just a yellow. Beckham's retaliation was more of a tap or flick, but he still should not have done it. I thought the referee could have given Beckham a yellow, but he did not!

Simeone had brought about his side's early lead in the sixth minute, when England's goalkeeper David Seaman mistimed a challenge and Simeone left his leg out for the fall and was given the penalty from which Gabriel Batistuta scored. Even then Simeone, a fiery coach these days, asked the referee to book Seaman.

Then Alan Shearer equalised with another penalty in the tenth minute, before eighteen-year-old Michael Owen scored a wonder goal six minutes later after a pass by Beckham. Javier Zanetti then made it 2–2 on the stroke of half-time.

England battled on bravely and in extra time and right near the end did have the ball in the net but it was correctly ruled off for a foul on the goalkeeper Carlos Roa when England's defender Sol Campbell headed in what would have been a heroic winner. Defender – something I had to correct Hoddle on in the live postmatch interview on the pitch. I was being escorted down the touchline to do the interview and was level with the disallowed decision.

I had to put some tough questions to the England head coach particularly with the Beckham sending off. We had 23.8 million viewers watching our coverage on ITV, which at the time was the biggest UK television audience for a single channel for a live football match.

You never think about figures when you are appearing on those shows even if you are aware of a potential high figure. It is just as well. When you are performing, you must concentrate on what you are seeing, what others say and not think about the size of your audience. It's something with experience that your conscious learns to deal with, but your subconscious may be different. It took me a few early years to cope with it.

The dramatic penalty shoot-out saw England eliminated yet again, as they had been in 1990. This time the Argentinian goalkeeper, Carlos Roa, saved penalties first from Paul Ince and then David Batty, who had never taken a penalty before in his career. Seaman had saved the opening penalty from Hernan Crespo.

Our commentator Brian Moore was beating himself up for putting his co-commentator and great friend Kevin Keegan on the spot before Batty's penalty attempt, asking Keegan if Batty would score. What could Kevin answer except 'yes'? We consoled Brian while Keegan, ever the top man, told Brian it was not a problem. All in the heat of the moment.

Poor Beckham was castigated by many back home; the worst instance was the awful burning effigies of the man who was to be England's saviour and captain; he was to score the heroic last-gasp winner in a World Cup qualifier against Greece to send England to the 2002 World Cup in Japan.

CHAPTER EIGHTEEN

OVERCOMING A STROKE

My last World Cup was to be in 2002, with the final stages in Japan and South Korea. I was based in Japan with England.

An indelible mark was left on my life on 2 February that year. As previously mentioned, I suffered a stroke, which put my chances of working that June in real jeopardy.

I had already suffered three TIA (transient ischemic attacks, or 'mini-strokes'), which had put me in hospital twice, the second time by ambulance. I was released on the condition that I saw Professor Adrian Williams privately. The problems, as it turned out, had been building up for several years. I had suffered unaccountable dizziness and feeling rough without any doctor discovering why. Unfortunately I had just shrugged these symptoms off.

After the latest TIA, my wife begged me not to go to Manchester to cover the United–Sunderland match for ITV. I compromised by going the night before by train and was booked into the Lowry Hotel in the city centre.

I ordered room service and suddenly, lying in bed, I could hardly feel my legs. The next morning I went to the bathroom feeling sick and terrible and could not stand up. I dived onto my bed and rang Jeff Farmer, who was the editor of that night's highlights show.

'Jeff, I feel terrible and cannot do the show.' I explained what had happened and Jeff, knowing me so well, knew it was serious for me to pull out. I told him, somewhat foolishly, that I needed to get back to Birmingham, where I was under a specialist. He booked Archie, a private driver in Manchester that ITV Sport used. Exhausted, I fell asleep, until Archie woke me up near Birmingham Airport. He did not know where I lived.

It turned out that I had suffered an actual stroke while I was asleep in the car and I was shocked to discover that the right side of my body was paralysed and I could not speak. I used my chin to tap my number into my phone and threw it forward to Archie, who spoke to my wife for directions to our house nearby in Solihull.

Then Katie rang Professor Williams, who thankfully on this Saturday had his phone on. He asked Katie to drive me to the Priory Hospital in Edgbaston, where he would meet me in a private ward room. He confirmed it was a stroke. This is where the supply of blood to the brain is reduced or blocked completely. It prevents the brain tissue getting oxygen. It is obviously very serious.

I just wanted to sleep. I can only describe the feeling as like having flu many times over. I recall Professor Williams telling Katie that I might need a big operation with a bypass, although he wanted lots of X-rays first. He said no visitors, apart from her. (You'll remember that my good friend Ron Atkinson nonetheless made an appearance, which was greatly appreciated by me if not my angry wife!)

As it happened, I did not need any operations. What was very important, however, was to get my speech back as soon as possible.

Stroke victims do need a speech therapist in asap. When mine arrived the next day, both she and I were very surprised. She did not know before arriving who the patient was going to be. I was in the same situation re. her.

It was Penny-Anne O'Donnell, the daughter of friends of mine. I had given the speech at her eighteenth birthday ten years earlier. She was to save my speech and career.

Penny-Anne was excellent, and by the end of the week I was talking properly again. The physiotherapist also visited me and within days had me walking up and down the nearby stairs. I was on the mend.

After a week of intensive X-rays, it was decided I could go home. But I would need fifteen weeks of exercise, diet, no alcohol, a bit of golf and lots of walks.

My emotions, though, were playing havoc, and I was soon crying as I read lovely letters coming in from Brian Clough, Mike Ingham, Alan Green from BBC Radio, and many more. It was like reading my obituary before I had died. Phone calls from the England goalkeeper David James, Terry Venables, Sir Alex Ferguson, Trevor Francis and lots of others were moving me to tears again.

Moving forwards, Brian Barwick sensibly decided I had to prove my fitness before he would allow me to the World Cup.

Professor Williams had advised I did not drive, as that may have been one of the many factors that contributed to my stroke. The pressure of TV; drinking too much wine, smoking Cuban cigars, high blood pressure that had been detected a long time ago and the fact that I had a family history of strokes were obvious others. Central TV always treated me brilliantly, and I was able to choose a driver called Paul Young.

When I recovered, I picked a European Champions League

match at Old Trafford for my first game back because I knew that Sir Alex Ferguson, who had rung me three times during my recovery period, would help me as ever that night. It was 10 April and the second leg of the quarter-final with Deportivo de La Coruña. United had won the first leg 2–0 in Coruna eight days earlier with David Beckham scoring a terrific opening goal.

Well, even though it ended up being a victory for United, the game did not go quite as planned; David Beckham suffered an injury on the far side from my position between the team benches. He was the victim of a heavy tackle by Deportivo's Aldo Duscher.

I moved as quickly as I could as David was taken to an ambulance in the players' tunnel. I jumped in the back and asked the club doctor Mike Stone what the injury was. He said that he thought David had broken his metatarsal.

I didn't have a clue what a metatarsal was, let alone the ability to spell it, so I asked the doctor what it was. He said that it was a bone in the foot, and with that the ambulance sped off to the hospital.

I messaged to our control scanner van where for the first time everyone, as well as most of our viewers, heard the word 'metatarsal'. There are five of these bones in each foot. Sir Alex explained that England's captain was probably a doubt now for the World Cup.

This injury takes four to six weeks to heal and then there is usually two weeks of rehabilitation. So both of us were doubtful, although in the end I am delighted to report that both of us were there on 2 June for the opening group match against Sweden. David leading out the England team; I in my position as match reporter.

Going back to Manchester, however, this 'fitness test' match for me at Old Trafford was still a hectic night. United did win the second leg 3–2, with Ole Gunnar Solskjær scoring twice and Ryan Giggs once. Deportivo had two players sent off in the second half – Lionel Scaloni and Aldo Duscher.

After I had done all my post-match interviews, I climbed back into my car, exhausted, and asked Paul Young to drive me home.

Being married with three lovely children, I perhaps had my priorities wrong in developing such an obsession with making the World Cup! But I have always put work first, although you are certainly soon forgotten after you die! Thankfully I was nowhere near that point, but I had a lucky escape with my health, and not for the last time.

I convinced Barwick that I was fit enough to travel and work in Japan. Beckham was to do the same but his best man, Manchester United's right-back Gary Neville, was not in the same position. Gary had broken his foot and could not recover in time.

Gary and his brother Phil have always been media friendly and interested in speaking to us, despite the football writers being quite cruel during the 2000 European Championships, dubbing them 'the ugly brothers', for instance. Out of order.

It had been the same with Graham Taylor when he was the England manager. As the son of a football writer, Graham was always helpful with the media, but it did not stop *The Sun* dubbing him, cruelly, a 'turnip head' when England failed to qualify for the 1994 World Cup. Talk about the hand that feeds you. Criticism may be merited, but not personal insults.

I was very friendly with Gary and Phil's father, Neville, who was also their agent. I talked to Neville about Gary being on the ITV panel in London for this World Cup. And it happened. When I moved to Sky in 2004, I soon persuaded Neville that Gary should

My two-year folly as owner and developer of the Solihull Barons. On the left of me is Chuck Taylor and on the right is Barry Skrudland, who, believe it or not, was sacked for being too violent. An ice-hockey player!
Author collection

Jack Charlton, a playing and managerial legend who was great fun but refused orders from the ITV bosses to call me Gary; he always called me Gerry!
Author collection

After filming a documentary with her, I cheekily asked the Queen Mother to pose for a picture with her former jockey Terry Biddlecombe and my TV film crew.
Author collection

My proudest day: receiving the MBE at Buckingham Palace with my wonderful family. From left to right: Neil, Katie, me, Claire, Laurence.
© Palace Photos

One of the three interviews I did with Muhammad Ali. I used to sneak out of boarding school to watch Ali's fight highlights; who would have thought I'd end up interviewing him? Author collection

The ITV talent for the 1998 World Cup in France. Has there been a better punditry line up in the history of television? Author collection

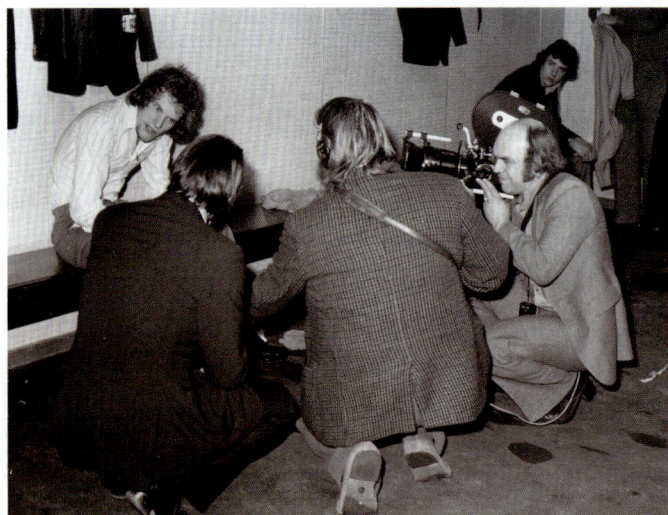

Interviewing Andy Gray when he was a playing star; he later became a television punditry giant. Author collection

Me and Jimmy Greaves, the footballer who turned into a television legend. He started his career with me.
Author collection

Interviewing great friend, wonderful personality and brilliant footballer Kevin Keegan.
Author collection

26 October 1973, the best day of my life: marrying Katie. Author collection

With the England manager, Bobby Robson, at the Azteca Stadium in Mexico City for the 1986 World Cup.
Author collection

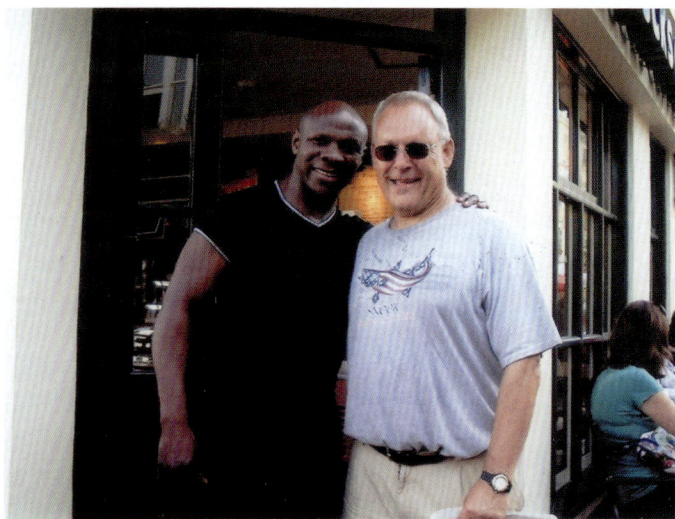

With one of the key characters in my TV career: the unpredictable, one-off Chris Eubank.
Author collection

Aston Villa's goalkeeper Nigel Spink, after his heroics as the young substitute in the 1982 European Cup final.
Author collection

With David Beckham at the 2002 World Cup in Japan. Not that he was ungrateful, but he left the bonsai on the table! Author collection

One of the few interviewees from whom I never asked for a contact number! Author collection

Interviewing Muhammad Ali again after being knocked down by a car on my way to the Variety Club lunch in 1979. Author collection

In the middle of a famous moment: Brian Clough had just told Trevor Francis to take his hands out of his pockets. This was a couple of years before he signed Francis as the first million-pound footballer. Author collection

With Aston Villa's European Cup, their manager Tony Barton, and my colleagues Jeff Farmer, John Killeen and Sid Kilby. Author collection

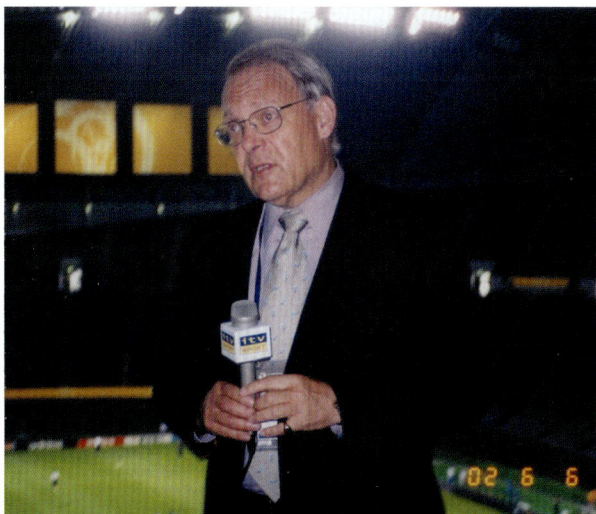

Presenting as a reporter in Sapporo, Japan, during the 2002 World Cup.
Author collection

With the great Sir Alex Ferguson outside Château Lascombes after a wine-tasting session in Bordeaux.
Author collection

With one of our finest athletes Sebastian Coe, who became a great friend at the 1980 Moscow Olympics and went on to achieve even greater feats, such as helping to bring the Olympics to London and moving up from Sir Sebastian to Lord Coe. Author collection

The last of the seven interviews I did with the greatest footballer of all time, Pelé. Author collection

Sitting on the Aston Villa substitutes bench at the 1982 European Cup final. The injured goalkeeper Jimmy Rimmer is on the far left, and the gap next to me is where the substitute goalkeeper, Nigel Spink, had been sitting.
© Bob Thomas Sports Photography / Getty Images

cross too and that I could help facilitate the move. The Sky Sports deputy managing director Andy Melvin agreed and met and signed Gary. The rest is history. Gary is brilliant.

On 1 September one of England's great displays was the 5–1 thrashing of Germany in Munich's Olympic Stadium – the last time the German national team played there. Michael Owen scored a hat-trick with goals added by Steven Gerrard and Emile Heskey.

I went to Munich as the guest of sponsors Nationwide and re-member walking from the hotel to the stadium with Alan Ball Jr and Jimmy Armfield, listening to their experiences with Sir Alf Ramsey. Bally recalled his debut for England against Yugoslavia in Belgrade. The England manager was a man of few words. Before the game, he just said: 'Welcome, Alan.' He did not give group half-time chats, preferring to speak to individuals. During the interval, he sat with Ball and asked if the player thought that the captain Bobby Moore was a good passer of the football, then a great passer and finally 'possibly one of the best passers of a football in the world?' Alan agreed with all three, to which Sir Alf responded: 'Well, in that case, would you please stop taking the f****** ball off him?'

Jimmy chipped in with the fact that he was captain for Sir Alf's first match. He did not speak before the 5–1 thrashing by France but enquired of Armfield afterwards: 'Do we always play like that, Jimmy?'

Sir Alf was cutting at times.

The laughter and thrill of England's great performance was to be saddened by a phone call from Ron Atkinson. I had reported the match for talkSPORT and then hosted the phone-in show. When I finished, I received an urgent message to ring Ron. He told me that our commentator, Brian Moore, had died earlier that day at his home aged sixty-nine. A great commentator and an absolute gentleman.

So we were off to Japan for a friendly in South Korea. ITV and the BBC were allowed to stay in the England luxury Westin Hotel on Awaji Island. I travelled from London with Trevor Brooking, a lovely man who deserved his knighthood after great service as a player for England and West Ham. He did a fine job too for the BBC, and he was going to work with my old schoolmate John Motson.

Conscious of the fact that I was still recovering from a stroke, my producer Simon Moore protected me as best he could, sending me down to the hotel spa to relax once I had finished my interviews and reports. There I would meet up with one of the FA members, my great friend Doug Ellis, the chairman of Aston Villa. I soon got stronger.

Back in the 1996 Euros, the FA's David Davies had introduced press officers. Access had always been easy before then, but David was clever and built a media marquee at the England training camp at Bisham Abbey and divided it into sections of press and radio/television. There was always plenty of food and tea/coffee/soft drinks for the journalists, but the control of access to managers and players had begun. I understand that the media has massively expanded these days, but the press officers at one or two of the bigger clubs will often try to sanitise the statements/interviews.

There are, in fairness to the clubs, huge demands these days from so many media outlets, including news channels and online websites. Club media offices have needed to expand; the days of there being just twelve trusted journalists have long gone.

It isn't my problem these days, but I was left very angry in 1996 at the Euros when Gareth Southgate missed the penalty in the semi-final shoot-out between England and Germany at Wembley; Gareth was happy to talk to me (I had been invited by Gareth to his wedding the following year), but the FA press officer prevented the interview.

I have to say though, Paul Newman was in charge of the FA press office by 2002 and he was really helpful. We got most of what we needed, although we were kept well away from the players the rest of the time. There was a 'neutral ground' coffee bar, and I spent quite a lot of time there talking with Sol Campbell.

The England manager at the time was Sven-Göran Eriksson, and I never could work him out. He was always friendly and had a lot of success around Europe. His manager/agent Athole Still was a long-standing mate of mine from our Olympic days, and he certainly did a good job for Sven on the financial side.

I first came across Sven in Europe when he was in charge of the Italian team Lazio and interviewed him after a European match in Rome. He was most helpful on interviews. Like many Scandinavians his English was excellent.

He certainly arrived in England with a good football reputation, later taking charge of Manchester City and my team Leicester, where I used to have a post-match drink with him in his manager's office.

His romance with the Italian–American lawyer Nancy Dell'Olio was well reported. I met Sven and Nancy several times and was quite fascinated by their relationship. Sven was certainly a charmer and a gentleman to deal with.

I liked Japan, but the language was a real problem. Not many people there spoke English and it was difficult to work out signs.

Away from Japan many people of course do speak English, which has meant that the British are spoilt, and many of us do not speak other languages. However in France, Spain and Italy you can usually work out shops, signs, drinks, airports and some foods and so on; since the phonetics of Asian languages are so different, I found navigating Japan nigh-on impossible.

Thankfully I had an Oxford University graduate called Alex, who spoke perfect Japanese, as my interpreter. He was great fun.

This World Cup lasted from 31 May to the final on 20 June. It was the first World Cup to be hosted jointly, the first in Asia and the first outside the Americas and Europe. Both South Korea and Japan had ten venues each – many newly built for the tournament. There was no World Cup venue in Tokyo – the first time a capital of the host country did not have one.

There were some early shocks. The holders France were knocked out of the group stage collecting only one point and failing to score a goal. The second favourites to win the tournament, Argentina, were also eliminated at the group stage. The South Korean team had an incredible run, managing to reach the semi-finals after beating the likes of Portugal, Italy and Spain in the process. There were plenty of stories to report!

On the pitch England qualified for the knockout round of sixteen by finishing second in their group. They were level with Sweden who had scored two more goals. At the draw, their group had been labelled 'the Group of Death', since it contained Sweden, England, Argentina and Nigeria.

England drew their opening match with Sweden in Saitama with Sol Campbell giving England the lead in the twenty-fourth minute.

We then travelled to Japan's northernmost island for the second game against Argentina, which would take place in the indoor Sapporo Dome with the top referee Pierluigi Collina in charge. He was considered the best in the game and went on to officiate the final.

This was a match with many chances for both sides, but it was decided a minute before half-time when Argentina's Mauricio Pochettino (Chelsea's head coach at the time of writing) brought down Michael Owen in the penalty box. David Beckham smashed home the game's only goal from the spot.

England's goalkeeper David Seaman made a great goal-line save from Pochettino in the second half. England won against Argentina in the World Cup for the first time since 1966 and in Motty's words 'laid the ghost of both 1986 in Mexico and 1998 in France'. For Beckham, it was revenge for the Simeone red card incident in Saint-Étienne. This time, Simeone was on the losing side.

England needed to avoid losing in the final group match, and they shared a scoreless result with Nigeria in Osaka, Japan's second city. It was Denmark in the knockout stages next – the round of sixteen in Niigata. I had high hopes for England and they won 3–0 with goals from Rio Ferdinand, Michael Owen and Emile Heskey. This was a good England team that, across the competition, was putting away goals from their powerful central-defensive pairing of the talented Sol Campbell and Rio Ferdinand, as well as the usual suspects!

So to Brazil in the quarter-finals. A lot of critics thought the World Cup winners would emerge from this tie in Shizuoka. I was doing a reporting job on this one from high up behind one goal.

Michael Owen put England ahead after twenty-three minutes. Could England beat Brazil in the World Cup at last? Early days in this match of course.

Ronaldinho was to feature big time in this match. Two minutes into first-half stoppage time he went on a dazzling run before laying off a pass to the unmarked Rivaldo on the right whose cross-shot nestled in the left-hand corner. One-all.

Then five minutes into the second half, Ronaldinho had a free kick a long way out on the right and floated it directly over David Seaman, who had come off his line anticipating a cross, and into the top corner of his net. Two-one.

Then seven minutes after that, Ronaldinho was red carded by the Mexican referee Felipe Ramos for a tackle on the England defender Danny Mills. But the scoreline stayed the same, despite Brazil being a player short for the rest of the game.

It was deflating. Brazil went on to win the World Cup for the fifth time by beating Germany 2–0 in the final at Yokohama with both goals coming in the second half by their striker Ronaldo, who finished up with the Golden Boot as the tournament's top scorer with eight goals.

My job in the final was to find a top football name for the pre-match interview. I asked my good friend Sir Bobby Charlton, the 1966 England hero and a director of Manchester United. I had seen a lot of Bobby during our coverage of Manchester United. He agreed to walk around the stadium to my interview area and gave me a really good chat before the start of ITV's live coverage.

The night before the final I had dinner with John Motson, which had become a World Cup tradition for the two of us. I had covered seven World Cups for ITV; Motty had done even more for the BBC. Both companies knew we were in the same year at boarding school and so were happy for us to go ahead. Motty was fussy about food. I told him I love the raw Japanese fish. He therefore booked an Italian. It was another memorable and rather boozy dinner with my great friend, but an Italian restaurant in Yokohama in Japan? I ask you!

Meanwhile I did not realise it at this time, but two years later I was to leave ITV and join Sky Sports for an extension of my presenting career.

CHAPTER NINETEEN

THE FINAL STINT AT ITV

My school days at a private boarding school had taught me the art of leadership and how to get the best out of people. I was captain of the school's rugby first XV and turned several ordinary players who had come up from the second and third teams into part of a fit, winning machine.

When I was at Westward TV it was not long before I was making the decisions on the sports coverage. After my move to the major station ATV, I soon became sports editor and then assistant head of sport to Billy Wright.

When Central TV took over the Midlands franchise, the region was split into West Midlands based in Birmingham, East Midlands in Nottingham and South Midlands in Abingdon near Oxford. I became head of sport in Birmingham while continuing to present. Trevor East, who was to play a major part in my network presenting career, was in charge of Nottingham.

Sadly, the unions played up on the move from Elstree to Nottingham, despite Central trying desperately hard to accommodate their members. There was a story of Central even offering to pay for a nervous goldfish to be transported to a staff member's new home!

So, the opening of the Nottingham station on 1 January 1982 was delayed. Nonetheless, I needed to get to work on assembling a new team for the franchise. I had agreed to use Nick Owen as a presenter in Birmingham, but before long he left to become a great success with another ATV news presenter, Anne Diamond, in the new ITV breakfast show at TV-am. Trevor East also left for Thames TV on his way to a fine management career as head of ITV Sport, then deputy managing director of Sky Sports, moving on to be director of sport at Setanta Sports. When the latter folded, he helped form Pitch International – the TV production company that also does a multitude of other things, such as licensing football rights.

Trevor and I occasionally had our differences. We were both ambitious, but most of the time we were a great partnership. We moved regional coverage to new heights. I continued to develop even more when he left to be one of the original three hosts of Chris Tarrant's amazing *Tiswas* Saturday morning show.

As it stood then, the only team member that I would be taking over from Central TV to the new Birmingham franchise would be production expert John Killeen. A crucial appointment would be the sports editor.

Jeff Farmer, who I've mentioned throughout this book, was at the time the *Daily Mail* Midlands' football reporter, back in the days when the nationals had regional football writers. Jeff was a brilliant journalist and was the *Mail's* No. 2 football writer to Jeff Powell. He came from West Bromwich and was always very proud to have done so. When he retired he became a non-executive director of West Bromwich Albion, the club he had supported his life entire.

Jeff gave me a lift to Nottingham Forest one day when he was on the *Daily Mail*. I asked him what his ultimate career goal was. He said he wanted to be a sports editor.

I was delighted when he accepted my offer in 1981 – a few months before Central went on air. Jeff did a great job for me, and I went on to 'hire' his services for ITV network sport, as assistant to first Trevor East and then Brian Barwick. He also became ITV's head of football.

Jeff was in his forties when he joined me, having been an established writer all his professional life. It was a brave decision on his part. He was always a good sounding board for me. While he left me to deal with confrontations and did not take risks like I did, he would steady me up and make me think again on quite a few occasions.

Trevor thought it was the wrong decision to take Jeff on at his age after only newspaper experience, but he soon came to appreciate Jeff's ability and told me his initial reaction was wrong. Jeff and Trevor were to get on really well, so I was doubly pleased.

I needed another presenter and two new reporters. I approached Bob Hall, who was presenting the rugby league shows for both Granada and Yorkshire TV. I rang Paul Doherty, the head of sport at Granada, for permission, but he refused, saying Bob was under contract. I rang Bob's agent, Paul Vaughan, to explain, but Paul said he had not received a contract from Yorkshire TV, who it turned out had neglected to issue it when asked to do so by Paul. Bob Hall therefore became a presenter in my new team.

I now needed two reporters. First, I signed Barbara Slater, the British gymnast who had carried the British flag at the 1976 Montreal Olympics. Barbara, the daughter of the famous Wolves centre-half Bill Slater, was good and went on to become the director of

BBC Sport (the most powerful position in our profession). At the time of writing, she is due to leave the post in a few months' time.

My other choice was Tim Russon, the presenter who followed in Jim Rosenthal's footsteps at BBC Radio West Midlands. He was a real hard worker, and I have always believed attitude is a key factor.

The final post went to our dispatch motorbike rider Mike Inman, who spent Saturdays under our feet watching our football productions and was keen to be involved. I gave him the production job as a trainee. It was an emotional appointment for me and Mike turned out to be a key player in my successful bid years later to win the ITV football production contract. These days Mike is a Premier League matchday manager.

Mike, like all my team, was very loyal. However, I developed a problem with Killeen, who took me for an industrial tribunal claiming constructive dismissal. I had grounded him after coming to the conclusion that his expenses were out of control. I said he would have to clear expenditure with me in future, which I thought was reasonable, as did the industrial tribunal panel, who dismissed his claim after four days. John was not sacked. But he made his resignation before the tribunal, and we had accepted. It was a great shame; he had been an important member in the early days of the team.

Jeff Farmer was great fun and company. He sadly died in retirement aged seventy-nine in October 2018 after a brave two-year fight against cancer.

Bob Hall died suddenly from a heart attack in May 2022 in his mid-seventies. We were shocked at his passing. He was a good professional presenter who did an excellent job for me.

Besides those days with Trevor East, my other partnership that was to make great strides was with Paul Doherty, who was head of sport at Granada Television. Paul Doherty was very innovative in television, covering a whole range of sports shows, including showing all the goals in his area within minutes of the final whistle. He had an up-to-date scores show, which was the forerunner to Sky's *Soccer Saturday*.

He was also responsible for bringing a lot of talent through like Ian St John, commentators Clive Tyldesley and Rob Palmer, Elton Welsby, Ron Atkinson, Martin Tyler and Alistair Mann. Doherty did not pull any punches and told it as it was. It made him unpopular in some circles, but that never bothered him. He was a great operator.

Most importantly, he taught me a lot about the politics of ITV's different companies and how to challenge the London Weekend Television/Thames TV dominance.

We would attend monthly heads of sport meetings in London. One day, Paul asked me to have dinner the night before one such gathering. Doherty explained that the two London companies' sports heads got together before these head of sports network meetings to agree decisions, and now we should do the same.

When I was in Manchester for a big fight, the director of the TV coverage, Ted Ayling, said to me the night before that he was taking the team involved out for dinner (all London Weekend colleagues) and that he did not want to see me again until the fight. I was left alone in the Midlands Crowne Plaza Hotel. I was really upset and called Paul Doherty, who lived in Manchester, to join me.

Paul and I were talking in the lobby when the others returned. LWT Sport's No. 2, Stuart McConachie, was clearly unsettled at seeing us deep in conversation. I was sad when Stuart died quite young as a recluse in the south of France, but at work he did me no favours. I think he was getting wind of what was about to happen.

The thing to understand about ITV sports broadcasting in those days is that Central and Granada TV were paying the lion shares of the ITV budgets, but our team were frozen out of ITV sports network productions, with London Weekend in particular filling every slot apart from some video editing.

Paul and I decided it was time to try and get a fair share of the production spoils as in those days we had sizeable regional sports TV teams. We had already asked for this, but our London counterparts had resisted.

Our managing directors got to work. Andy Allan at Central and Steve Morrison at Granada finally got their opposite numbers to agree to put the sports out to tender.

I rang Paul and suggested that we go for the football production together. I was really surprised when he said: 'No – you just go for it.'

After all that effort to get a chance like this, I could not understand his decision. He would not give a reason.

So, I went to see Clive Jones, the boss of London News Network, which was owned by the London companies. Clive was keen on a joint bid for the football production, but he eventually told me that Greg Dyke, the chief executive of London Weekend Television, said he did not need Central and that he should go for it on his own.

Why was Dyke so confident? I asked Andy Allan to make sure it was a level playing field. It probably was, but Andy made sure of it at his level.

This meant that I had to bid for production on my own. I had never prepared or written a tender. I knew that the outstanding sports director John Watts would be a key factor in establishing where the production rights for football landed. He by now was working for the independent production company Grand Slam Sports. I also thought Mike Inman, who had risen from dispatch motorcycle rider to production chief in my Central team, would be important too. Central also owned a highly rated outside broadcast company called 021, which was led by Ed Everest.

So I met the Grand Slam Sports chairman Ronald Allison, once the Queen's press secretary, who was keen to make a joint bid. But I learned later that two of his team were more inclined to go with London News Network and Clive. However, Derek Brandon backed his chairman and fought hard to take up my approach, which was what happened.

At an interview with the ITV bosses, which was part of the tendering process, Inman and Watts were impressive. The ITV production boss, the incredible genius Roger Philcox, asked the right questions and they were fielded well by our team, including Everest.

The head of ITV Sport was now Bob Burrows, and while he was decent in most aspects he kept chipping away on the money, taking the best of offers from the other bidders to try and get the price down for whoever won it, which I did not think was completely fair. However, apart from that, the process was very well-handled in my mind. We got there and won the tender.

Andy Allan, a large man, jumped up in the air with delight and then said I should go for the boxing contract as well as the football one we had just landed. But I told him: 'No. This all happened because London would not share, and if we started looking for more, we would be just as bad. Football is the top one, so let someone else go for the others.'

I rang Clive Jones and told him of my decision and said he could have 021 and any of my people. I also said that I would use his studios and some of his team for the football.

It proved to be a good decision. Clive ultimately won the boxing tender, and you never know where people will finish up. Three months later, Allan left for Carlton TV in London and Clive Jones was the new Central TV managing director and my new boss! We have stayed good friends and I attended Clive's second wedding reception in Home House in London. He is now Sir Clive Jones.

I like Greg Dyke. He saved TV-am with Roland Rat. He was Director General of the BBC and when he was the managing director of LWT he was a very good head of ITV Sport. I agreed with some but not all of his decisions – I think that one in particular contributed to ITV losing the top division of football.

The chief executive of the newly formed Premier League was Rick Parry. During the process of allocating broadcasting rights, there were suggestions that Sky, the new kids on the block, may be involved. Parry originally wanted the BBC to continue with Saturday night highlights show *Match of the Day*, ITV to continue with a live Sunday afternoon *Big Match* and the fledgling Sky Sports to have Mondays. Dyke would not have it, despite pleas from me and Trevor East. 'We need to blast them out of the water,' he said. I understood his position but did not agree with it.

Then on the Friday before the clubs voted on who they wanted to have coverage, Parry rang Greg to say that he could not recommend ITV to the clubs. Greg rang Trevor and me to explain his phone call with Parry and then asked us to ring all the chairmen in our areas to ask them to vote for us. It was a bit late, but we did our best.

All I recall was the Coventry chairman saying he would.

Nottingham Forest told me their secretary, Paul White, would be going straight to the London meeting from holiday. As it turned out, they did not vote for us, which was their right of course, Sky got the Premier League and the rest is history.

I wanted the Football League and we had eight clubs in the Championship in my Midlands region. Greg at this stage was not interested. I then hatched a plan to show live Sunday afternoon matches, just in the Midlands, when Midlands clubs played each other. Our commercial department, who sold the advertising, liked it, and so did my bosses. But could I get a deal done? I offered £30,000 for the home clubs and £10,000 for the away team. It did not seem much even then, but these were huge and record sums for regional sport, which normally had tiny budgets. But could I get the clubs to agree?

They had no other TV to show their pitch-side advertising or provide exposure for their sponsored shirts. The trouble was, they all wanted different things. Oxford, Peterborough and Swindon wanted the coverage. David Sullivan, joint-chairman of Birmingham City, only wanted me to cover his club in away matches. But even though I eventually got the deal over the line (and the Football League's Lee Walker and Trevor East were a great help), the Leicester chairman, Martin George, had missed the meeting while on holiday, and he soon told me he would have blocked the deal. Thanks, Martin – although he never told me why? I assumed he wanted more money. I did not ask him, because the deal was done!

I nearly blew it, though, at the final meeting. At what would have been my fifth and final attempt at securing the broadcasting rights for inter-Midlands matches, I laid on dinner in a private room at the Hyatt Regency hotel opposite our Birmingham studios. I left

Lee and Trevor with the eight clubs and waited for ages, fearing it would not happen.

I had quite a few drinks to pass the time, and when I was called in, I jumped the gun by angrily having a go at everyone after misreading the situation.

Lee said: 'Hold on, Gary. You're leaning on an empty door. The clubs have agreed.'

I apologised. Lee said later: 'Don't worry. They all like you and actually thought it was funny!' Thank goodness. The deal went on to be a great success.

Dyke had, in my opinion, generally good vision and judgement. But I did not agree with his call to drop the very popular *Saint & Greavsie* show. His reasoning was that we had no football. I disagreed. I thought it would have survived well, but it was not my call. He also dropped wrestling, saying that the image was not right. But ITV in my book was in the ratings business. Wrestling was a big draw. Perhaps it was an image problem. I do not know.

When Billy Wright reached sixty-five, he had to retire, because he was a staff employee and those were the rules. He was controller of sport for Central. I was called in a few months earlier, and when I walked into Andy Allan's office, he stretched out his hand to shake mine, saying: 'Congratulations, you are my new controller of sport.'

My first question was: 'I love Billy; does he know?'

Andy said: 'We all love Billy and it was his idea to do it now, before he retires.'

Sir Jack Hayward and I were the last two people (outside his family) to visit Billy at his home in London's Whetstone a few days before he passed away. I was grateful to Sir Jack. He owned Wolves, and after Billy retired he made him a Wolves director. Billy loved it and even attended youth team matches. They renamed a stand at Molineux Stadium 'the Billy Wright stand', and it was opened by a very proud Billy with his family on the pitch.

After Billy died they built a statue of him. Joy Beverley, his widow, asked me to represent her on the statue committee. Another member was a Wolves legend, their outstanding striker John Richards. The local councillors wanted the statue erected in the Mander Shopping Centre. John and I argued strongly that it had to be at the main reception at Molineux. Luckily we won the day, and the statue stands proudly at the ground admired by everyone who passes it.

Back at Central, where I was now controller of sport, I had to reorganise my team in Nottingham. I promoted Steve Lambden to sports editor. I lost one presenter, Keith Daniell, to the corporate world, where he has made a huge success of his own company. I also decided that while I wanted to keep the other reporter, Dennis Coath, I needed a female host as well.

I had met Sarah-Jane Mee when she worked for a public relations company in Manchester with her agent, Skylet Andrews. I had given her a screen test in Oxford and she was obviously a natural, but she needed to understand the business. I suggested she went to a big company and learned production. I would have trained her in Oxford, but Tim Russon clearly wanted to be a one-man band there. I understood that and he worked very hard. I promised Sarah-Jane and Skylet I would come back for her.

Sarah-Jane went to Sky Sports News and worked on production, but they would not use her on-screen. So I kept my word and was delighted when Sarah-Jane joined us. After I left she became Central's No. 1 sports presenter and then rejoined Sky to present their

Saturday night football highlights show before being switched to present Sky News.

At the turn of the century, Clive Jones was keen on diversity, particularly in our recruitment, and he instructed me to find some suitable candidates. I asked Steve Lambden and he recommended Manish Bhasin, who worked for BBC Radio Leicester. The BBC at the time did not seem interested in using him on TV. I gave him a screen test. After thirty seconds I stopped it, as I was so impressed. I offered him the job and more money than he was earning at the time. He asked for twenty-four hours to think about it. I told him not to take any longer! He rang me back twenty-three hours later to accept.

I put the two of them together. Sarah-Jane and Manish were simply outstanding. In time, Jon Holmes, a longstanding and trusted friend of mine (agent for Gary Lineker and others), asked me if he could have my blessing to take Manish to the BBC, who now wanted him back. He was to have a fantastic role in the popular *Football Focus* programme. Of course I agreed. I am proud of what both Sarah-Jane and Manish have achieved as indeed I am of the various production people I started who have gone on to top jobs in the industry.

Everything seemed to be going well. Trevor East had made me the No. 1 network football interviewer quite a while earlier. I was covering boxing and other sports and enjoying life.

But, nothing lasts for ever. Granada TV and my owners Carlton TV were getting together to form what was described as a merger. But in my view it appeared that Granada were making all the decisions, and it soon felt more like a takeover. My immediate boss by then was Ian Squires, who kept telling me not to keep calling it that!

Granada's Charles Allen soon visited our studios and my department. I had a feeling that I knew what was coming. Paul Doherty had felt that Allen liked redundancies, and when Paul departed Granada he had felt like a victim, even if another executive had done the deed in a meeting.

I was management as well as a presenter, so I could not relay my fears to my department. I needed confirmation and we had programmes to make and broadcast.

I was fifty-nine and was facing compulsory retirement at sixty-five, but I had no mortgage, owned a huge pension and no debts. I could see the writing on the wall. High salary, successful sports department but, I believed, on the wrong side of the merger!

So I decided to go to London to first talk to Clive Jones in his office and then have lunch with Vic Wakeling, the managing director of Sky Sports.

I had known Vic since my arrival at ATV in the early '70s. Vic was the deputy sports editor on the *Birmingham Evening Mail* and their boxing writer. I sat next to Vic at boxing events and always had a fine relationship with him. We got on well in my Central days when we swapped material when needed. He would let me have Sky footage to show only in our region and I would give him items such as Birmingham City–Aston Villa matches before Sky was formed.

His deputy was Andy Melvin, who I discovered later was the person who had suggested my move to Sky. When Andy was a director at Scottish Television he worked on a *Fight Night* outside broadcast I presented from Scotland. On sponsors' media trips abroad, we often went on long walks and enjoyed confidential conversations about the industry. I was to owe them both, particularly Andy.

When I arrived in Clive's office on that London trip, he told me that I needed to leave Central. He planned to do the same in a few months. I told him I was on a one-year notice period either way. That was because I had been headhunted three times during my Central days – first by ITN after the 1972 Munich Olympics, then by International Sport and Leisure, a marketing company based in Switzerland, for the 2002 World Cup and finally by the American National Basketball Association (the NBA) to be their European person based in Paris. I had turned all three down. Clive had been aware of the last two approaches. The last two were executive roles which I did not really want, because I would not be involved with TV programmes, which was my love.

I told Clive that I had one year left before completing my final salary pension. Clive said I should leave when I wanted to after I told him that I wanted to make sure my thirty-strong team were properly compensated (only three were to be kept). Clive repeated that I should leave when it suited me and confirmed that Carlton would pay me the year's pension and wages plus all my holiday money that I had not taken.

Then I left for Langan's Bistro for lunch with Vic. I told him that I was officially 'retiring', but in reality I had no intention of doing so, even if my ITV days looked over.

Vic told me that Sky wanted me. I asked him what he wanted me to do. He said he'd like me to present and in particular a chat show. I had a high profile, having appeared quite regularly in front of millions of viewers, an audience that the satellite station could not yet command. I had also built up a great contacts book. He added I had gravitas.

He said he would not offer me the job until I had actually left ITV. I told him that I wanted a short rest and to take my wife, Katie, to the USA for a long holiday. He said that was fine. I was leaving ITV in August and would like to start at the end of September.

Finally I asked him about whether I needed an agent, as I had never had one. I had not realised that Vic did not really like agents. He bristled: 'I will pay you more than they would be able to get you!' And he did!

So a career move and just presenting at fifty-nine years of age. I was so happy, but I wanted to look after my team. So I made sure everything was settled financially before I left.

Central gave me a great dinner with colleagues from both London and Birmingham at the Hotel du Vin in Birmingham, for whom I am coincidentally now an ambassador.

I had enjoyed and was grateful for a week short of thirty-six years with ITV. I was to feel the same over fourteen years at Sky Sports. I have nothing but gratitude – fifty years in front of a TV camera is incredible, and it is an achievement that is unlikely to be beaten by many!

At Sky I was to cover darts, greyhound racing, snooker and boxing. In the studio I hosted the football phone-in *You're on Sky Sports*, plus nearly 200 editions of *Time of Our Lives* and *Sporting Heroes*.

I am often asked what my two favourite sports are. Easy: football and boxing. In the next chapter, those many years in boxing, from Muhammad Ali to regional *Fight Night* and many more stars and fights. From London to Las Vegas and more venues around the world. Ding dong!

CHAPTER TWENTY

WHY I FELL IN LOVE
WITH BOXING

Boxing has always fascinated me. My father liked cricket and boxing. He would often talk to me about Walter Neusel, the German heavyweight who fought several top British heavyweights in London at the old Harringay Arena and the Empire Pool at Wembley, as it was known in the 1930s and early 1940s.

He also fought the likes of the German Max Schmeling, losing first and then beating him. Schmeling also won and lost the world title against the legendary American Joe Louis. Neusel was a blond six-footer who died aged fifty-six in Berlin from a heart attack but was rated as the sixth greatest pound-for-pound German boxer.

During the Second World War, my dad had breakfast with Freddie Mills, a successful British boxer, when they were both in the RAF – Mills was there as a physical training instructor. After the war, my father would also recall Freddie's challenge of the USA's Gus Lesnevich for the world light-heavyweight title.

When they first fought in May 1946, Mills was floored in the second round and twice in the tenth before the fight was stopped;

Lesnevich therefore retained his title at the Harringay Arena. But in July 1948, a fit Mills won the title by beating Lesnevich on points, after the holder was cut badly in the first round and dropped twice in the tenth.

Mills often fought against heavier opponents and was almost too brave for his own good. He was an all-out attacking boxer who retired after taking a real pasting three years later at London's Earls Court Arena against Joey Maxim, another American. The doctors found that, during the fight, three of Mills's teeth had been knocked out and one of them had been embedded in his gums! Maxim was twenty-seven years old; Freddie was thirty.

Freddie was a popular man who dabbled in showbiz and owned a West End nightclub. He was found dead in an alley behind his club on 24 July 1965. It has never been concluded whether his death was a suicide or murder by the crime syndicates he was in debt to. He was just forty-six.

He had experienced too many hard fights with a professional record of 101 contests, 77 wins (55 by KO) 18 losses (7 by KO) and 6 draws.

I was fascinated by my dad's stories and started to read everything I could about the great champions, who I was in fact to meet over the years: names like Willie Pep, who the greatest featherweight of all time, and Jake LaMotta, who was known as the Raging Bull. Robert De Niro won an Oscar for playing LaMotta in the movie *Raging Bull* in 1980. I got LaMotta to sign my son Laurence's DVD of the film and my copy of his autobiography.

I met Pep in the USA when former boxer and then manager/matchmaker/promoter Mickey Duff knew I was covering a fight. Duff took me as his guest when he was inducted into the Boxing

Hall of Fame. I arrived at the venue on my own and was lost. This oldish man asked if he could help and guided me to the function. Along the way I realised that my guide was Willie Pep. What a fighter – 241 contests, 229 wins (65 by knockout) 11 losses and 1 draw. The world champion from Connecticut was ranked the No. 1 featherweight of all time by the International Boxing Research Organization in 2005, while the Associated Press named him as the No. 1 featherweight of the twentieth century. Being a boxing anorak I will tell you that Willie Pep's real name was Guglielmo Papaleo!

I met Jake LaMotta and his *seventh* wife in London at a fundraising dinner that Frank Warren had arranged for Michael Watson in London's Park Lane. An extraordinary man! He wore a Texan hat throughout dinner. I had a photo with him and I acted like a fan!

His great rival in the '40s and early '50s was Sugar Ray Robinson, arguably one of the greatest boxers of all time. You might argue Muhammad Ali, who I was fortunate enough to interview several times, is 'the Greatest'. Ali was certainly the biggest personality and most famous boxer of all time, but Robinson was an incredible middle and welterweight. At his prime he had a record of 128 contests (54 stoppages) 1 defeat and 4 draws. He finished with 174 wins (109 by knockout) 19 defeats (only 1 by technical knockout) and 6 draws, stretching from 1940 to 1965.

Like my late parents, I am not religious. Usually one seems to inherit religion and politics from their parents, so, when I went to boarding school, I found the compulsory twice-on-a-Sunday church services a bore. Culford School was a Methodist School, and while Motty went to their service I was an attendee at the Culford Church of England, which was situated within the school grounds.

I suppose I was a disgrace. I used to spend some of my pocket money on boxing autobiography books on the historic world heavyweight champions, and I'd go to church services with them tucked inside the bible. I never got caught. I recall sitting on the hard wooden pews while the dreary sermon was delivered, read- ing the stories of Jack Johnson, Jack Dempsey, Gene Tunney, Max Schmeling, Max Beer, James J. Braddock, Joe Louis and Jersey Joe Walcott, stretching from Johnson in 1908 to Walcott in 1951.

Little did I know that I was to meet Joe Louis in Nottingham in the '70s and, years later, Jersey Joe Walcott in Atlantic City. The latter was a bit embarrassing.

The USA promoter Lou Duva was promoting at Trump Castle with his new Olympic silver medallist Riddick Bowe having his second professional fight. He was keen on ITV signing Bowe, which eventually did happen through Bowe's manager Rock Newman.

Duva gave me and Jeff Farmer ringside seats to watch Bowe. We were there to cover a contest the next day for our series *International Fight Night*, which some of the ITV companies in the UK screened.

Jeff was getting a little agitated because the old man sitting di- rectly behind us could not control his walking stick and was acci- dentally poking Jeff through the back of his seat.

Just before the start, with Jeff really peeved, the ring announcer, Michael 'Lets Get Ready To Rumble' Buffer, started introducing some of the personalities at ringside. Then for the finale, Buffer said: 'Ladies and gentleman – last but not least, let's give a special Trump Castle welcome to a man who is so great, they even named this state after him [we were in New Jersey; Buffer's line was not true but great nonetheless!]: the former HEAVYWEIGHT CHAM- PION of the WORLD, Jersey… Joe… WALCOTT!'

The packed crowd went potty and Jeff yelled at me: 'Gary, Jersey Joe is here!'

At which point we turned round to set our eyes on him; two guys lifted the old man with the walking stick to his feet and Jeff, without batting an eyelid, shook his hand and said: 'Jersey Joe, Jeff Farmer from England. It is an absolute pleasure to meet you.'

And I went into fan mode and asked him to sign my fight order sheet!

I revealed earlier in this book how my mate George Zeleny and I used to break the school curfew to go down to the cricket professional Johnny Boughton's house in West Stow next door to one of the exits of the school to watch highlights of Muhammad Ali's fights the previous day. Little did I think I would conduct three individual TV interviews with him in the years ahead.

The first time was when his own book came out. He was in London staying at the Hilton Hotel on Park Lane. He had taken a whole floor for his group and I was invited to his suite to interview him on his balcony. Besides the film crew I took my father and one of my best friends, Lorenzo Ferrari.

The second time was more dramatic. In 1979, Ali was coming to Birmingham and the Variety Club of Great Britain (the children's charity now know as Variety) had booked him to be the guest of honour at the then Night Out venue. It was a 800-seater dining/cabaret venue where I had seen the likes of Roy Orbison singing. I had also compèred a heat of Miss ATV, swimsuits and all, on the stage.

Now the best of all. As a Barker of the Charity I was asked to compère and interview the world champion. Before the luncheon I had arranged to interview Ali with a film crew in the nearby

Stephenson Street near New Street Station. The police kindly brought all the traffic to a halt for the actual interview. It was more to protect the VIP visitor than my interview!

Sadly a driver lost control of their car and hit me in the thigh, sending me flying into the air and landing outside the Ladbroke's betting shop. My ATV crew thought I was going to die and stopped filming in shock. The local news programme *ATV Today*, which I was due to appear on, had to buy some stills off the *Daily Express*. (Some of the national newspaper agency photographers were there because of Ali.)

I remember two things in particular – thinking that I needed to keep conscious in case it was more serious than it turned out to be and that I might never come round again. I was also being dragged into the Ladbroke's shop by my great mate Peter Lorenzo (a top sportswriter in his day). Peter, father of the broadcaster Matt Lorenzo, was the public relations chief of the gambling company and was really worried that I might die under a Ladbroke's sign. That is what mates are for!

I was concerned about my wife Katie and our young kids (our daughter Claire was four and our twin boys Laurence and Neil were two). I need not have worried. My parents were living in a small village near Huntingdon called Hilton. A local farmer heard about the accident on the radio and ran to tell my mum and dad, who rang Katie. Meanwhile, my secretary was trying to break the news gently to Katie, who said: 'Olivia, I already know he is going to hospital in an ambulance, but he is going to recover!'

In hospital the doctors/nurses put me through the X-Ray machines twice. I was in pain, but I had very tough thighs from my rugby days; there was intense internal bleeding but nothing broken. They told me I needed rest for a few days.

Meanwhile Bob Warman, another of my closest friends who presented the local news show at ATV and then Central for many years, was really very worried. Not so much about me (although he cared!) but the fact that he was being rushed in to replace me. He knew nothing about boxing and still dines out on what happened next.

I stupidly told the hospital I needed a pair of crutches and that I was discharging myself. I did not want to miss hosting Muhammad Ali.

I got a massive cheer as I walked into the place on those crutches and Bob told me later he had never been so pleased to see me.

I did the interview and talked to Ali as he doodled on his paper napkin. I later auctioned it for quite a lot of money for the charity.

Meanwhile I was exhausted at the end of the luncheon. I taxied home and slept for twenty-four hours. But it was worth it. My thigh was painful once the painkiller wore off, but eventually it was back to normal.

I had first met Ali at a Variety Club function in London at the film premiere of a movie based on his life. So now I wondered if I would interview him ever again.

I did and it would be for the last time. I was asked by two businessmen to join them at a casino in Moseley in Birmingham for a luncheon. Alan Manning owned two casinos in Birmingham – the one we met in and another in Edgbaston. He was with a mutual friend, Harry Rubin, who was one of the best charity auctioneers that I ever met. He was a wheeler-dealer and great fun.

They were to bring Ali to Birmingham again and wanted me to compère and interview Ali at a charity dinner to raise money for the Jewish National Fund. I agreed on the condition that I had Ali live on my 6.20 p.m. sports slot in Birmingham within the Central News programme, which had big viewing figures in those days.

They agreed and invited me to join Alan in his Rolls Royce collecting Ali from Heathrow Airport. Ali was to travel in another Rolls.

So we collected Muhammad from Heathrow Airport. On the way to Birmingham, Ali wanted a soft drink and to go to the toilet so we pulled into the Bear Hotel in Oxfordshire's Woodstock. The restaurant was packed, so we took Ali into the hotel bar. But the hotel staff, including all the waiters, joined us. Ali, starting to slow up after all those hard latter fights, was doing magic tricks with cards.

The hotel manager soon arrived and began pleading with us to leave so he could get the chefs and waiters back to their posts; the hungry diners were getting impatient.

When we got to our studios, I was joined by our commentator Reg Gutteridge because I knew Ali loved Reg more than any other media person – including the BBC's Harry Carpenter, with whom he had a great on-screen relationship. During our interview, I put it on Muhammad that he was not well and we were worried about him. He disputed it, but a year later he admitted he had big problems. It was described as Parkinson's, but I thought it was worse than that.

That interview was featured in ITV's documentary *When Muhammad Ali Came to the UK* as the first time it was suggested that he had problems more than just Parkinson's.

I was to see Muhammad Ali twice more before he passed away in June 2016 aged seventy-four. The Mike Tyson v. Francois Botha fight took place at the MGM Grand in Las Vegas on 16 January 1999. Tyson won by knockout one second before the end of the fifth. Reg Gutteridge, Jim Watt and I were there for ITV.

The next day was Ali's fifty-seventh birthday and he had breakfast at the hotel with Reg Gutteridge and Muhammad's fourth wife, Lonnie. He invited Reg to his ranch, but Reg said he had to get back to London. So Ali explained that the MGM were throwing a dinner that night in a private room to celebrate his birthday. He invited Reg and his wife, Connie.

His wife was not on the trip, so Reg asked me to come in her place. The other guests were Mike Tyson, who sat with Ali and fifty of the Casino's top high-rollers (mega-rich, big-time gamblers) and Reg and me. Gladys Knight sang 'Happy Birthday'.

Then Ali and Tyson went and sat on two stools and invited the fifty high-rollers to form a queue (or 'a line', in American speak!) to have their photo taken with the two legends.

I stood up and Reg said to me: 'Oh my gawd. Please tell me you are not going to do what I think you are going to do?' I nodded and joined the queue. I survived, moved in when it was my turn and the photos were laid out on the table once they had been developed. Unbelievable!

The last time I saw Muhammad was so sad. There was a big lunch at Stoke City that I was booked to compère. I sat with my good friend Peter Coates, the chairman of Stoke City, and we waited and waited for Ali, who was not at all well. He was sitting quietly with his wife in another room; they would not bring him out. He could no longer write his autograph, which he had always been brilliant at doing for everyone.

When he did emerge an hour or so later than expected, he sat at a table and suddenly vomited. He could not be interviewed by me. I had filled in the time talking to former world champion John H. Stracey. It was a sad sight and not how I want to remember one of the greatest sports personalities of my lifetime. In my opinion, he should not have been there.

In his career Ali came back three times to win or regain the world title. His career is so well known, with two mega fights with Joe Frazier – the first time was his first defeat in what was billed as 'the Fight of the Century' at Madison Square Garden, where Frank Sinatra got ringside with a photographer's pass.

Ali got his revenge over Frazier in 'the Thrilla in Manila', before beating George Foreman in 'the Rumble in the Jungle' as these big fights began to go around the globe.

When he was known as Clay, he came to London in 1963 and, in a fight at Wembley, almost lost to Henry Cooper. He was hit by 'Henry's Hammer' (Cooper's left hook) in the closing seconds of round four and was in real trouble. But his corner man Angelo Dundee called Referee Tommy Little over in the sixty seconds break to explain that the seam on his right glove was torn, and there was a delay while a new glove was fitted. That delay allowed Clay to recover and went out to stop Henry quite quickly on cuts.

Henry was prone to cuts and Ali beat him the same way in 1966 when Cooper challenged for the world title at the Arsenal football ground in Highbury.

Many years later promoter Frank Warren took Dundee, Reg Gutteridge and me to lunch at the J. Sheekey fish restaurant just of St Martin's Lane in the Leicester Square district. Dundee told us he realised Clay was out on his feet so Angelo produced a knife or razor and slashed the glove to buy precious time. It saved Clay from defeat.

Despite his sad end, Ali was a great part of the history of boxing and sport in general. When he was sharp he was clever, bright, and his baiting and wind-ups of opponents were loved by a worldwide public, who probably at times wanted to see this 'braggart' beaten. But the effect he had on people and the large crowds wherever he went was something to behold.

Nicknamed 'the Greatest', he was, in his pomp, one of the most famous people in the world.

In my opinion he was surrounded by hangers-on who were prepared to let him pick up the tab, but apart from his faithful photographer Howard Bingham, none of them were to be seen in his demise.

Back to my early days covering the sport, and after covering the Laud brothers' professional fights and hanging around with the yet-to-turn-professional Joe Bugner (who was to fight Ali twice without winning), I was off to London to be ringside for several fights, including a bantamweight British and Empire championship (it's now called the Commonwealth championship) fight between Scotland's Walter McGowan and Liverpool's Alan Rudkin on 9 September 1966 at the Empire Pool, Wembley. It was very close, but McGowan, despite cuts, won. It has stayed in my mind among the hundreds of fights I was to watch during my fifty years with ITV and Sky; two little men in a hell of a scrap.

Rudkin was to have three attempts at world titles in Japan, Australia and Mexico, but he could not quite pull it off. McGowan became the world flyweight champion.

I left London for Westward TV, but there was little to interest me in professional boxing down there. It was a different matter when I moved to ATV in the Midlands, where boxing was thriving.

CHAPTER TWENTY-ONE

BOXING IN THE MIDLANDS

The hottest boxing property in the Midlands when I took up the ATV sports presenting job in the early '70s was Jackie Turpin Jr – the nephew of the former world middleweight champion Randolph Turpin. But Jackie never fulfilled his promise and admitted to me recently that he felt the full pressure and expectations of the famous Turpin boxing family name.

His mother Betty pushed Jackie and even cycled alongside him when Jackie was doing his road running. In the end he packed it up when the British Boxing Board of Control revoked his licence after a heavy beating in his last fight. The licence was later returned, but Jackie did not want to make a comeback and worked in circus boxing booths before becoming a professional wrestler.

Jackie had been voted Young Boxer of the Year in 1971 by the Boxing Writers Club, which is based in London. The Turpins were all from Leamington Spa in the Midlands. Randolph won the world middleweight title in 1951 when he outpointed the mighty Sugar Ray Robinson in a national headline fight at London's Earls Court. But it was a tragic end. After losing the return in the USA, Randolph got into financial troubles and was eventually found dead in his flat. His death was ruled a suicide. There is a statue of him in Leamington Spa.

My relationship was with Jackie Jr. I was asked to be godfather to his son, John Matthew Turpin, who at the time of writing is fifty years old. I am sorry to report I was not good in that role and did not recognise him when we recently attended the funeral of wrestling TV star Tony 'Banger' Walsh in Leamington.

It was, however, a reunion when he introduced himself and his mother, Heather.

Jackie Sr, brother to Randolph, was a Midlands featherweight champion, and his other brother Dick was the first black man to win a British title when he became the middleweight title holder.

The Jackie I knew was a handsome, exciting fighter with a fearsome punch. He had a great start and soon became a big favourite at the Wolverhampton Civic Hall. Just before I first met him, he had stopped Al Romano in the second round on an ITV show.

Sadly, he had a weak chin. He could dish it out, but was so vulnerable at taking it. His career at welterweight and super-welterweight came to a sudden end when he was knocked down three times against Jim Devanney on 29 October 1975 and the referee Frank Parkes had to stop the fight.

These days Jackie lives in sheltered accommodation in his hometown. His ex-wife Heather has remarried, but relationships all round are good. But the boxer who never quite made it does not enjoy good health. I still ring him from time to time.

Going back to Leamington, I helped a potential new hero from the area: 24-year-old Commonwealth Games heavyweight champion Lewis Williams. He is twenty-four years old and 6ft 6in. with a real chance.

Jackie Turpin's manager was George Middleton, the same as his uncle Randolph, and his promoter was Alex Griffiths from Wolverhampton.

I had good days attending the Griffiths promotions but eventually we fell out over a TV interview which was his own fault.

In those good days I attended and enjoyed his shows, apart from Jackie's defeat. But we were to fall out after Griffiths tried to bully me after a studio interview with boxing manager George Biddles.

I struck up a good relationship with Biddles, who loved to do TV interviews. Danny McAlinden, a Northern Irishman who had moved to Coventry as a teen (managed by Middleton) fought Jack Bodell (managed by Biddles) of Swadlincote in Derbyshire for the British and Commonwealth titles on 27 June 1972. I arranged with Alex Griffiths to have the contract signings for the fight live in the *ATV Today* studios.

It was a terrible, brawling contest in the open air at Villa Park. Bodell was a spent force and was knocked out in 1 minute 31 seconds of round two by a swinging punch from the Irishman. McAlinden's supporters stormed the ring to round off a crazy night. Bodell retired from boxing after what proved to be his last contest.

Biddles had become a manager in 1927 and ran it from his snack bar in his home city of Leicester. His boxers fought regularly and most of them had many contests. His first world champion was Hogan Bassey in 1957.

He was certainly a good talker and agreed for Richard Dunn to challenge Muhammad Ali for the world heavyweight title in Munich. Ali wanted an easy fight after the Thrilla in Manila and the Rumble in the Jungle. He got it against Dunn on 24 May 1976, with the Yorkshire man down five times in five rounds. That was as far as it went, with Dunn earning £52,000.

I saw Biddles and Dunn promoting the event live on an American TV show with Biddles (answering the question of how he secured the fight) stating that he could persuade turkeys that Christmas was good for them. There was a shot of Dunn next to him nodding in agreement!

McAlinden's next fight was against Willie Moore from the USA. There had been several Willie Moores! Which one was this?

The contest was scheduled for the Solihull Ice Rink on 12 December. Just before the fight, I was interviewing George on my Friday night sports slot on *ATV Today*. I asked him about McAlinden's upcoming contest. George said: 'Nobody in the know seems to know anything about this opponent.'

It was true, but I was surprised to get a phone call as soon as we came off air. It was the promoter Alex Griffiths. 'I am going to sue you,' he threatened. 'You have ruined my show.'

I was shocked and upset. I was a year into my career at ATV, twenty-seven years old and four years into TV. I would now have handled his threat far differently to the way I did then. I would now have rumbled what Griffiths was up to.

As it was, I went to see Tony Flanagan, the executive producer and power behind these shows. He rang Alex and told him off for his words to me. He said to Alex to come in on Monday and be interviewed by me to put his case. We would record it for legal reasons.

After the call Tony turned to me and said: 'I want him stuffed. Find out about this boxer and arm yourself with the facts. This opponent looks dodgy to me. Alex is trying to get cheap publicity for the promotion by putting the wind up you.'

I went home to my flat and rang Neil Durden-Smith, whom I had worked with in the Munich Olympics that summer.

I knew he had boxing connections, but I was not quite sure who with. I told the story to Neil, who told me he had the man if I would pay £50. I said I would pay it myself and gave Neil my home number as I had to face Griffiths on the Monday. This was before mobile phones.

I remember it clearly. A man called Dick Reekie rang me the next day: 'I have the SP [starting price, i.e., his fee]. Have you got a pen?'

I cannot remember the actual facts about Moore now and he is not on Boxrec, which is the boxing bible for records. This Willie Moore's record turned out to be very poor. Nothing like the Alex Griffiths promotion poster! He had also suffered a detached retina and was suspended over in the USA.

Dick added: 'The documents are on their way from New York and will be couriered up to you.'

Wow! I was in pole position and ready to 'stuff' Griffiths as ordered. I did not stop to think why Neil's man had gone to so much trouble, but I was to find out later that a rival promoter was behind it.

On the Monday, Alex Griffiths strode confidently into my studio at ATV in Birmingham. The videotape was rolling and the red light came on: 'Alex, this is your poster. Are the facts about this American boxer correct?'

When he said that it was, I put a caption with Moore's correct record up. Griffiths was surprised at my revelation. I then brought up the suspension through the detached retina. He was now shocked and floundering.

He stormed out at the end and we never spoke again. I took a call from his partner, the famous veteran boxing promoter Jack Solomons, who verbally threatened to ruin me.

I politely said: 'Mr Solomons, I respect all the great world title fights and other promotions you have staged in this country, but you are an old man now, and your time is over. I do not appreciate this call.'

The actual contest attracted a tiny crowd. Local TV shows were very powerful at that time when millions did watch television.

Some time afterwards, I took a call from boxing guru/promoter Jarvis Astaire, who was a rival to Solomons. (He has sadly now passed away.)

'I believe you owe me a favour,' he said. The penny dropped. He had been involved in the Willie Moore find-a-fact operation. Dick Reekie was manager of the Terry Downes betting shops.

I agreed. Astaire (who I was to get on with well in later years, despite his being a rival promoter with the BBC to ITV and Frank Warren/Barry Hearn) explained that he was a director of William Hill bookmakers and they were staging their 'Golden Spurs' racing awards at the Hilton Hotel in Park Lane. 'The only winner not coming is your friend, the jump jockey Bob Davies. Please make sure that he attends.'

I rang Bob, for whom I ghosted a column in *The Sun* newspaper. He said that he had a ride at Fontwell. I explained how important it was for me that he attended 'the Golden Spurs' to collect his trophy and that I would pay his racing fee. Like a true friend, he said that he was not bothered about that particular ride and that he did not want my money. He would attend the awards.

I was still relieved to see his photo with his trophy in the next day's *Sporting Life*. There is no such thing as a free lunch, or in this case a free 'saving my arse' favour!

I attended many good fights at all levels, including world championships. Many good boxers came out of the Midlands. The unluckiest one was Warley's Pat Cowdell. Pat had so much talent but came across two of the best featherweights and super-featherweights of all time in Salvador Sánchez and Azumah Nelson.

I am still friendly with Cowdell and we have shared many dinners and laughs over the years.

For instance, when Pat was European champion, the British Medical Association were asking for a ban on professional boxing. I interviewed him at his home on the subject. I loved interviewing him because he always gave me plenty of name checks!

In his Black Country accent, he said: 'All I know, Gary, is that I am 9st 4lbs, Gary, I do not smoke or drink, I run nine miles a day, Gary, and I go to bed early. My doctor, Gary, is 18st, Gary, he drinks half a bottle of whiskey a day, Gary, and smokes twenty cigarettes a day, Gary. He tells me what I am doing is dangerous!' Classic Cowdell.

When Pat fought Salvador Sánchez in the old Astrodome in Houston, Texas, he took him all fifteen rounds. The judges made it a split-points decision to Sánchez, but Pat, honest as ever, told me it should have been unanimous. He had lost. But it was a ferocious contest, and Cowdell showed just what a super boxer he was against the best. I have always claimed that Pat was the best British boxer never to win a world title. He fought the best in the world at the time and two of the best of *any* time.

Sánchez would have been the greatest featherweight of all time if he had not been killed in a car accident in his native Mexico at the young age of twenty-three. He had been the unbeaten WBC champion from 1980 to 1982. He had beaten all the top contenders, including future champion Azumah Nelson with a TKO (a technical knockout, where the referee waves the fight off because they believe the losing fighter can no longer safely continue) in the fifteenth round at Madison Square Garden in New York. Three weeks after the Nelson contest, he was killed on an early-morning drive on 12 August 1982 while driving his Porsche 928 sports car on a federal highway in Mexico. He loved fast cars and died instantly.

His professional record was 46 contests, 44 wins (32 by knockout), 1 loss and 1 draw. He won the WBC title with a TKO victory over Danny Lopez in the thirteenth of fifteen rounds in Phoenix, Arizona on 2 February 1980. He successfully defended the title nine times, with Cowdell being the challenger on 12 December 1981.

The day before the contest I met Sánchez briefly in the Astrodome car park after interviewing Cowdell. Sánchez looked chiselled and ready to go,

Pat was relaxed and in a good mood as I interviewed him for *ATV Today* back home. We sat on the edge of the ring as it was being constructed. I had bought an expensive big Texan hat and was wondering how I could justify it on my expenses! So at the closing of the interview, I put it on my head and asked Pat: 'What do you think of this hat, Pat?'

He quipped: 'Well, Gary, I am just surprised they found one big enough!'

As an amateur, Pat won a bronze medal at the 1976 Olympics in Montreal after earlier winning the gold at the 1974 Commonwealth Games in New Zealand. He was also a bronze medallist at the 1975 European Championships in Poland. He collected several ABA titles before turning professional in 1977.

As a professional he had 42 contests of which he won 36 (19 by KO) and lost 6 including 2 world title challenges. The second of these was against Azumah Nelson at the Birmingham NEC Arena on 12 October 1985. Cowdell was past his peak by then and, challenging in front of his own supporters, was hit in the first round by a left uppercut that knocked him out.

I interviewed Pat in the ring, but he was in tears, so the interview did not last long either.

Sad though the ending was, the build-up to that fight brought some amusing moments too. At first we thought Pat might challenge the American Rocky Lockridge who won both the WBA (World Boxing Association) and IBF (International Boxing Federation) super-featherweight titles – I was the interviewer at the latter when he beat Barry Michael, who retired in the eighth round at Blazers Nightclub in Windsor on ITV.

Earlier he had fought Julio Llerena with a knockout in the sixth round of ten in a non-title outdoors contest in the impressive Castello Sforzesco in Milan. ITV's boxing promoter Frank Warren had arranged for Jeff Farmer, Pat, my best friend Lorenzo Ferrari and me to be ringside for the contest with Frank on 29 July 1984.

I decided that Jeff, Pat and I should travel to Lorenzo's home in Salsomaggiore Terme, a spa town in the Province of Palma. It was about seventy miles (113 kilometres) from the boxing venue.

Jeff, Pat and I were sharing a big bedroom. Pat was in training so went to bed early. Jeff and I went out on the town with Lorenzo. On our return to the room, we were rather worse for wear and stumbled over poor Pat in the darkness and woke him up!

The day after the Milan trip we took Pat up to the town's bowls club. The locals were excited to meet Pat. European sports fans are not so insular as Brits and they had all seen the Salvador Sánchez world title fight with Pat on Italian TV three years earlier. This was obviously years before the likes of Sky and TNT in the UK. So they wanted him to play bowls in their top team against the likes of Jeff, Lorenzo and me. A good crowd gathered to see my team get thrashed.

Afterwards, they brought out a good spread of local food – prosciutto crudo on bread, parmesan cheese and local wine. We told Pat that, training or no training, he had to eat the food and drink the wine. He told us: 'It's boot-iful!'

The hosts were too generous, and Pat was too polite. My everlasting memory of the world championship challenger was of Warley's finest mooning out of my soft-top car on the M1 on our journey back from Heathrow Airport. Then I carried Pat into his home over my shoulder, watched by his lovely but astonished wife Inger!

Pat always blamed Jeff and me for his first-round knockout by Azumah Nelson!

It was Nelson that was finally named as his next world champion opponent. So I decided to take the two Pats – Cowdell and manager/trainer Lynch – to Miami Beach in Florida, where Nelson was to meet Juvenal Ordenes in defence of his WBC featherweight title at Tamiami Park in Miami.

I received a sponsorship for the flights from Poundstretcher airline and booked the three of us into Frank Sinatra's favourite hotel, the Fontainebleau Hilton in Miami Beach. Now renamed the Fontainebleau Miami Beach, it is an oceanfront luxury hotel with a great swimming pool.

Somehow (and certainly not deliberately) I had been given the wrong date, and we arrived a week early! The two Pats trained on the beach while I filmed with an American police car in mock pursuit at my request.

The actual boxing took place on 6 September 1985 and Nelson retained his WBC title in the fifth round. The Cowdell challenge was on, and Pat celebrated by pushing me into the swimming pool as we filmed!

So to Birmingham, and sadly the big fight only lasted two minutes and twenty-four seconds. My wife, Katie, was working for a hospitality company, and when she sat down at ringside all she saw was Pat being counted out!

Nelson, like Sánchez, was an exceptional fighter and made six successful defences of his featherweight title before winning the WBC super-featherweight title. He then successfully defended that title nine times.

The year before his challenge to Nelson, Cowdell won the European super-featherweight title by beating the reigning champion Jean-Marc Renard from Belgium at the Aston Villa Leisure Centre in Birmingham. Pat took the unanimous points decision.

It was live on ITV, and I interviewed Cowdell in the ring afterwards. I put it to him that, although he had taken a long lay-off, it was an easy win for him.

He stuffed me with his reply: 'It might have been easy for you, Gary. I saw you at ringside smoking your big cigar. It was bloody hard in here, mate!'

I was relieved to hand the show back to our presenter Dickie Davies in London.

Over the years I covered many boxers who were made in the Midlands, like Larry Paul (first British champion at light-middleweight),

Tony Sibson, Robert McCracken, Richie Woodhall, the exciting Kostas Petrou and Shaun Cummins to mention just a few.

The one that I had high hopes for but did not fulfil his potential was Errol Christie. I was deeply saddened when I learned of his premature death from lung cancer in June 2017 aged just fifty-three.

Errol, from Coventry, was a brilliant amateur boxer who captained England in 1980, became ABA champion the next year and is the only British boxer to win all ten amateur titles.

He turned professional with manager Burt McCarthy in 1982, and that is where I entered his life and career.

Errol won his first thirteen fights as a middleweight – all but one inside the distance. He looked so exciting at twenty years of age. I recall going to his twenty-first birthday party at McCarthy's home.

Having spotted Errol's potential I formed a relationship with McCarthy and persuaded him to let me put highlights of Errol's fights on my Central TV shows.

Then I thought up the idea of Saturday afternoon live boxing on ITV's *World of Sport*. I may have gone on to have my difficulties with Stuart McConachie after this, but in this period he was 100 per cent supportive of everything I did. He backed my idea, but in the long run it just did not sit easy on a Saturday afternoon. Recorded wrestling did, but not live boxing.

For the first episode, I put it to Burt that Errol should be the star. McCarthy was excited at the prospect. He booked Errol to fight at the Willenhall Social Club in Coventry for Saturday 15 October 1983 and ITV were ready to go.

The fight was scheduled straight after a big horse race from Newmarket. And that is where the trouble began.

First of all Christie's fast-growing reputation and power – eight wins out of eight and only one going the distance – meant that, as Burt was discovering, no one wanted to fight him. I joined in using my contacts. Burt was up all night and making himself ill with worry.

In the end, Frank Warren stepped in and, through the manager Doug Bidwell, he produced Welshman Doug James as the opponent for an eight-round fight. Burt and I were both mightily relieved. Frank has always been a good friend to me and to this day continues to deliver the goods.

So to the day of the transmission. The next problem was, as we were getting James ready to enter the ring first, there was a long delay before the Newmarket race was able to start. I had to keep promising the boxers that they would be walking 'any moment now'. It seemed to take an eternity, but eventually we were ready to go.

Referee Paul Thomas had to rescue a brave James after one minute of the fourth round.

Christie then won his next four on the trot and all inside the distance, before running into a shock defeat. This happened on ITV, with Frank Warren now promoting his contests. The date: 19 September 1984 at the Britannia Leisure Centre in Shoreditch. The opponent: Jose Seys from Belgium, who was eight pounds heavier than Christie and stopped Errol in forty-six seconds when referee Larry O'Connell had to call it to a halt. It was Errol's first defeat since he was fourteen years old.

I took some stick from at least one tabloid newspaper for telling Christie in the ring interview: 'Let's face it Errol – you cannot take a punch.'

Despite that cruel observation we stayed good friends, and I was pleased when Errol bounced back to win his next seven contests and all inside the distance.

Then came the Wembley Arena meeting with Mark Kaylor for the final eliminator for the British middleweight title on 5 November 1985 and it really was fireworks.

The fight had a nasty build-up. The pre-fight press conference at the Stakis Regency Casino in London brought an angry argument between the two boxers and then punches were thrown. Christie thought the word 'black' was used – Kaylor denied it.

The British Boxing Board of Control fined Kaylor £15,000 and Christie £5,000. This was not one of the fake incidents that often happens in boxing build-ups today.

There had been racial tension and inter-city riots earlier in the year, so this incident was not welcome. There was a sell-out crowd at Wembley. It was a National Promotions event, which meant it was being promoted by Mickey Duff and his team and was being shown on the BBC. I was given a ticket by Burt McCarthy, and there were plenty of extra security and police drafted in.

Kaylor was looking to regain the British title in a must-win for both camps. The winning bid to stake the contest was £82,000 – a record at the time.

Christie was down in the opening seconds but recovered to put Kaylor down towards the end of that first round. So it carried on, with Kaylor down again in the third but recovered to hurt Christie again, who was hanging on and so it went on, until Christie's brave effort to stay in the fight was finished in the eighth when Kaylor's hard right put Christie down and referee Harry Gibbs waved it off. Kaylor was the stronger puncher and they embraced at the end in respect to each other.

Christie had run out of both energy and ideas. He was twenty-two and, although he went on to collect more wins, two stoppages against Michael Watson and then Trevor Ambrose in the third and second rounds respectively meant it was time to retire in 1993 with a record of 41 contests 32 wins (26 by KO) 8 losses (7 by KO) and 1 draw.

He never achieved what he and his team had hoped for. It was all so sad in the end, but not as sad as his death from cancer at such a young age.

The last time I saw Errol was in a street in Manchester. We hugged each other and he thanked me for my support and friendship over the years.

The series *Fight Night* was conceived by Paul Doherty, head of sport for Granada Television in Manchester. I was the presenter and head of sport for Central TV. The two franchises were to partner on the show.

Paul managed to get other ITV companies to join us. All of them were north of London, including Ulster TV in Belfast and Scottish TV in Glasgow. Tyne Tees and briefly Yorkshire TV were among the others.

We used ITV's promoter Frank Warren, who brought in promoters like Jack Trickett in Manchester, Pat Brogan in Stoke, Alex Morrison in Glasgow and Paddy and Tommy Lynch in Birmingham.

Young, new and established boxers were on the bills. Nigel Benn even topped the Glasgow *Fight Night* on one show, while Terry Marsh did the same in Manchester.

It was all going well, until Frank Warren suddenly wanted to increase the fees. Paul called me to a meeting saying we could not afford it. Was I prepared to walk away? I said that, although Frank and I were good friends, business was business and yes, we should move on.

Before Paul told me how he planned to book fights moving forward, I asked him if he now believed the denial that Frank and I had given when he'd accused us of something that had shaken and angered us both.

Paul had been told that Frank had been paying me money. I have never taken a bent penny in my life and trust and integrity are vital to me – remember how crucial they were to my relationship with Ferguson and others. Obviously we both denied it when it was put to us after a show in Belle Vue, Manchester. I did not even know what any money would have been for!

'Now,' I said to Paul, 'as we've decided to move on from Frank, do you believe me when I say I never took a penny from him? I would not have been able to take that decision if Frank had paid me money.' He said he believed me, and I demanded to know who had told him.

It turned out that it was a high-profile member of London Weekend Television. I then went and confronted that person high up in their office. He denied the accusation, but when I told him my source he gave me the lame excuse that he had heard I'd been taking money from Frank from a fledgling company in Soho.

I left thinking, but unable to prove, that this was another anti-regional move.

Meanwhile Paul produced a new matchmaker to work for us in conjunction with independent promoters and sought my approval and backing. He was Charles Atkinson, a failed professional boxer but a brilliant coach with a great knowledge of the sport. He had done incredible things for international boxing in Thailand and produced six WBC world champions there, including Sot Chitalada, who stopped Britain's Charlie Magri on a cut left eye on 20 February 1985 at London's Alexandra Palace. It was the Thai's first defence of his flyweight title.

Atkinson matchmade some great fights and *Fight Night* continued to do well every Thursday fortnight.

Bob Burrows was head of sport at Thames TV and was close to Warren. He was upset that we had walked away from ITV's promoter even though we had no complaints about Frank except that we could not meet his financial demands. In fairness, he had done a good job for us.

There had been no other regional boxing, but Thames suddenly announced they were going to do their own version of *Fight Night* called *Seconds Out*.

In spite of this new competition, we survived until several of the regional companies started to drop out of showing boxing altogether, and we were left, budget-wise, only being able to afford to do *International Fight Night*, with Paul buying overseas rights cheaply. I was off to Thailand, the USA, Japan, Milan, France and other venues on a regular basis.

Paul bought a fight between René Jacquot, the reigning WBC super-welterweight champion from France, and John 'the Beast' Mugabi from Uganda, who was managed by Mickey Duff. The fight was at an open-air fun fair called Mirapolis at Cergy-Pontoise in the Paris area.

Although I was a rival in the boxing business to Jarvis Astaire, Mickey Duff and Terry Lawless because of my ITV connection and friendship with Frank Warren, I got on really well with the three of them, all of whom were involved in the fight between Jacquot and Mugabi.

So I stayed for three days in the same hotel as them in Paris. Duff was furious that Doherty had paid only $2,000 for the fight because no other overseas TV wanted it. He banged on about it, but I kept telling him that it was not his promotion and none of his business.

The actual fight on 8 July 1989 was awful. Jacquot took one punch, or so it seemed, and then fell down, claiming that he had twisted his knee after slipping on the canvas. The veteran big-fight referee Arthur Mercante Sr from the USA started a count, while Jarvis Astaire, who was sitting next to me at ringside, was yelling at him to stop the fight. Arthur was still counting while he was shouting back: 'Three... Shut up, Jarvis! Four...'

It was comical. It was all over in the first round after just two minutes and fifty-three seconds.

I climbed into the ring to interview Duff, who was hugging Mugabi as the new champion. Then Duff spotted me and ran over, saying: 'You ripped them off to buy the fight and in the end you paid too much!' before he ran off again.

I laughed my head off – a great line!

I also made, for the only time, the *It'll be Alright on the Night* bloopers show, which got an enquiry from the famous *Dick Clark Show* in the USA.

It was lucky that the episode of *Fight Night* was recorded, as after I finally interviewed Duff I turned to the camera to introduce the back-up fight when a French TV person, who was trying to get me out of the ring, deliberately stood in front of my camera. I lost my cool and whacked him. Although, they had to freeze the shot on the bloopers show. Good times.

CHAPTER TWENTY-TWO

THE EXTRAORDINARY
CHRIS EUBANK

The late Jarvis Astaire once said to me: 'The BBC and us have got Frank Bruno and Harry Carpenter and ITV have got Chris Eubank and Gary Newbon.'

I would not quite put us in the well-known 'Know what I mean, Harry?' Bruno/Carpenter class, but I certainly had an interesting relationship with Eubank. I liked him and appreciated that he was in the high TV ratings bracket with millions watching his fights, but he could drive me crazy at times with frustrations away from the TV screen.

I mentioned earlier that the four people on and off the TV who had the biggest effect on my career were Brian Clough, Sir Alex Ferguson, Jimmy Greaves and Chris Eubank.

Just as I did not get off to a good start with Sir Alex, it was the same when I first met and interviewed Chris.

ITV's *Midweek Special*, made by Thames Television, showed the defence of Chris Eubank's international title (not a full world title) against Argentina's Eduardo Domingo Contreras at the Brighton Centre near Eubank's home. I was to be the interviewer.

It was 25 April 1990. I popped into Eubank's dressing room to introduce myself and received a cool reception, which was fair enough as he was preparing to go into the ring a little later.

The fight was a big disappointment, with the Argentine intent on spoiling the party and Eubank who was twenty-three at the time was initially not able to cope, but by the end there was no doubt about the result with Eubank winning nearly every round on the scorecards.

I was quite aggressive in my interview. I told Chris that I thought if he kept producing displays like that, he would never win the world title. Eubank replied: 'That tells me you know nothing about boxing.'

I am told Chris played that tape over and over again before his first contest against Nigel Benn. It worked.

Eubank appeared to be arrogant, but in reality he was an approachable, personable guy who just loved his fame and being recognised.

Some time after that first meeting, by coincidence both of us were in the Metropole Hotel at Birmingham's National Exhibition Centre for unrelated meetings. Chris sought me out for a chat. He asked me if we could work together rather than have another Brighton episode. I said sure, but only as long as he accepted that I was not his PR machine. It began an excellent professional relationship that, in regards to big-TV fights, finished in Belfast on 21 May 1994.

It was Eubank's return fight with Ray Close for his WBO (World Boxing Organization) world super-middleweight crown at the King's

Hall. Our commentator, Reg Gutteridge, was in Venice for the wedding of his daughter so presenter Jim Rosenthal switched to that role and I moved from interviewer to presenter with Barry McGuigan.

I was staying at the Europa Hotel in the centre, while Eubank and his team were at the Balmoral Hotel on the city outskirts. He asked on the morning of the contest for me to come and see him. He had something to say.

There were rumours circulating that Chris was leaving ITV for Sky, and I feared that he was going to mention it in our live transmission.

I arrived in his suite and sitting there were his promoter Barry Hearn, his trainer Ronnie Davies and Eubank himself, sprawled across a chaise longue. I told Chris that if what I heard was true, I would never forgive him if he told our viewers about Sky, live on air. He said that the switch was true, but he would not mention Sky. All he wanted to do was thank ITV. I calmed down.

A little later, Eubank asked me how many of his fights I had covered. I told him that night's would be the eighteenth. He asked me what I would remember most.

I told him that I was very grateful to him because in the first fight in Brighton, he told the viewers and me that I clearly did not know anything about boxing. But after a recent fight he had told me that he'd taken a comment I made as a real compliment, since it was coming from such an expert on the sport. 'So,' I said, 'in the course of seventeen contests with you, I went from knowing f*** all to becoming a real expert!'

I was being rather sarcastic, but the three of them thought it was hilarious and Eubank was laughing so much he fell off the chaise longue.

Some of the stories first, and then the pick of his fights, in a career of 52 bouts with 45 wins (23 by KO) and 5 losses (4 of those in his last 6 contests). There were two draws – one was the controversial decision in the second fight with Nigel Benn, which I thought the latter won.

The eccentric Eubank was unpredictable. After his win over Benn in their first fight, I was in the ring interviewing him when suddenly he used the opportunity to propose to his girlfriend: 'Karron – marry me!' It certainly threw me. He was married that year.

I am told that he went to Paris at Hearn's invitation, upgraded the booked suite at the Four Seasons Hotel and filled it full of flowers, which he subsequently discovered he was allergic to and had removed. He also had a Rolls Royce on standby at the hotel! He said he lived rather lavishly.

On his return he presented Hearn with a bill of around £20,000 for the weekend. Barry said it was impossible to spend that much in the weekend. Eubank replied: 'You gave me the rope and I hung you.' In fairness to the lovable Eubank he then split the bill 50/50!

The most frustrating encounter I remember was his defence of the WBO world super-middleweight title against the American Ron Essett.

The fight was to be in Portugal, and it would be staged in the Quinta do Lago golf course car park. Barry Hearn had the tree in the middle removed and built a mini arena around the boxing ring. The dressing rooms were situated about 100 yards away or so in the country club.

I wasn't originally scheduled to be involved with this fight; I was with the Scotland team for the 1992 European Championships in

Sweden. But after they were knocked out, I was phoned and told I would be going to Portugal to meet a floor manager and engineer to cover the fight. My brief was to be in charge that end and do the interviews.

On the day of the fight, I was asked to interview Eubank at lunchtime live into *Saint & Greavsie* from the side of the swimming pool at the hotel. What should have been a simple task turned out to be really hard work.

I had to collect Eubank from his suite and take him to the interview position. Using the lift it should have taken two minutes at the most. Knowing Chris, however, I allowed half an hour.

Arriving at his room I was greeted by Chris: 'Ah, I am glad you are here. I want your opinion on what shirt I should wear.'

He pulled back a roller door in the wardrobe to reveal a lot of brand-new, smart designer shirts. He fancied the white one, which would have been wrong. With the bright sunshine it would not have suited the camera, but I could not find the right words so we debated for a few minutes as to which he should wear. I eventually got my way. The clock was ticking and he disappeared into the bathroom for a while with a black shirt.

We eventually got to the side of the pool with eight minutes to spare. But my relief was short-lived. Chris announced he had to go back to the room. Why?

'Because this watch does not go with this shirt. I'd planned to pair it with the white shirt.'

In frustration, I said: 'Chris, just keep your bloody hand down on the table,' at which point he said: 'If you are going to swear at me, I will not do this interview.' I said: 'Correct, I am so sorry. I apologise.'

In my earpiece I heard the production assistant in London: 'Three minutes to the live cross to Quinta do Lago.'

Suddenly, because of the fierce sunshine, Chris pulled out a pair of sunglasses from his pocket and put them on. They were reflectors, and all I could see was my cameraman behind us and me! I asked Chris to take them off, and we wasted a minute explaining the problem. He asked for a moment while he adjusted his eyes to the bright light.

'Twenty seconds to Gary,' I heard from London. I told Chris that we'd be going live any second now, and I suddenly thought: 'What am I going to ask?!'

Experience got me through, and as ever Chris was good value!

When it finished, he invited me back to his room for a chat, but I declined and made him look puzzled as I said: 'Thanks, Chris, but I am going to go and lie down in a darkened corner! I am knackered.'

I eventually sorted out ringside tickets for the Leeds United football manager Howard Wilkinson and one of his top players Gary McAllister, who were on holiday in the area. They had just won the Football League title – the last season before the Premier League began.

Racecourse owner and multi-millionaire property developer Stan Clarke – a great friend of mine – had also flown in at my invitation.

So to the fight on 27 June, and it was full of the usual Eubank drama. All was going smoothly as we went on air live on a Saturday night on ITV – or so we thought!

The floor manager got Essett into the ring with his manager Mickey Duff. But then there was a delay. A frantic floor manager reported to the director that, across in the country club dressing room, Eubank was skipping, wearing only his jock strap and protector cup, while his trainer Ronnie Davies was having a shower! The floor manager had pleaded with Eubank to come out, who stated quite firmly: 'I am not going to the ring until my trainer has finished his shower and gotten dressed.'

Some presenters, with no pundit to turn to, would have frozen, but without sounding too clever I had plenty of experience filling thirty minutes on live shows, and I'd had quite a time doing so at the Benn–Barkley fight.

We still did not know how long the delay would be, so I turned to Duff, who claimed that this was typical Eubank, employing deliberate delaying tactics! Actually it was not, and eventually we got what turned out to be a forgettable, boring contest over the twelve rounds.

Chris retained the WBO super-middleweight title for the third time with a unanimous points decision. The judge's scorecards were 117–112 points, 117–113 and 118–110.

After five more successful defences, Eubank and I travelled to Berlin for the challenge of the German-born Graciano Rocchigiani at the Deutschlandhalle on 5 February 1994.

The day before the contest, London asked me to take Eubank out filming in Berlin for opening shots for the live programme. I asked Eubank and he dressed up in his monocle and jodhpur, which are horse riding leggings and tights worn with boots. Chris told me he wore them so that people would be sure it was him.

I chose the Brandenburg Gate, an eighteenth-century neoclassical monument. It is the most famous sight in Berlin.

I asked Eubank to walk through it while we filmed him. Obviously recognising him in advance of the fight, the passing motorists were banging their horns in anger; I imagine they weren't happy at the sight of the man who was to fight their homegrown star strutting through their landmark in all his finery.

He said to me afterwards: 'I think they loved me,' to which I replied: 'Sorry to disappoint you, but they hated you, Chris!' He looked puzzled once more.

When it came to fight time, Chris entered the hall to loud boos and jeering. He then stood at the edge of the ring, paused and jutted his chin out in defiance! Programmes and the odd bottle came flying at him. Chris was standing right above our ringside commentator Reg Gutteridge, who yelled at him: 'Chris, for God's sake get into the ring!'

It was Eubank's thirty-eighth professional fight (his ninth defence of the WBO super-middleweight title) and he was unbeaten. He had won all of them apart from his previous two, which had been draws.

He was to win this one in Berlin comfortably by a unanimous decision, but I felt Eubank should have stopped the German. I put it to him that he had lost his 'killer' punch. The tragic fight with Michael Watson, which I will come on to in another chapter, had left an effect on Eubank, who, despite his eccentric ways, is a decent human being with feelings.

The next day I flew home to be greeted by a phone call from a great pal Colin Hart the experienced and much respected boxing and athletics writer for *The Sun* newspaper.

'Hallo, mate. I'm afraid I've rung to stitch you up. The paper want to do a piece on your remark to Eubank in the ring – the one that he had lost his "killer punch".'

I was surprised and even more so the next day when the back-page headline in *The Sun* was 'TASTELESS'. 'Killer punch' was a common boxing term in those days.

That night I was at a boxing dinner in London and the famous veteran referee Harry Gibbs told me: 'I think *The Sun* took a real liberty with you.'

I thanked Harry for his concern but said I was fine; the only thing that annoyed me was they did not use a picture of me! He laughed and thought my comment about the photo was so funny that he went around the room telling a few people.

I will come on to his super fights with Michael Watson, Nigel Benn and Steve Collins in further chapters, but I have a couple more stories about the eccentric Eubank.

The first involved an interview in Brighton, when Eubank kept my editor Jeff Farmer and me waiting while he had his hair cut for the chat. What was different was that he had flown the hairdresser down from Lancashire and left me to pay the bill!

Then after my wife had an unexpected dinner in Cardiff with the great tenor Luciano Pavarotti and his promoter for the night at the invitation of a friend of mine called Rod Gunner, I was asked by his record label representative (a posh chap who lived near Harrods in Knightsbridge and was another guest) if I happened to be driving to London the next day.

I told him that I lived in Solihull, but I was driving to talkSPORT studios in Oxford Street the next day to present a show. I said my wife Katie and I would be delighted to give him a lift.

On the journey I was asked what Chris Eubank was really like. I was about to explain when my phone went. It was on open talk back (speakerphone), and I remember we were passing signs to Reading at the time: 'Gary, it is Christopher Eubanks here [his birth name is Christopher Livingstone Eubanks]...'

I didn't need to say another word until we reached Oxford Street. Eubank rambled on about the meaning of life. I thought: 'Will he ever shut up?'

We reached Harrods, and I quietly got my passenger out with his luggage. I apologised to him. He replied: 'No, no. It was quite fascinating. Remarkable chap.' As I returned I quietly asked my wife: 'Did he notice?' She shook her head. When we got to Oxford Street, I told Chris that I had to go, and he sounded quite disappointed.

Susan Hearn, the wife of Barry, gave Chris the tag 'Simply the Best', from the Tina Turner song. Inspired choice.

Chris Eubank was one of the best.

Someone asked me if I have any ambitions left. My answer: 'I have had a great life and I just want all my children and grandchildren to outlive me. I ask for nothing else.'

So I was devastated for Chris when he suffered any parent's worst nightmare; one of his sons, Sebastian Eubank, drowned. How do you ever live with that? I cannot imagine. ITV and Sky's outstanding boxing co-commentator Jim Watt has lost both of his children and the late ITV head of sport John Bromley lost a son in a car accident in Birmingham. It makes me go cold thinking about it all.

Eubank was a fine, brave boxer with a great chin. Nigel Benn was also brave, with a massive punch and an attitude of 'have gum shield will travel round the world'. He was certainly different from Eubank and at times he was difficult – a complete contrast to the Nigel of today.

But I always admired him in the ring. He comes up next.

CHAPTER TWENTY-THREE

'THE TEAR-UP', NIGEL BENN

Nigel Benn was an exciting, brave fighter who would fight anybody and anywhere. His form could be a bit like our professional relationship.

He would be angry with some of my questions and give me a bollocking, or he could be lovely and give me a hug, as he did in the ring in Rome after a result in his favour. Mind you, it ruined a suit I had bought that day, but the damage was not caused on purpose.

His anger came out at the Brentwood Centre in Essex after outpointing Lenzie Morgan over ten rounds on 26 October 1991.

I questioned an aspect of Benn's performance that night and he lashed into me. Fair enough.

Then after the tragic Gerald McClellan fight on 25 February 1995 at the London Arena, he told me to shut up, saying: 'We are always listening to you,' cutting me off when I was trying to alert *everyone* that McClellan was collapsing near me.

Benn also said, referring to McClellan: 'They sent him over to bash me up.' That may have been true, because he and his then handlers were acting difficult and unhelpful with all of us. It was a time when Ambrose Mendy was no longer involved, and I missed his co-operation. Frank Warren and Don King were the promoters.

The ruined-suit job came on 2 October 1992 in Marino, Lazio. Benn stopped Mauro Galvano because of cuts that forced the end of the fight after the third round to take his WBC super-middleweight title.

After Galvano was unable to continue, there was confusion and controversy as to which way the fight was going to go. Promoter Barry Hearn got involved and persuaded the officials to go to the WBC rules. When it was announced that Benn had won he hugged me in delight. I had bought a very expensive designer suit in Rome that afternoon. The oil and sweat on Benn's body ruined it and I was never able to wear it again. Mind you, that was hardly life-changing!

Chris Eubank was at ringside to challenge Benn for his new WBC title and put Eubank's WBO on the line as well. Benn first beat Nicky Piper with a TKO in the eleventh round in London, then Galvano in the return with a unanimous points decision in Glasgow, and then stopped Lou Gent in four at Earls Court.

Benn fought five times in the USA. He beat two USA boxers – first Doug DeWitt in Atlantic City in eight rounds on 29 April 1990 to win the WBO middleweight title. Then on 18 August that year at Bally's Casino in Las Vegas, he beat Iran Barkley to retain the title in one round under the three-knockdown rule, whereby a fighter wins by knocking their opponent down three times in the same round. This rule was being applied by the WBO at that time.

Promoter Bob Arum had told me before the fight that the employment of the three judges was an unnecessary expense and he was right. They hadn't been required at all and the fight was over. That is what Benn did to Barkley.

I, however, was left with a huge amount of time to fill, so I told Benn's manager, Ambrose Mendy, that I needed help.

Mendy told Benn to attack the British Boxing Board of Control for taking a percentage of his purse but not sending a representative to the fight. In the live televised interview with me, he did just that by ripping up his boxing licence in anger – or at least everyone thought he had, and the story made headlines back home.

· When Benn was brought before the Board for bringing boxing into disrepute, he produced the licence intact. With slight of hand Benn had actually torn up a strip of a cereal packet. He was like a magician. I was close up and I did not spot the switch.

Mendy was a fascinating character who has been in and out of jail on convictions over the years. I always liked him and he was always respectful and polite in my dealings with him. He never let me down. I was still surprised one day when he rang me from his latest sentence in prison to offer me a fight. I asked him where he was phoning from and he said: 'The Governor's office.' What an operator.

Benn and Eubank shared a few things. In my opinion, they both went on too long. Both also lost to the Irishman Steve Collins in the twilight of their careers.

Benn's last two fights were both against Collins. The penultimate one brought a TKO defeat in the fourth round to Collins for the latter's WBO super-middleweight title in the then NYNEX Arena in Manchester on 6 July 1996. Then on 9 November that year, in the same arena for the same title, Benn was retired at the end of the sixth round.

Eubank lost for the first time in his career when Collins out-smarted and out-psyched him to take the WBO world super-middleweight title in Ireland with a unanimous points decision. That was 18 March 1995 in Millstreet, Ireland, and then he lost to Collins again on 9 September the same year for the same title near Cork in Ireland.

I did not cover of any of those Benn–Collins or Eubank–Collins fights. I always rated Collins. It was a golden time for UK and Irish middle and super-middleweight boxing. Michael Watson, Eubank, Benn and the Irishman Collins.

Benn's record was 48 fights, 42 wins (35 by KO) 5 losses (4 by KO) and the one draw with Eubank, which as previously mentioned I thought Benn had won, and so did he. His losses were those against Collins and before that against Watson, Eubank, and Thulani Ma-linga losing his WBO title by a split points decision over the twelve rounds on 2 March 1996 at the then Telewest Arena in Newcastle.

To keep his career in proportion, three of those five defeats were in his final contests at the end of a hard and at times fierce career. He was one of the most exciting boxers ever, and I had huge respect for his bravery.

Both Benn and Eubank enjoyed brilliant careers overall. They are British boxing legends.

Benn's first defeat to Michael Watson, like Eubank, came after a long unbeaten run to start his career.

But for his terrible injuries, which I will cover in the next chap-ter, Watson could have been the best of the lot, but we will never know. It is a subjective view. Mine is that Watson would have out-classed them both.

In retirement, Benn greeted me warmly and with a hug when he was still living in England. He has found peace with God and seems content with life. He deserves that and is now based in Australia, returning occasionally to watch the professional boxing progress of his son, Conor.

Nigel competed as a professional from 1987 to 1996. He tried to make a comeback at fifty-five, but the BBBoC put a stop to that. There have also been suggestions since that Benn and Eubank would get it on again, but nothing came of that.

The Dark Destroyer, as Benn was called, held, like Eubank, the world title at two different weights and also the Commonwealth title.

For one period, Benn and Mendy were outside the two main promoters, who at the time were Warren and Hearn. I went behind ITV Sport's heads and spoke to the chairman, Greg Dyke, and said: 'Benn is exciting and he is stuck with no one to fight against. I can get his next fight cheap.' Dyke, a good mate over the years, could see the attraction, so he gave me the backing.

I said to Mendy: 'I can pull it off for you, but I need a promise that Nigel will fight on my *Fight Night* series.' They promised and kept their word on that, and Nigel fought on an Alex Morrison bill, beating Mbayo Wa Mbayo with a second-round knockout at the Kelvin Hall in Glasgow.

That was 28 March 1989. On 8 February of that year, 'my fight' was his previous bout, in which he knocked out Michael Chilambe to retain his Commonwealth title in only sixty-seven seconds of the first round at the Royal Albert Hall!

On reflection the profile of Benn was good for *Fight Night*, but the network production was not good in terms of the coverage of the actual contest. However, Benn and Mendy kept their word and they benefited by getting back in the swing of things with the Watson fight at Finsbury Park.

I was privileged to then be a ringside reporter from the start of the '90s onwards for Benn and Eubank. As a professional boxer you have to be so brave to get into the ring. It is a dangerous sport and you do put your life and brain on the line. The next chapter illustrates this point so clearly.

Benn and Eubank were still to be involved in winning fights throughout the upcoming decade, but it is a dangerous sport and they were to inflict life-changing injuries on their opponents. I was working as usual in our commentary position with Reg Gutteridge and Jim Watt and then in the ring for the post-fight interviews, with millions viewing live on ITV as the tragedies unfolded.

CHAPTER TWENTY-FOUR

TWO TRAGIC FIGHTS

The 1990s brought four epic and then two tragic fights involving Nigel Benn, Chris Eubank, Michael Watson, and Gerald McClellan.

Benn was unbeaten in twenty-two fights when he met Michael Watson in a venue in Finsbury Park in London on 21 May 1989. Both were first-class fighters and it was made for TV. Benn was defending his Commonwealth middleweight championship, which he had won thirteen months earlier.

Going into this one, Michael had won all but two of his twenty-three professional fights – losing to James Cook on points over eight rounds and drawing with Israel Cole in a technical decision when Cole was cut from an accidental head clash in the second round.

Benn had won all his fights inside the distance. He was definitely in the explosive-boxer class. He was relaxed about Watson's good record. He said of Watson that he was a lovely man who was good-looking and extremely polite; he praised him for the fact that he did not mouth off.

Benn thought it would be an easy day at the office. He was so wrong.

Watson's manager was the shrewd Mickey Duff, who told Watson to cover up and let Benn burn himself out. Michael's team were smarter on the night. Watson survived the early attacks, hurt Benn in the fourth round and knocked out an exhausted Benn in the sixth. Benn was too tired to beat the count.

Benn then went to the famous Fifth Street Gym in Miami to discover what he really needed to do. Watson challenged Mike McCallum, who was known as 'the Body Snatcher', for the WBA middleweight title at the Royal Albert Hall the following year, but he had been trying to balance against illness and a broken nose in training. He was stopped in the eleventh round.

Watson did have two more unsuccessful world title shots which I covered at ringside – both against Chris Eubank. For the first, I went to the press conference at the Grosvenor Hotel in London's Park Lane.

We stood for a while chatting on our own while Eubank dominated proceedings. Watson and I always got on well and had an emotional hug and reunion at the British Board's 2023 awards at the Brewery in London's Chiswell Street.

The first fight was at the Earls Court Exhibition Centre in London on 22 June 1991, and the WBO middleweight title was on the line. Eubank won on a majority decision. It was so close – too close for me, and I had Watson winning it. The judges gave it to Eubank 116–113; 115–113 and 114–114.

The rematch was a few months later on 21 September for the vacant WBO super-middleweight title outdoors at White Hart

Lane. Watson was clearly ahead in the eleventh round when he put Eubank down with a right punch. Eubank got up and hit Watson with an unbelievable uppercut that sent Watson reeling back; his head hit the ropes.

The referee Roy Francis stopped it in the twelfth, at which point Watson collapsed in the ring. The tragedy of what followed was to change the standard of safety measures that are taken in British boxing. Astonishingly, there was no ambulance or paramedic at the event. Doctors rushed from a dinner event minutes later, but during that time there was no oxygen to give Watson.

I interviewed Eubank in the ring. Eubank said that he wanted Watson tested. I misunderstood what Eubank meant, thinking he was referring to a drug test or the like, but he actually meant he wanted to somehow take a measure of the tremendous strength of Watson.

I went home not realising quite how serious events were after the chaos that followed. It did not take long to discover that Michael was having to fight to stay alive.

Michael spent forty days in a coma and underwent several operations to remove a blood clot on his brain. Eventually Michael regained consciousness and began the long road to recovery, which entailed a lot of time in intensive care and rehabilitation. He was in a wheelchair for six years, but with steely determination he regained his speech and some movement. Incredibly, he completed the London Marathon in April 2003, walking two hours each morning and afternoon for six days and raising money for various brain and spine charities in the process.

Chris Eubank, who was emotionally affected by Watson's injuries, and Peter Hamlyn, the neurosurgeon who operated on him, were by his side when he crossed the finishing line.

We will never know what Watson would have gone on to achieve. His record was 30 fights; 25 wins (21 by KO) 4 losses and 1 draw. The Queen awarded Michael the MBE for services to disability sport and in 2012 he was a torchbearer for the Paralympic relay.

Watson is very religious and bears no grudges against Chris Eubank or boxing. He is a truly wonderful person.

The very first action the BBBoC took was to ban me from doing post-match interviews in the ring, and for the next fight I covered I had to do the interview in the boxers' dressing room, as if the Board's negligence was my fault. One winning boxer went mad at me, thinking I was ignoring him; he didn't realise I was banished to his dressing room!

The other tragic fight was the WBC world super-middleweight contest at the London Arena just under four years later, on 25 February 1995 at the London Arena in the Docklands, between Benn and the fearsome American Gerald McClellan.

Benn had been proving difficult. McClellan was a two-time world middleweight champion – holding the WBO version from 1991 to 1992 and the WBC from 1993 to 1995. Benn was now the WBC super-middleweight holder.

McClellan was a fearsome puncher and had produced some of the best first-round knockouts in the history of boxing. His 31 wins had 29 by KO, and before this fight he had just 2 losses.

He was training at the Peacock Gym run by brothers Tony and Martin Bowers from a real boxing family. I was assigned to film and interview McClellan. He looked so strong and I recall him talking to me about his two pet rottweilers.

So to the night with around 10,000 packed in the arena and millions more watching live on ITV.

The atmosphere was noisy and a little hostile. McClellan was the bookies favourites at 1–3. The event was a joint promotion between Frank Warren and the American Don King who was McClellan's promoter.

McClellan had told me he would produce a vicious knockout and indeed within thirty seconds or so of the first round, Benn was knocked through the ropes and landed on the protection cover on my TV monitor at ringside. I found myself trying to push Benn through the ropes but not making a fist of it. Our commentator Reg Gutteridge exploded: 'Someone is trying to help Benn back. They have parked the rules at the gate here,' but he stopped when co-commentator Jim Watt lifted his headphones and said in his ear: 'It's Gary!'

It was a brutal fight and there are rumours that McClellan told his trainer Stan Johnson that he wanted to quit. The trainer denied this.

The brutal tit-for-tat fight continued as a fierce spectacle. Benn was doing well until McClellan knocked Benn down again in the eighth to take that round.

By the tenth round I realised McClellan had never been past eight rounds despite this being his thirty-fourth contest. Benn connected with a right that forced McClellan down on one knee until he got up on the count of seven. But soon after Benn dropped him again with another right and McClellan was again on one knee but allowed the referee to count him out.

At first we thought Gerald had quit, as he walked back to his corner and collapsed on his back.

Meanwhile I was trying to get in the ring – I had been allowed back for a while now to do the post-fight interviews – but I was hindered by a security man. I told him what I was doing. I had never seen him before, but he said: 'Sorry, Gal,' and held up the rope for me. I did not know who he was.

At the end of the year I discovered that he was a friend of Benn's called Tony Tucker, who, along with two other men, was shot dead in a Range Rover in Rettendon on 6 December, allegedly in connection to drug trafficking. It was known as 'the Essex Boys' murders.

Once in the ring I started interviewing a fairly wild Nigel, but I noticed McClellan (out of TV picture range) collapsed on the canvas, and all I could think about was the Eubank–Watson ending. I tried to shut Benn up without success with him ranting: 'We are always having to listen to you.' I wanted to somehow alert my director to what was happening.

In the confusion and my anxiety to return to the presenter Jim Rosenthal, I accidentally called McClellan 'McCallum', who had been on the bill earlier (WBC light-heavyweight champion McCallum had retained his title against Carl Jones). I got well hammered in the newspapers, particularly in the *Daily Telegraph*, for saying: 'Something is happening here to McCallum.' Ah, well; it goes with the territory.

Due to the new regulations by the British Boxing Board of Control after the second Eubank–Watson fight and the 1994 death of boxer Bradley Stone, the medics were present and placed McClellan in a neck brace and gave him oxygen.

Both fighters were taken rapidly to the nearby Royal London hospital where a brain surgeon removed a blood clot. McClellan spent almost two weeks in a coma and it was several months before he left hospital.

I spent several hours outside the hospital feeling relieved to discover Benn was just exhausted but fearing for McClellan. Benn was distressed and said his heart went out to his stricken opponent. Benn added it was a fierce but fair fight, but no one could imagine such a great sporting event could end so sadly.

Thirteen million had watched ITV's coverage and the channel put a block on any repeats for a long while. After one more contest, ITV pulled out of boxing for four years.

The after-effects for poor Gerald McClellan are that he is blind, struggles greatly with comprehending what little he hears, has memory problems and is in a wheelchair, though he has regained the ability to walk a little with a cane. He still needs full-time care.

Less than two years later Benn was out of boxing following those two losses to Steve Collins.

Benn–McClellan is the greatest, most brutal fight I have ever covered, but the thought of the outcome still makes me shudder, even after all these years.

Before that there had been the two epic Benn v. Eubank contests in Birmingham and Manchester respectively. The first fight was the better of the two, but they drew big audiences both at the NEC Arena and then Old Trafford, with, as ever on their big fights, many millions viewing on ITV.

So let me turn the clock back to Benn–Eubank I. The date and venue: 18 November 1990 at the National Exhibition Centre in Birmingham. It was a ferocious contest for Benn's WBO middleweight title in front of an excited full house.

In the build-up to the fight, Benn and his advisor Ambrose Mendy discovered he was over the weight limit. They blamed false scales in their nearby hotel room. Mendy rang me to arrange the use of a local gym for Benn to run off the extra pounds. I was having a personal training session with the former goalkeeper Paul

Barron at a city centre gym and arranged for Benn and Mendy to go there. I later heard that Benn fell off a running machine.

Come the night of the fight and there were accusations of some dirty tricks being played against Eubank. There were dirty towels in Eubank's dressing room, which would have been abhorrent to him. Then on the way to the ring, his walk-in music, 'Simply the Best', was sabotaged. His promoter, Barry Hearn lost his cool, but Eubank, always the calm one, quietened Hearn, saying: 'Barry, I will give the boy a good spanking.'

I was ringside with the executive producer Stuart McConachie, our excellent and regular statistician Bob Mee and the commentators Reg Gutteridge and Jim Watt. Everyone had been looking forward to this special, all-domestic encounter between two exceptional middleweight boxers, and we at ITV were no exception. It was a big fight for us all.

We all knew this would be something special and it was. We smiled as Chris spent half the first and second round breaks strutting around the ring.

In the end Eubank wore Benn down, but Eubank was in pain and in the post-match interview he revealed to me that he was suffering from a cut tongue and mouth.

Four seconds from the end of the ninth round in one of the most memorable fights in UK history the then world's No. 1 referee, the USA's Richard Steele, rescued the courageous Benn, who was really out on his feet against the robes. Steele halted the fight and Eubank was the winner!

It was a humane decision by Steele. Each boxer's immense and painful courage was never in doubt.

I could see and hear Eubank's agony in that immediate interview.

It had been a non-stop battle to the end. Even so Eubank never ceased to amaze me and threw me mentally off balance when he suddenly, during my interview, chose to propose to his girlfriend Karron: it is worth repeating! 'Karron,' he said, looking into our camera, 'marry me!'

And she did, the next month. They had four children – Chris Jr (himself a world champion boxer), Sebastian, Emily and Joseph – during their fifteen years together before Karron divorced him in 2005.

Benn was gracious in defeat after what at times had been a genuinely acrimonious build-up, telling me in his interview: 'Whatever I think of Chris Eubank, I have nothing but respect for the way he fought tonight.'

Eubank was to reign world champion for over five years and no one beat him for his first ten years – and never at the middleweight class.

That unbeaten record was threatened twelve fights and nearly three years later with the rematch on 9 October 1993 in front of 40,000 fans at Old Trafford, in what was to be the last time the Manchester United ground hosted a boxing promotion. At stake were two super-middleweight titles: Eubank held the WBO belt, while Benn held the WBC. This unification meeting for the two world titles was not as spectacular as their first meeting and this time the result of a draw was controversial.

The build-up was fascinating. Barry Hearn set up the fight, but finances were tight, so Don King was invited to be involved, as was Frank Warren.

The three of them hosted a pre-fight dinner in the French restaurant at the Midland Hotel, where we were all staying. I took my wife Katie to the fight. King always took a shine to Katie, who likes the fine arts and drama. He quoted Elizabethan/Shakespearean sonnets to her. On the way back to our room, Katie said that she was impressed, although they were not quite accurate!

King always called me 'Gary Newbon, the Voice of ITV Boxing'. He did it sometime later, when we met with Warren after ITV had lost Frank's promotions to Sky Sports; the witty Warren corrected King by saying: 'Gary has lost his voice.' A great line!

I had asked Warren for the return Eubank–Benn contest if sports-mad super violinist Nigel Kennedy could play the National Anthem in the ring before the contest. Kennedy, a good friend over the years and an Aston Villa fan, is eccentric at times and played a weird version. I do not think Frank was too impressed!

The fight went the distance. It was a split points decision. The judges' scorecards: Carol Castellano (USA) 113–114 Benn; Harry Gibbs (England) 115–113 Eubank; and Chuck Hassett (USA) 114–114 draw. It was close, but I scored the same as Mrs Castellano. Benn clearly agreed and rushed out of the ring in utter dismay and refused to do the interview.

Mrs Castellano was a boxing judge for over twenty-five years and is one of the best judges in the world.

As it happened the draw worked out well for Hearn. At King's insistence Barry had given the American the option on the next fight to clinch his backing and when he heard King boasting to the media about it Barry informed him that he only had the option on the winner – not the draw.

Hearn had got lucky!

CHAPTER TWENTY-FIVE

THE PRINCE

One of the great characters in British boxing was Brendán Íngle, who turned out four world champions from his Wincobank gym (a church hall) in Sheffield. They were Johnny Nelson, Junior Witter, Kell Brook and Prince Naseem Hamed. He also trained six European, fifteen British and six Commonwealth champions. His sons John and Dominic carry on the legacy.

Brendán had an odd sense of humour and gave some of his fighters 'stage names'. For instance, Clifton Mitchell was a heavyweight from Derby, and he called him 'Paddy Reilly'. Others included 'Slugger O'Toole' (real name Fidel Castro Smith) and 'Kid Galahad' (Abdul-Bari Awad). I would look at them and think – 'What?'

Íngle was from Dublin; this unusual Irishman passed away in May 2018 aged seventy-seven. He lived near the gym and was once asked to do some community work by the local vicar because the local youths were out of control. He organised a weekly dance and then opened the boxing gym. His boxers were taught footwork, brilliant defences and leaving their hands free to attack.

I gave Johnny Nelson, one of Íngle's fighters, a rough interview after his attempt to win the WBC cruiserweight title against Carlos de León at the City Hall, Sheffield, on 27 January 1990. We televised it live on ITV. The fight finished in a draw – and was one of the most boring fights I have covered. I told Johnny in so many words that he should change his nickname 'the Entertainer' as this performance was certainly not entertaining!

In fairness to Johnny he went on to win the WBO world title and successfully defended it fourteen times.

Johnny has never held it against me and stayed a good mate both in the gym and for future interviews; we went on to work together at Sky Sports, where he is a long-time and accomplished pundit in their boxing team.

Of special interest to me in that Sheffield gym was a bright young amateur called Naseem Hamed who was dubbed 'Prince' by Brendán Îngle. He was sent to the gym as an unruly seven-year-old by his Yemeni father and was a boxing champion by eleven years old. I used to watch him develop when regularly visiting the gym to interview Îngle and his other boxers.

He turned out to be one of the most exciting and best British boxers I have ever seen. Lennox Lewis is the best British heavyweight and I will say more on him later in this chapter.

One day I was talking to Mickey Duff of National Promotions. He complained that he could not sell Hamed's contests to the BBC. I will spare the top executive's name, but Duff claimed: 'They didn't want an Arab name as a boxer on their bills!'

Can you imagine the reaction to that today?

Anyway, I said nothing but reported that back to Trevor East, who now held a senior ITV position in London. Trevor backed my judgement on how terrific Hamed would be and told Frank Warren about our conversation. Frank said he would sign him if ITV would televise Hamed and Trevor agreed.

We started at the Leisure Centre in Mansfield and Hamed soon picked up the European bantamweight championship. He was flashy, athletic and entered the ring with a somersault over the top rope; he also wore leopard-print shorts. Later in his global TV career he was to enter on a flying carpet and perform other spectacular stunts.

He was a hard-hitting southpaw with a one-punch knockout power. With his slippery, hands-down style he was difficult to hit and went on to win thirty-six of his thirty-seven professional bouts with thirty-one of them by knockout.

He was so relaxed. When he fought Sergio Rafael Liendo at the Forum in Livingstone on 4 March 1995 I invited my daughter Claire, who was at nearby Edinburgh University, and a group of her student friends to the boxing. They were thrilled to be taken into Naseem's dressing room prior to the fight and he welcomed them all and had a photo taken with them.

Hamed went on to be a multiple world champion and was even selling out promotions before his opponents were announced. He wowed New York and was responsible for a new young crowd of followers to the sport.

Two things then happened. First of all, Frank Warren split from ITV to sell his promotions for a lucrative sum to Sky Sports. Then eventually Naz, as he was known, left Warren for his brother Raith to handle his affairs. He also fell out with Ingle.

He changed his trainers twice – the second one being the great Emanuel Steward in America. Hamed did make a lot of money, but he was not in the best of shapes for his penultimate contest, which brought his only defeat – he fought against the legendary Mexican Marco Antonio Barrera at the MGM in Las Vegas.

Steward had been complaining that Naseem was not training properly and had been watching videos of his earlier opponents and not the recent ones for whom Barrera had been on top form. The result was that the Mexican won a unanimous points decision over the twelve championship rounds.

Hamed had one more fight, which he won with a unanimous points decision in his favour, but clearly it was not the Hamed we knew, and he sensibly retired.

That should not detract from what he achieved as Britain's best-ever featherweight and the impact he had on boxing as a whole, especially with young supporters.

He had a set-back when he was jailed for fifteen months for dangerous driving after a terrible car accident that gave life-changing injuries to the victims in the car he hit.

But he is still wealthy and appears to be enjoying life. I had lunch with him three years ago near his home in the Virginia Water area. I have always liked and admired Naz and he has a special place in my career, as do the promoters Barry Hearn and Frank Warren, who remain good and valued friends to this day. Like Eubank and Benn, Naseem has a son who has just joined the professional ranks.

I first met Warren when he was promoting ITV shows through Thames Television and their head of sport, Bob Burrows. Frank was promoting at the Crest Hotel in Bloomsbury Square. The early TV shows featured Joe Bugner in 1982. Joe was thirty-two years old then. He knocked out Winston Allen in three rounds on 28 October before stopping Eddie Neilson in the fifth round when the Swindon heavyweight had to retire in the contest with a cut eyebrow.

The big London promoters known in the boxing cartel were Harry Levine, Mike Barrett, Jarvis Astaire, Mickey Duff and manager Terry Lawless. This lot had the London scene sewn up in their favour with restrictions on venues, times, live TV screenings and so on. Young Warren spent a fortune on lawyers to successfully fight all these barriers.

He successfully brought many world title promotions to the UK and ITV. I have always enjoyed a great relationship with him. I persuaded my programme controller at Central TV, Andy Allan, to deal directly with Frank one day to buy the Colin Jones (from Wales) v. Don Curry (of Fort Worth Texas) world title fight at the National Exhibition Centre in Birmingham. Allan was powerful enough to be able to do a deal with Frank and so we did the production with my sports editor Jeff Farmer as editor of the programme.

The night before, I hosted a dinner party at a club called 64 in Birmingham's Hagley Road for the American boxing promoter Bob Arum, Frank and the head of ITV Sport John Bromley, plus a few others.

The fight did not last the scheduled fifteen rounds on 19 January 1985. Curry, the reigning WBA and IBF welterweight world champion, extended his unbeaten record to 21–0 when Jones had his nose cut so badly across the bridge that the referee had to bring in two Birmingham doctors who asked the referee to wave the fight off early in the fourth round. Those doctors were the Aston Villa club doctor David Targett and a Solihull medic called Michael Abdou.

The disappointed Welsh fans started throwing things into the ring, so Paul Doherty helped steer Colin Jones towards me so I could interview him. Jones was so disappointed after working so hard for the challenge and said he would have gone all fifteen rounds but for the cut. He said it was the first time he had ever been stopped.

Meanwhile Frank was to manage and promote many more world champions and European, British and Commonwealth title fights. He also dealt with what I (and many others in the boxing community) would describe as the Mickey Mouse belts – international, silver or whatever.

A *Fight Night* show at Stoke was the WBC international super-featherweight championship featuring Robert Dickie at Stoke on Trent. It was in 1988 and five months after Dickie had won it in March. This time he lost when stopped by Tunisian Kamel Bou Ali, who went on to be WBO world champ.

Frank and some of my network colleagues at Thames Television took the mickey out of the title, claiming in a derisory manner that it was the Freight Rover Trophy (football's non-league trophy competition at the time). It was not too long that other promoters, including Frank, were staging these international championship contests as indeed they still do today!

Warren was smart, inventive and a quick thinker, with a sharp sense of humour that has made me laugh many times. He has lasted the distance; he's still going very strong as a promoter and has, as I write, most of the world's top heavyweights in his ranks, including Tyson Fury. Since those early days he has always enjoyed and deserved TV coverage.

He also coped with some of my tough interview questions to his boxers, although the tables were sometimes turned on me! There was a memorable incident with Terry Marsh in his IBF world light-welterweight title challenge to American Joe Manley in a circus tent in his hometown of Basildon, which was live on ITV.

Marsh was challenging for the IBF light-welterweight title. Although Marsh was unbeaten (as he continued to be for his career), I thought Manley would retain his title. The date: 4 March 1987.

An hour before the fight I had to record an interview with Marsh in the nearby Crest Hotel, which was the dressing room for the boxers. While we were waiting, Marsh asked me if I thought he would win. What do you say to a question like that before the boxer fights? I replied: 'Of course you will, Terry.'

Come the fight and Marsh, brilliant as ever, stops Manley in the tenth. I get into the ring, and my first question to Marsh was: 'Well, that was quite an upset wasn't it, Terry?' To which he replied: 'That's not what you told me an hour ago, Gary. You said I would win!' Stuffed!

Two years earlier in October 1985, Marsh won the then vacant European light-welterweight title in a deserted Stade Louis-II arena in Monaco live on ITV's *World of Sport*. I was taken to see the fight by ITV. I got on well with Marsh and the day before he asked me to join him on a very long walk around Monaco, which included going through the iconic road tunnel on the Formula One circuit, and we walked round the boats in the Marina.

I remember Terry talking about his days in the Royal Marines before he became a professional boxer. He served in Northern Ireland in the Troubles and told me of his experiences.

I always enjoyed the Marsh fights. He successfully defended his new world title once and then retired undefeated, citing epilepsy.

The next I heard of Marsh was when he was arrested on the charge of attempted murder of Frank Warren, who had issued a libel writ at the time against Marsh for a comment on TV. Marsh was acquitted at his trial after being on remand for ten months. The police have never charged anyone else. Warren knows who shot him – the gunman was masked at the time with a balaclava on his head – but says where he comes from you do not grass on people.

The gunman fired two shots at Warren. One went round his body like a bagatelle. His great friend the lawyer John Botros, threw himself across Frank like a bodyguard. It all happened outside the Broadway Theatre in Barking before a Warren promotion there in November 1989.

Frank lost half a lung and was off for a considerable period, which had a massive impact on his business, including the London Arena, a project that he had been one of the leads on. It is testimony to his business sense and determination that he made such a comeback. Ironically, talking of comebacks he booked Frank Sinatra to sing at the Arena. Frank, by the way, did not win the libel case against Marsh.

When the London Arena was almost open, Frank showed Don King and me around it. Don was worried about a coach he had ordered to bring his guests from Heathrow after they had flown in from the USA. They were to attend the world title fight at Wembley that Warren and King had arranged. I asked Don who the guests were, and he told me they were members of the jury that had recently acquitted him at a trial. As he used to say: 'Only in America!'

In my dealings with Frank, I used to love his matchmaker, Ernie Fossey. Even when a promotion was falling apart, Ernie would assure you: 'It will be a good fight!' He would do so even when he could not tell you who was fighting! It was a sad day when Ernie passed away in September 2003. He was a boxing man for six decades from fighter to matchmaker. He is attributed with saying: 'The art is to make the opponent's manager think he's got half a chance, when I know full well he has no hope.'

Warren is always generous at restaurants etc. Not long ago I met Warren and Botros at a Kensington restaurant. I wanted an interview with Frank and wanted to buy him lunch. There was nothing for him to gain, but he still insisted on paying at the end, leaving the waiters a huge tip. His real friends are friends for life.

I am so pleased that Warren has experienced massive nights in Las Vegas with Tyson Fury, whose career Frank has really put on the map. His sons are now involved in his boxing business, Queensbury Promotions, but I am sure Frank will always be there to guide them.

Barry Hearn's son Eddie has made a big impact too in the boxing world with lots of champions, including Anthony Joshua. Eddie is now running the Matchroom business, which Barry started a long time ago, beginning with snooker.

I do not know Eddie really. I have just met him a couple of times at Sky Television. But Barry and I go back many years to the days of a young Steve Davis when snooker dominated the BBC and ITV screens. These days we sometimes speak together at corporate events – he is brilliant at that as well! – and as I write, we have a podcast and speak at lunches.

There is no doubt Barry is a promoting genius. He has kept snooker going and expanded its global involvement as the sport's world chairman these days. He turned darts into the second most watched sport on Sky Sports, as well as providing a large chunk of their shows over the years.

He actually sold Sky the sport of fishing, with the competitive *FishOMania*. He involved Matchroom with pool, golf and gymnastics and entered boxing with big success through Chris Eubank as well as staging the fight between Joe Bugner and Frank Bruno, which attracted over 30,000 at White Hart Lane and millions more on ITV.

He has provided Sky Sports with many hundreds of sporting hours.

I was in his car a long time ago when he explained he was buying Leyton Orient football club. I asked him if he was mad, but he knew what he was doing and his purchase included the ground. He can smell money.

He is very rich with a great insight on life and business and the spark and personality to make him an outstanding orator in demand. He is worth millions and that helps him not give a damn if people do not like his opinions. I never get tired of listening to him. He knows how to enjoy his money too.

His wife, Susan, is smart too and breeds racehorses – some winning big races.

Barry has survived heart attacks, which do not appear to bother him too much, although he seems to learn to take breaks including fishing round the world and a holiday home in an exclusive part of the Caribbean; when he visits, he is far from the richest person there!

I have had one run-in with Barry; it was over advertising on boxers' shorts, when I was the senior person at an ITV show. It was daft in my book that Formula One drivers could wear all the advertising on their hats and clothes, but they would not allow it in boxing because, as the logic went, it was just two people in a small ring! But I was a company man and had to stick by their policies.

On this occasion I refused to let the fight go out in the UK because Jake Matlala was wearing advertising on his shorts. He was defending his WBO light-flyweight title – he was the shortest world champion ever at just 4ft 10in.

However, I was quite happy for the fight to go live to Baby Jake's home country, South Africa. This happened at the Everton Sports Centre in Liverpool on 13 April 1996. Barry slagged me off deliberately in earshot of the press at ringside – and ITV made him apologise to me, which he did. However, the apology was not really necessary and the incident certainly did not affect our relationship, which is still strong today.

Mind you, Barry had the last laugh that night, because while the Matlala fight was good our top of the bill was a quick knockout!

I had never fished in my life until Barry, who has a persuasive gift of the gab, entered me for his *Target Sports Stars Fishing* show on ITV 4. He said I would enjoy my first ever fish… And he was right (again!).

Barry says he can smell money, as he did when he first saw darts. He is for taking big fights to Saudi Arabia or wherever the money is on offer. The Essex boy and his best mate, snooker legend Steve Davis, have done very well.

Lennox Lewis is the best heavyweight to come out of England. He was born in London but left when he was twelve. This was where I had a problem with him in his early days as a professional, and we did not get on until I made my peace later on. Now we are fine.

The problem for me was that Lennox won a gold medal in the 1988 Seoul Olympics for Canada and spent a lot of time there and in Jamaica. Yet when he turned professional he reverted to Britain and manager Frank Maloney.

But he can of course rightly claim that he is British as he was born here and spent his early years in England.

He became a fine world heavyweight champion. I covered many

of his early contests for ITV and some of his world title fights –
three of them at ringside for talkSPORT.

Lewis was the last Briton to be undisputed world champion and
only the seventh Olympic gold medallist to go on and win the professional title as well.

He fought fifteen boxers for the title – the fifth most in history –
and they included the likes of Evander Holyfield and Mike Tyson.
I covered both the Evander Holyfield fights for radio – the first at
the iconic Madison Square Garden, which was given as a draw, but
I made Lewis the winner – and the return, which Lewis won on
points at the Thomas and Mack Centre in Las Vegas.

I was given a ten-hour live slot by talkSPORT in Vegas. One of
my hour-long fillers was fascinating, as I got to speak with Budd
Schulberg, the American screenwriter (and sportswriter) who
wrote the Academy-Award-winning screenplay for *On the Water-
front*, which starred Marlon Brando when it was filmed.

Lewis only lost two out of forty-four fights, and those happened
when he took his eye off the ball in some way. The first time was
losing his WBC title to Oliver McCall on 24 September 1994 at
Wembley, being stopped in the second round. In the return contest
McCall lost the opening three rounds, refused to box in the next
two and, incredibly, started crying in the ring. The referee awarded
the fight to Lewis.

Then on 23 April 2001 Lewis was knocked out by the 20/1 un-
derdog Hasim Rahman in South Africa. Because of the time difference and the need to accommodate the lucrative American TV
audience, the main event took place at 5 a.m. local time.

Lewis again won the rematch, knocking Rahman out on 17 November in the fourth round.

Thereafter it was winning all the way, but not without incident. He knocked out Mike Tyson on 8 June 2002 in the eighth round, but Tyson had to pay Lewis $335,000 out of his own purse for biting him at the pre-fight press conference. Tyson was to have some form on biting!

I saw a quote from George Foreman saying Lennox was the best heavyweight of all time. That might be disputed by others, but he was certainly great and fought and beat the best of his time, including Ukraine's Vitali Klitschko, Briton's Frank Bruno and all the others I have mentioned.

His record when he retired in 2004 was 44 contests 41 wins (32 by knockout) 2 defeats (both by knockout) and that 1 controversial draw against Evander Holyfield.

I made my peace with Lennox during a long interview in the Docklands at the Four Seasons Hotel, which I did for talkSPORT radio.

Then in my series of great legends for Sky called *Sporting Heroes* I did a wonderful hour with Lennox during the 2012 London Olympics. He said it was the best he had ever done and asked if he could use a copy for his website. Sky Sports agreed and I felt really flattered. I have done more interviews with him since.

My wife Katie sat in on the Sky interview. She is not a boxing fan but said Lennox was the most impressive boxer she had ever heard in my career. She can be hard to please!

I still love boxing and go to some shows, particularly in the Midlands. I have struck up a close professional relationship with matchmaker, manager, promoter and trainer Jon Pegg. He and Charles Atkinson are the two most underestimated boxing experts I have come across. Pegg took a journeyman boxer Sam Eggington to winning a version of the world title as well as being involved in the British Boxing Board of Control's 'Fight of the Year' award two years running.

The Eggington story – born in Birmingham; lives in Stourbridge – is a rag to riches one. He only took up boxing because he was married with two children and was made redundant as a forklift driver. Barry Hearn provided him with the early TV platform and money.

Defeat never harmed Eggington's reputation. As I write he has lost just eight of his forty-two fights winning the other thirty-four around the welterweight and super-welterweight divisions.

He has held the IBO (International Boxing Organization) light-middleweight title; the British, Commonwealth and European welterweight titles and is always involved in Rocky Balboa-type fights! However, once he retires I doubt you will ever see him involved in boxing again. My view is that he is in it for the money.

CHAPTER TWENTY-SIX

FRIENDS IN SPORT

Covering sports as a journalist/tv presenter, you are often having to go back to the same people for interviews or information. If you like them and vice-versa you tend to build a type of friendship. I have done that over the years and value that friendship and trust.

It is also impossible to write about all my mates in sport – people like Harry Redknapp, Glenn Hoddle, Sam Allardyce, Lord Ian Botham, Dennis Amiss, Phil Taylor and Willie Carson, for whom I ghosted a column in *The Sun*. There are so many others, like one of my closest friends in football, the Burton Albion chairman Ben Robinson. Maybe another book sometime. I could fill another one easily but I think one volume is enough!

But there are other stories that I will squeeze in!

I always found the late Graham Taylor a class act. He was a full-back with Grimsby Town and Lincoln City but rose to be manager of England.

I spent a lot of time with Graham as a manager, broadcasting pundit and on corporate speaking events. He managed famously for Elton John when he was the owner of Watford, Doug Ellis at

Aston Villa and Sir Jack Hayward at Wolverhampton Wanderers, among others.

I remember the first time I met him. It was a foggy winter night in December, and he had driven all the way from Lincoln to appear on my live sports programme in our Birmingham studios for a three-minute interview. Lincoln, who he managed, were on the edge of the ATV region in those days.

I worried for him driving home in those conditions and thanked him for the effort he had made for just three minutes. He said it was all worth it to get his club in the spotlight on a popular programme watched by many in the Midlands.

The next time I saw him was in 1977. I had helped arrange a trip for ninety-eight men through the Midlands Football Writers to watch England play Italy in Rome. It had been suggested to me by the Aston Villa manager Ron Saunders as a 24-hour trip so that the managers could get back for training. In the end the only manager who came was Graham Taylor. One of his directors came as well and tried to pay for Graham, but his manager insisted he paid for himself, saying he was going as a fan!

Years later when he was the Aston Villa manager he was with me at the Cavalieri Hilton Hotel high above Rome. We were both part of ITV's team covering the 1990 World Cup in Italy. He was being offered the England job but thought his chairman would be difficult. As both were good friends I offered to take them out for lunch to discuss it.

Doug Ellis, being the businessman he was, was true to form to start with. I was getting frustrated towards the end of lunch and probably had drunk a little too much wine. I started having a go at the chairman before Taylor kicked me under the table. I had mis-read it, and Taylor got the go-ahead in the end. We laughed about it later. Indeed I laughed many times with Graham.

When the tournament reached the semi-final and England were to play West Germany in Turin, ITV had not got enough rooms in that city, so they put Graham, our commentator Brian Moore and me in the Hilton in Milan some ninety miles away.

Graham and Brian who were good pals and had arrived the previous night to me. Brian, one of life's gentlemen and the doyen of commentators, explained to me that next door was a 'nice little Italian restaurant that did a nice piece of fish with a quiet bottle of white wine', and we were going there.

On the short walk there a chuckling Graham pulled me back and quietly said: 'This is what you are having to eat. Brian ordered for me last night and he will do the same for us this evening.'

Graham was right, and I started laughing when it happened. Mind you, like his commentaries, Brian was spot on.

I have known Kevin Keegan since he was a young player at Liverpool, where I used to interview him for ATV's regional football show *Star Soccer*. I then followed him to Hamburg for the semi-final of the European Cup against Real Madrid.

He was a regular ITV pundit and then co-commentator. In Mexico City, I discovered a lovely striped shirt and soon others were buying the same ones from the same shop. Kevin was highly amused and told everyone I was wearing a deckchair. He was prob-ably right. It looked like a replica!

Kevin and I had plenty of fun over the years and we only had one cross incident, which I innocently walked into. There was a fiery match at Highbury between Arsenal and Newcastle, who were managed by Kevin.

Earlier that day Terry Venables had resigned as England manager over a contract dispute. This was before Euro 1996, for which Terry was in charge and took England to another semi-final against West Germany, where we lost the penalty shoot-out. That night, when Arsenal played Newcastle, Terry was our pundit at Highbury.

Following Terry's resignation, Kevin was the favourite for the England job. I put that to him in the immediate post-match live interview, and in response he pushed a waiting Arsenal player, Ian Wright, towards me and said: 'Talk to him,' which I did.

I was puzzled by Kevin's reaction. It would have been a simple answer for him; my question had been: 'What about the links to you for the England job?' I and any other interviewer worth their salt would always have asked that question, given the day's rumours. So I went into the Newcastle dressing room with a VHS of the game that we always gave each manager and he tore into me. His striker Alan Shearer looked puzzled. I suppose I should not have gone in there.

The press asked him the same question later that evening to underline the point that any journalist would have asked Kevin about the England job; he had been installed as favourite!

Because I valued our relationship I decided not to make the same mistake and left it alone. Months later I was at Euro 1996 with my family in the ITV production pen. Suddenly Kevin appeared from nowhere and jumped on my back and kissed my neck.

I was so relieved. I explained to my wife later what had happened at Arsenal but underlined how important my friendship with Kevin was to me. I had been with Brian Moore for lunch at the Keegan house with Kevin and his wife Jean outside Newcastle before Brian, Kevin and I went to Middlesbrough for ITV's coverage of the League Cup.

I was so pleased when he eventually got the England job but felt his anguish and disappointment after the 1–0 home defeat to Germany in October 2000 with the booing on the way to the tunnel and his sudden resignation as we waited to interview him.

Kevin was a brilliant player who won every honour in the game apart from the European Championship and World Cup. He loved his Liverpool manager Bill Shankly and was a loyal and trusted colleague and friend. We still talk on the phone from time to time. He is an outstanding and very funny after-dinner speaker.

Another long-term relationship is with Howard Wilkinson, who won the Football League as manager of Leeds – the last season before the Premier League began.

He had just formed, with Graham Taylor's help, the League Managers Association, which had broken away from FLESA (a body which represented all executives, including managers) and it did not look good when, as the new LMA chairman, he was suddenly charged with insulting a linesman.

The match involved: Sheffield Wednesday 1–6 Leeds United on Sunday 12 January 1992 live on ITV.

In the match, I was the touchline reporter between Trevor Francis, the Wednesday manager, and Wilkinson. I was absolutely freezing!

I heard Wilkinson shouting and maybe swearing at his full-back Tony Dorigo. The linesman on that side accused Wilkinson later of swearing at him!

Howard asked the *Daily Mail* writer David Walker and me to be his witnesses at the FA disciplinary hearing.

At Howard's request, I found a camera shot that was not used on transmission that showed the linesman involved a long way up the pitch from the dugouts!

Howard was relieved to have rightly been found not guilty. The linesman to my knowledge never officiated in the top division again.

I mentioned the Aston Villa chairman Douglas Ellis earlier. He was a very good friend right up to his death, and I was always his guest in the directors' room whenever I went to see his club during and after his time as chairman.

He earned the nickname 'Deadly Doug' by firing a lot of managers, but actually his ratio was exaggerated. He was very determined and could be ruthless, but he was more appreciated for what he did for the club *after* he sold it.

There were some great stories about him. I was witness to several, but my favourite was after they had beaten Liverpool at home at last after quite a few years. Doug only had men in his boardroom in those days and he kept toasting their win. I was standing with Sir John Smith the Liverpool chairman and his club secretary Peter Robinson and after several toasts we all felt Doug was over doing it.

Suddenly in came Nigel Kennedy, the wonderful violinist who was a football fanatic, with his instrument in its case.

'Gentlemen,' said Doug excitedly, 'our No. 1 supporter, the great violinist Nigel Kennedy, who would not join me in the directors' box to watch the match, but he is here. In honour of our wonderful win over Liverpool, would you please play your latest classical offering?'

Nigel as ever played beautifully to a relieved round of applause. Doug, however, could not finish there. 'Last week, Nigel, you came to our house in Four Oaks and after my wife Heidi had cooked us supper you played [he named a classical piece that I can't recall now]. I wonder if, in honour of our wonderful win today, you could play it again?'

Nigel chuckled and then said: 'I have just played it, you pr***!' Doug did not bat an eyelid.

I did test our relationship once over an interview. Doug had the foresight to appoint the first overseas manager in the top division to succeed Graham Taylor in 1990. He was Jozef Vengloš from Slovakia. He had spent his playing career as a midfielder with Slovan Bratislava and had managed many clubs and countries, including Australia, Czechoslovakia, and Malaysia. He was only with Villa for the one season but did go on to manage Slovakia and Celtic. He could not fulfil the chairman's hopes as Villa finished two places above the relegation zone.

One of the closing home matches was featured on ITV's *Midweek Sports Special*. I was asked by London to interview Doug (after what was Villa's latest defeat) about Vengloš.

Doug agreed on the condition he was not asked about the manager's position. I had to ignore this and asked him about where Vengloš stood. Ellis angrily took off his glasses and replied that he had agreed to this interview on the condition he did not have to talk about the manager's position.

I asked what I thought was a clever follow-up question: 'Fair enough, but can you confirm Dr Vengloš will be here next season?' The reply: 'No.' Ellis promptly left.

After I finished my work I thought I had better make it up with

Doug – which I did before too long because I knew that he loved being on TV.

So I went straight to the Boardroom where, as usual, I had been Doug's guest. The only person there was the former Minister of Sport Denis Howell, watching the TV. I asked him if he knew where the chairman was and Denis came up with a great line: 'Trying to avoid you.'

When Ellis reached seventy, the club decided to throw a big luncheon for charity at the Metropole Hotel in the National Exhibition Centre complex. The comedian Dave Ismay, a mutual friend, came to see me and said he had two questions: 'Will you co-host the luncheon with me and what do you present a rich man with everything as a present?'

I told Dave it would be an honour and that Doug once told me he would love to have a Villa Park stand named after him.

That has been air-brushed out of selected memories, but I would take an oath that is what occurred in that conversation. Tom Finney, the Preston North End and England legendary winger, was Doug's hero and attended to present Doug with a model of Villa Park with the stand duly named as it is today.

It was a memorable lunch. Doug had made his money from travel and pioneered package holidays in Majorca. Jasper Carrott, the wonderful Brummie comedian, came on dressed as Doug's first air hostess with suggestive humour!

Then Lorenzo, the popular local Italian restaurateur, came on dressed as Doug's first pilot. Quite a day.

Years later at Doug's funeral, David Dein, the former Arsenal director who brought Arsène Wenger to the London club, revealed that he sat next to Ellis at FA meetings. One day, Doug asked David if he could help him with a suggestion. He had his stand but did not know what to call the other stand. Dein suggested: 'Why not call it "the other Doug Ellis stand"?' Another great line!

Ellis had fallen out with his son Peter. They knew I was friendly with both of them and it was not a problem. I invited both to my seventieth birthday lunch at the Hotel du Vin in Birmingham.

Villa is a different club these days and I am sure they are on their way towards the top of the Premier League – certainly the top six. But I have great memories of this big club over the years with the players and an outstanding relationship with club secretary Steven Stride.

Another character who is sadly missed is Jim Smith, who managed Birmingham City, Derby County and Oxford United among others. He was the one who sold Trevor Francis to Nottingham Forest to make him Britain's first million-pound footballer in 1979, as previously mentioned.

He was often the butt of Ron Atkinson's humour, as many of us were, but, like Ron, we all loved the Bald Eagle (Big Ron created that nickname after *The Muppet Show*).

Smith unwittingly gave me two scoops. Media life was so different and far easier in those days. Access to managers was never a problem.

I was doing an interview in Smith's garden in Solihull at the start of the 1978–79 season. I quizzed him about the Blues' lack of signings, and he blurted out 'our new left-back Alberto Tarantini', who had just played in the Argentina team that won the World Cup in 1978.

He went: 'Oh dear, we have not announced that yet!'

Tarantini was twenty-three and played for Boca Juniors until a contractual dispute put an end to his career there. Boca persuaded the other country's clubs not to sign him. So without a club Tarantini was on his way to Birmingham City, costing them around £300,000. For the record, he was not a great success. He had poor discipline and one particular foul on Manchester United's Brian Greenhoff was a shocker. Then on another match he went into the crowd to attack a heckler – an incident that finished his time at St Andrew's. He was soon on his way back to Argentina.

Move on to 15 June 1995 and Smith had by now become chief executive of the League Managers Association. By coincidence, we were both having lunch at the Feathers Hotel in Woodstock on nearby tables. Smith lived in Woodstock.

As controller of sport at Central TV I was meeting my Oxford reporter Tim Russon to discuss something at length. Jim was meeting John Campkin, who was one of the founders of the LMA, and Gordon Milne, who was a committee member. All three knew me so I went over to say hallo.

Jim said: 'You have done me again. I cannot believe it after the Tarantini incident.'

I had not got a clue what he was talking about, but thought I better not let on and just fished telling him: 'Jim, just like the Tarantini story, I have to do it!'

Jim then said that he knew I was friendly with Stuart Webb and you had better check with him. 'If Stuart says I can give you an interview, then I'll do it.'

So that was it. Smithy had the vacant Derby County job! So I rang Webb, who thanked me for telling him and asked what time I would use it. I said that it would be on our six o'clock show *Central News*. He said that he would bring the press conference forward from the next day to six o'clock and yes, I had his blessing to do the interview. Stuart finally asked me if the story had come out at his end or my end. Without explaining what had happened I assured him it was my end.

Tim Russon quickly got a camera crew from his nearby studios in Abingdon, and the interview was sealed.

As I was leaving, Milne called me over. He was the only one who had clocked what had happened and said with a smile: 'You always were a lucky bugger!' He was right. I was on many occasions.

Smith died in December 2019, aged seventy-nine. I joined a massive turnout for his funeral in the Woodstock Church.

Jim had been a member of my ATV All Stars' football team, who played away charity matches on a regular basis in the '70s and '80s, drawing thousands to watch because of the combination of pop stars and famous old footballers. The team also included singer Robert Plant, ELO drummer Bev Bevan, Slade's Dave Hill, Trevor Oakes from Showaddywaddy, comedians Jasper Carrott and Don Maclean, former footballers Ron Atkinson and Ron Wylie, boxer Jackie Turpin, TV's Nick Owen, Trevor East and me, with radio's Tom Ross and restaurant's Lorenzo Ferrari, who I pretended had played for AC Milan, the team he supported!

When ITV had a long technicians' strike in 1979, I arranged a huge football match between the Saturday morning cult programme *Tiswas* with Chris Tarrant and my ATV All Stars, with several guests including Stan Harvey (Edward Clayton) from *Crossroads*. I worked so hard on the publicity, and *Tiswas* was so huge in ratings that over 12,000 people turned up at the Nuneaton Borough ground. Bruce Rioch was the referee, and he had so many buckets of water poured over him that he played the following week in a European Cup match with a heavy cold!

It is important that people in the public eye help charities as much as possible. We have a duty to do that. The football game at Nuneaton was for the Variety Club of Great Britain's children's charity. These days I am president of the Lord's Taverners West Midlands charity and 2023 brings my eighteenth annual Christmas sporting luncheon at the Edgbaston cricket ground.

Coming up next, the times I made a right fool of myself... And some of the other sports I covered on a regular basis.

CHAPTER TWENTY-SEVEN

OTHER SPORTS

The other sports I covered for TV were speedway, greyhound racing, darts and snooker. There were plenty of stories behind those.

Speedway was for ITV's Saturday afternoon show *World of Sport*, apart from the Wembley world championship, which had its own recorded programme on the same Saturday night. Speedway had long gaps between heats and sat better on TV as a recorded show.

My involvement on it was when a lady from London Weekend Television made a mistake ringing me at ATV to book me to do the interviews for the network coverage of a White City meeting in London. It turned out that she had mistaken me for Barry Briggs, which in hindsight was quite an error – Barry was a New Zealander and former world champion four times – the last being in 1966.

Speedway was strong when I covered the sport in the 1970s and 1980s. Ole Olsen, Bruce Penhall and Kenny Carter were the three racers I got to know best.

Olsen and the glamorous American Bruce Penhall captained two local teams in the Midlands – Coventry Bees and Cradley Heathens in the Black Country. They drew big crowds in those days, but they no longer exist as either speedway or greyhound venues. A sign of the times.

Olsen is Danish. He, like the other three, won many titles, including the world championship three times in 1971, '75 and '78.

He began with Newcastle Diamonds, then in 1970–75 with the Wolverhampton team before spending seven years with Coventry, where he was the most successful. I covered his farewell meeting with thousands packing the Brandon village track on an emotional night.

Ole had a frustrating night one year in the Daily Express Spring Classic meeting at Wimbledon (where I was to present the Greyhound Derby final in years to come). ITV were there for *World of Sport* and Olsen suddenly quit halfway through in an interview with me. I persuaded him during our chat *not* to quit, so Ole said OK and went on to win the meeting! I was chuffed when *World of Sport*'s presenter Dickie Davies thanked me on air for getting Ole to change his mind.

Occasionally the odd rider would ring me at my studios for some technical advice. I would never have a clue but would stall while I asked our news dispatch motorcycle rider Mike Inman whose great knowledge would save the day – and my reputation!

Ole's success – too many trophies to list here – helped make the sport incredibly successful in his native Denmark, and he built and opened the 15,000 capacity Vojens Stadium, which has held two World Speedway finals. He lived up to his tag as 'the Great Dane'.

Bruce Penhall came from Balboa Island, Newport Beach in California. He became a double world champion in 1981 and 1982 before retiring aged twenty-five to become a Hollywood star in the TV series *CHiPs*.

Penhall, who looked like a blond, surfing beach boy, was a great rider. He was brought to England by promoters Dan McCormick and Derek Pugh to ride at the Dudley Wood Stadium in Cradley Heath. That was in 1978, and I soon became good friends with Bruce, who lived in Sutton Coldfield just outside Birmingham.

He became a great hit on the track aged just twenty-one. He was relaxed and very co-operative. In 1981, two nights before what was to prove to be the last World Speedway final to be staged at Wembley, Penhall recorded a really emotive interview at my ATV studios. He explained how both his parents, LeRoy and Barbara Penhall, had been killed six years earlier when their private plane had crashed. Penhall calmly said he would be inspired because he believed that his parents would be on his shoulder on every bend of the five heats.

It was an incredible final in front of 92,500 people. Former world champion Ivan Mauger was mentoring the British rider Michael Lee, and like most other riders he refused to let me interview them in the pits during racing. But not Penhall. He gave me the time between all his rides.

He came from behind to beat both Olsen and later another Danish rider Tommy Knudsen on the finishing line. His only loss of the night was to England's Kenny Carter and he still finished second in that heat when third place would have been enough to win the title.

Bruce made sure I got the first interview as he was being carried around the track.

Then the following year on 28 August 1982, he came to my home in Solihull to give me the story that he was quitting after the upcoming final in his home city of Los Angeles (which he also won).

The reason was the offer to play the role of cadet/officer Bruce Nelson in the final series of the NBC television series *CHiPs*. He went on to star in other roles.

My twin boys, Laurence and Neil, were aged five at the time, were used to seeing sports personalities in our house like Harvey Smith, Willie Carson, Trevor Francis, Ron Atkinson and so on. They never took any notice, but on this occasion they suddenly came into the lounge, jumped on the sofa and stared at Penhall. *CHiPs* was something they did watch!

Bruce went on to suffer another tragedy. His 22-year-old son Connor was killed by a drunk driver in 2012 while working on a freeway.

There was tragedy, too, in the story of Kenny Carter, another world-class rider, who at the age of just twenty-five shot his wife, Pam, dead and then turned the gun on himself. In doing so he left their two young children orphaned. It happened at their home, Grey Horse Farm in Bradshaw, Yorkshire.

ITN reporter Tony Francis knew I was close to them and phoned me just after I arrived in Mexico for the forthcoming World Cup.

A year earlier on 15 March, Kenny and his wife were guests at my surprise fortieth birthday party, which was organised by my wife, Katie, at the Birmingham Holiday Inn next to the then Central TV studios.

Kenny presented me with a TAG Heuer watch. He was sponsored by that company.

Earlier that year he broke his leg at the intercontinental final in Sweden. After I had finished my work, I accompanied Kenny and Pam to the local hospital. He was British champion at the time and so we asked him to be the co-commentator with Dave Lanning at the 1985 final in Bradford, as he obviously had to miss it through that injury.

Kenny was brash and occasionally outspoken, which did not make him popular in some circles, but I liked him very much. He would ring my wife, who was an agent at the time, with commercial ideas as he tried to promote himself.

One great story against me was when he came into our Central TV studio for an interview before riding in the Midlands. I finished the interview by congratulating Kenny on the birth of a new son. Kenny explained: 'We have named him after you,' to which I said: 'What, Gary?'

Kenny retorted to massive laughter around me: 'No, Wally.' Actually for the record, the boy is called Malcolm.

But what a tragic way for Kenny to end his and his wife's lives. It is too sad to speculate the reason. I often think about him as a friend and also what he could have achieved. The watch, which I still wear, is a permanent reminder.

I also covered motorsport, particularly motorcycling, because Mallory Park was in Leicestershire and Tom Wheatcroft had reopened Donington Park, also in Leicestershire.

I remember interviewing the Beatle George Harrison with former motor racing great Sir Jackie Stewart at Donington on a motor racing day. I interviewed Sir Jackie many times over the years at both ITV and Sky Sports.

Another legend world motorcycling champion who I worked with was Barry Sheene, and he was the closest contact I had in his sport. I would cover his super bike meetings at both Mallory Park and Donington. He would always win, give me plenty of interviews and invite me into his motor home at the tracks. Indeed he used to recall how I was sitting with him and his wife, the glamour model Stephanie McLean, when I got the call that my wife was going into labour with our twins. That was not quite true, but I let him stick with it as he really believed it.

Everyone loved Barry, whose riding number was seven. He was good-looking, humorous, outspoken, friendly and helpful, although I told him he smoked too much, which he ignored! He even had a hole drilled into the chin bar of his racing helmet so that he could smoke on the grid. Unbelievable.

He always had a special place for his father Frank, who was always at the tracks with him.

His charisma and looks attracted many people to his sport. He made a fortune from riding and from advertising, including TV commercials for the aftershave 'Brut', as did Henry Cooper and Kevin Keegan.

He was the 500cc world champion and would have won it more than twice (1976 and 1977) but for the American Kenny Roberts, with whom he had some great races.

Barry in the end was riddled with arthritis from two particular crashes when he retired in 1994 after fourteen years of racing. The first was in the Daytona 2000 in 1975 at 175 miles per hour. He broke his leg, multiple ribs, his arm, his wrist and his collarbone. When he came round in hospital the first thing he asked the nurse was whether he could have a cigarette!

Then seven years later at Silverstone in practice for the 1982 Grand Prix, he hit the bike of fallen Frenchman Patrick Igoa. It almost killed Barry and he had twenty-seven metal bolts put in to hold his legs together, and indeed save them, by orthopaedic surgeon Nigel Cobb.

When Barry was finally released from hospital, I was in the massive media scrum with cameras and notebooks, but he spotted me with my cameraman and gave me the first interview. Relationships and contacts are the heart of my business.

Barry, with his mind-blowing courage, came back from all of it to be dubbed the bionic man, although he always set off the X-ray alarms at airports!

The Sheenes eventually emigrated to the Gold Coast in Australia, where he developed a property business and commentated for Australian television.

Sadly the man with the regular smile, who made people smile, died from oesophagus and stomach cancer in March 2002 – eight months after it was discovered. He refused chemotherapy. He was just fifty-two years old. Another tragic story.

Darts and snooker next. I had often watched the News of the World Darts Championship on TV, but apart from *The Indoor League* (made by Yorkshire TV and hosted by cricket legend Freddie Trueman) I could not recall it being televised elsewhere. Snooker seemed limited to *Pot Black* on the BBC.

So with ATV's backing I set off to make them locally. First of all the Butlins Grand Masters, which ran from 1977 to 1986 and was just shown on ATV, which later morphed into the new franchise of Central TV on 1 January 1982.

I approached Olly Croft, who, with his wife Lorna, ran the BDO (British Darts Organisation).

He said that he could lay on the sixteen best players in the world if I could come up with the money, venue and TV coverage. The only stumbling block was the money, which I had to somehow scrape together. The venue was not a problem. I needed two days of filming to make fifteen half-hour shows – a knockout 501 down of first round (eight) quarter-finals (four) semi-finals (two) final (one).

My bosses would let me have the outside broadcast for two days (which was expensive with union restrictions, lighting, catering etc.) and commentator Dave Lanning. But nothing else. I was the presenter on the staff!

I had a problem: you could cover a sponsored event in those times but you could not create a sponsor. Strict TV guidelines with the Independent Television Commission.

That meant that I had a week to find someone to sponsor my event in a crafty way.

Coming into the last day and starting to feel panicked, I had a phone call from my greyhound trainer, Geoffrey de Mulder, who had the 1974 greyhound winner, Jimsun. More on my involvement in that feat later in this chapter. But the owners were squabbling over the winner's jacket. Spillers, an equine feeds company, were the sponsors, but the logo wasn't on the jacket. It was 2.30 p.m. when I finally got hold of Steve Gebbett from Charles Barker Lyons, the agency who were handling the Spillers account. I asked him if he could get another jacket made up, and he said: 'Yes, no problem.'

Miraculously, Steve then added: 'By the way, I have some spare money from Butlins, who want to sponsor a televised sports event. Any ideas?'

I tried not to sound too excited: 'Well, as it happens...' But I needed a fax to confirm, and quick (this was before emails!).

'It has to be with me by 5.30 p.m. tonight, otherwise my bosses say the event is off. Can you do it in three hours?' The fax arrived at 5.10 p.m. and the Butlins Grand Masters was *on*!

The first year of the darts was at the Sutton Coldfield Town Hall and was won by John Lowe, beating eighteen-year-old Eric Bristow in the final. Then we moved to the New Cresta nightclub above the Solihull Ice Rink, where I once got an autograph off singer Frankie Laine ('Rawhide' and all that) and another time was on top of the bill by interviewing Brian Clough there! And then we were off to the largest pub in the area – The Swan at Yardley.

John Lowe was runner-up the following year to Leighton Rees of Wales. Bobby George won it twice. Eric Bristow was a regular star, but the biggest character of the lot was Jocky Wilson. He drank a lot and was funny when interviewed!

We lost one year when a trade union pulled it at the last moment over a dispute in the drama department. I was furious as I sat with sixteen outstanding players for two days hoping in vain that the dispute would be settled.

Barry Hearn and the new stars formed the Professional Darts Corporation, and my series was soon history. I have to say the PDC and Barry's promotional genius have made darts huge. I actually hosted the first series of Sky Sports Premier League Darts, until I was the subject of a wrongful story about being unpopular with the players. This came from inside Sky, I believe. As it happens, I was the only one invited to a players' party in a Colchester pub and in years to come Phil Taylor made a round trip of six hours to appear on my *Sporting Heroes* series. Just occasionally, TV can be unpleasant.

So onto snooker and if beer, fags and bellies were the feature of darts then snooker was smart dinner jackets and slim players. Local businessmen Ian Townsend and David Hadley came up with the State Express Grand Masters – yes, it was named after the cigarette company. Tobacco had not been banned then. The venue was the Albany Hotel in Smallbrook Queensway in the centre of Birmingham. They had a big function room. It is now called the Birmingham Conference Centre.

The first tournament was in December 1978 and it was won by Graham Miles, a local professional from the Erdington district. The year before he had had his highest world ranking of fifth and had been beaten in the final of the world championship by Ray Reardon, 22 frames to 12. He also won *Pot Black* in both 1974 and 1975. He was always good fun to be with and made me laugh a lot. We had top players like the exciting, volatile and almost mad Irishman Alex 'Hurricane' Higgins in the tournament.

Two famous comedians at that time were Leslie Crowther and Arthur Askey. They were appearing in a local pantomime nearby, and as soon as they were off stage they would join us for the closing matches/frames of the evening.

Other good friends of David Hadley who came to watch were Led Zeppelin singer Robert Plant and drummer John Bonham, plus comedian Jasper Carrott.

I tried snooker locally for one more year. I did not have a sponsor. Barry Hearn rescued us with Padmore & Sons, who made the snooker tables with the padmore super crystalate. The venue was the West Bromwich Baths, and the first prize was £2,000, won by Alex Higgins.

Alex was presented with the cheque and I then spent a couple of unsuccessful hours late at night trying to help him cash it.

I used to see Alex at football matches as well and tripped over him filming once; I was going backwards into the Wolves dressing room before a match against Manchester United at Molineux.

I saw plenty of him of course on the snooker tables, as the sport became all the rage on both the BBC and ITV. I felt, by the way, that the game, rather like show jumping, became overexposed and the terrestrial companies, even with more channels, now do not cover snooker so much, apart from the BBC.

The BBC still do the world championship outstandingly well. I hosted a few screenings on Sky and made a decent documentary of Mark Selby, a fellow Leicester City supporter, who has been world champion four times. His upbringing was full of emotive stories. He is a top guy and we are still in touch.

Greyhound racing also played a big part in my TV and personal life. How did that come about?

As I've mentioned, in 1972 I was ghosting a column in *The Sun* for racing jockey Willie Carson alongside my television work. One cold day I was waiting by a big active fireplace at Warwick Races while Willie changed after his various rides. It was a flat and jumps racecourse then. Now it is jumps only.

Because I was on local TV most nights, two people approached me asking why I did not show greyhound racing. They were trainer Geoffrey de Mulder and top greyhound writer Norton Jones.

I explained that you had to show their sport live, as it was about gambling, and that ITV only had one channel then and it would have clashed with huge-rating soap opera shows like *Coronation Street* and *Crossroads*. I thought that would be the easy way and accurate way out.

Then they challenged me on how many times I had been to the tracks. I said I had been once, at Exeter County Ground. So they insisted I went to the Hall Green track for dinner with my fiancée, Katie (who is now of course my wife). Before the end of the night,

I had leased two bitches for local graded races called Alice Springs and Hopping Mad. They won sixteen out of twenty-eight races between them and I was hooked.

For a short while I thought the game was easy, but I soon found out that it was not after being involved as an owner of too many greyhounds to recall!

However, I was slightly involved in the 1974 Greyhound Derby winner Jimsun, trained by de Mulder and owned by his wealthy dad, Joe de Mulder, and Gordon Walker, the shrewdest judge I ever met. I was their lucky charm and responsible for putting the bets on. I wrote earlier about Sir Alf Ramsey's reaction when I was in Germany with him on the night of the final.

I was flattered by being asked to do the eulogy at Geoffrey de Mulder's funeral. He was a great trainer who deserved more than two Greyhound Derby winners. They were great days at Hall Green and we always joined the Boxing Day brunch meeting as a family. It is now a housing estate after becoming just one more casualty as a greyhound track.

Meanwhile the highly respected ITV horse racing presenter Brough Scott also presented the dogs for the Ladbroke Golden Jacket from Harringay. Plus, when the horse racing was abandoned through bad winter weather (and there was a lot of snow in those days), the greyhound racing standby service from the same track became the ITV7 – a famous accumulator in those days.

The *World of Sport* editor was Andrew Franklin, an expert on the horse racing scene. He was told by Brough that he no longer wanted to do the dogs as well. Andrew then discovered that I was an owner and offered me the job. I loved it.

On the Friday when the race was called off I would somehow

battle through the bad weather after hosting *ATV Sport* and stay overnight in London before getting an early morning tube to near the track. I would have to walk through deep snow to finish the journey. Reg Gutteridge was the commentator. Our boxing commentator had started his journalistic career on the *Greyhound Express* before joining the *London Evening News*.

Two memories of those days. In December 1981 I was in the USA at Houston, Texas, interviewing Pat Cowdell before his world title fight. I was just about to dive in a swimming pool in hot sunshine when I took a phone call from Franklin saying I had to get back to London because snow had gridlocked the capital and Harringay was the ITV7.

On the way to Houston Airport, I had a taxi driver who had never seen snow; I had to describe it to him. Travel was much easier. I was able to buy a KLM business flight to Amsterdam just before the gate closed and on arrival do the same thing on a BA flight that was the last to land before they shut Heathrow Airport. I had a quick shower and, armed with notes waiting for me, I was off to Harringay.

Ron Pollard, the bookmaking guru at Ladbrokes, was a terrific mate over the years, and he laid on an expert, once I got the greyhound role, called Alan Isherwood, who was a great judge.

But Ron pulled a trick on the leader of the Labour Party, Neil Kinnock, and me, which I did not notice until I read Ron's book many years later! Ron was a huge Labour supporter and his expert odds were on politics and Miss World. He always got them right!

He asked Neil to present the Ladbroke Gold Jacket final trophy. Ron suggested I asked Kinnock about the government's reluctance to abolish on-course betting tax. He told Kinnock that I could be a bit tricky and would put him under pressure on this subject. Kinnock's reply that they would campaign to abolish this tax forced the Tories to do it! Wow – all over a greyhound meeting interview!

When I got to Sky, their outstanding presenter Jeff Stelling was ready to move to another more high-profile programme, so I took over. Sky covered many meetings a year, including the Greyhound Derby at Wimbledon. I loved it and covered the event with a great, friendly team led by the kind producer Dave Lawrence, who lived for the sport and still has countless runners today. The director was Jerry Logan, who was excellent to work with on different locations including Shawfield in Glasgow and Dublin in Ireland.

The betting ring team was Dave Smith and Gary Wiltshire, who was known as 'the Belly from the Telly' as he was around 26st. in those days. Gary and I are still in touch. Gary is a bookmaker and lost £1.4 million as an independent when Frankie Dettori rode seven winners one day at Ascot. Gary sold everything to pay his debts.

Working with me was Jonathan Hobbs, another top greyhound expert who gave me so much help as the resident on-screen pundit. Julie Collier was the on-track interviewer and Errol Blyth was the excellent commentator with Darrell Williams having an all-round job.

There were two highlights that stand out for me.

Westmead Hawk is the best greyhound that I and many others ever saw. He won the Greyhound Derby in 2005 and 2006. There are a lot of rounds to qualify. He would come from the back with electrifying pace. He was sire to two more winners: Taylors Sky in 2011 and Sidaz Jack in 2013. Westmead Hawk, trained by the veteran Nick Savva, has been compared with the other legendary greyhound Mick the Miller and the Grand National horse hero Red Rum. He was owned by the amiable Bob Morton. Westmead Hawk features in Madame Tussauds!

I asked the Hawk's veteran handler if he would train a dog for me. He said he would only train a Westmead dog, so we flew to Waterford in Ireland to the Dunphy family stud. Westmead Hawk was standing there and Nick stood in a field. They let the dog out and he jumped all over his old trainer with emotive affection. I was quite moved.

The Dunphys kindly did a good deal for me to buy his grandson Droopys Greg. Droopys was the kennel name. Greg was just like his father, with a great ratio of winning runs on Sky, including a recording of Greg winning the Midlands Puppy Derby in 2011, coming from last at the first of the four bends to take it on the line from Shuttle Express. The first prize: £12,500.

Sadly before he was even in his prime Greg smashed a hock so badly he had to retire. We found him a new home with my wife's cousin, Andy Christie, and his wife, Jo, in plenty of acres down in Sussex. They called him Bolt and he had a happy life until passing away aged eleven years. He was a lovely natured dog with amazing speed. I never had a bet because he was usually odds-on with the bookies and on the tote and I had to hide my excitement when he won and I was live on TV.

The game has gone a lot. Closing Wimbledon to greyhound racing was a major blow.

But greyhound racing was good to me and I am grateful for my time on TV with it.

CHAPTER TWENTY-EIGHT

CRICKET AND ICE HOCKEY

Two sports that I love but did not really cover on television are cricket and ice hockey. My work on the former was restricted to working at Edgbaston by interviewing former Test cricketers for thirteen years in the two big hospitality suites at Test matches, plus interviewing the greats like Garry Sobers and Lancashire's cup heroes such as David Lloyd for Sky's *Sporting Heroes* and *Time of Our Lives* programmes.

I owned and developed the Solihull Barons ice hockey team for two mad but successful years.

When I arrived in the Midlands in 1971, I was soon going to cricket matches, watching some international greats steering Warwickshire so unbelievably close to the coveted county championship title – even though they drew on points with Surrey, the title went to them because they had won more matches.

Several West Indian heroes were in that team: there were batters (I hate that word) like Alvin Kallicharran and Rohan Kanhai plus spinner Lance Gibbs and wicket keeper Deryck Murray. There were also some fine English players, like openers John Whitehouse and John Jameson plus Dennis Amiss, who went on to be chief executive and is now club president. Dennis, his wife Jill, my wife Katie and I have all maintained our friendship. The pacemen were Norman McVicker and the club's all-round record wicket-taker David Brown with 1,165 first-class wickets.

The captain was A. C. Smith – a rather aloof fellow who most people, including me, eventually warmed to. He did a very good job.

The biggest achievement came in 1994 when the Bears pulled off the rare feat of a treble, which nearly became a quadruple. The team was led by Dermot Reeve (I did the auction at his testimonial dinner at the International Exhibition Centre) and had names like West Indies star Brian Lara, Ashley Giles, Tim Munton, Gladstone Small, Roger Twose from New Zealand, Paul Smith and wicket-keeper Keith Piper.

They won the championship for the first time since the 1972 season, the Sunday League over forty overs and the Benson and Hedges Cup over fifty-five overs. The one that got away was the NatWest Trophy, scheduled for sixty overs. Both cup finals were played at Lord's, and again it was against Worcestershire, but this time they lost by eight wickets.

The biggest individual achievement came from Lara who hit 501 not out in 1994 in a match against Durham at Edgbaston. It is still a world record score and enabled his county to declare at 810 for 4.

Amiss was chief executive and told me how Lara's agent, Jonathan Barnett, came to see him to ask if someone could do Lara's fielding, as he did not like it, and let him concentrate on batting. Dennis, ever the gentleman, calmly explained that cricket did not work like that.

I used to enjoy interviewing the Test greats at the lunch and tea interviews – there are too many to recall, but my favourite was Sir Geoffrey Boycott.

I am president of the cricket charity the Lord's Taverners in the West Midlands region. As I mentioned before, I have hosted eighteen annual LT Christmas charity sports luncheons with so many great names and friends supporting me: Gary Neville, Sir Clive Woodward, Kevin Keegan, Ricky Hatton, Eddie Jordan, Barry Hearn, Andy Gray, Martin O'Neill, Trevor Francis, Terry Butcher, John Motson and many more.

I also played cricket for the Lord's Taverners team for over twenty-five years. It was great attracting good crowds and playing with famous ex-Test stars from England and the West Indies and big names from show business like Chris Tarrant and Rory Bremner.

I played once at Edgbaston in a charity match and American pop singer Donny Osmond bowled out the legendary Imran Khan with a ball that shot along the ground. Khan was not happy and I had to explain to Donny what he had actually achieved!

I still love Test cricket the most. I've been hooked on cricket ever since as a young schoolboy I watched Cambridge University against the West Indies and marvelled at a high ball flying toward Wes Hall on the boundary. He took a swig from a young spectator's fizzy pop drink and then took the catch off a University batsman. Hall of course never took his eyes off the ball. That was my kind of guy.

The other sport I loved but never covered was ice hockey.

One day in 1982, a service-man called Steve Small was mending our washing machine at my home. He asked me if I liked ice hockey and I told him I loved it. I had grown up watching Wembley Lions on the BBC in the '50s with commentary by Alan Weeks. He said he was secretary of the local team, the Solihull Barons, and they needed help.

Fifty people used to watch. The players were all English and they paid to play, hiring the ice and equipment and sorting their own travel.

I agreed to be chairman and owner only if I had full control. I soon got sponsorship. They were bottom of the bottom league in British ice hockey – then the Second Division. Their net-minder, Chris Pugsley, had been banned for life after being found guilty of violence (unusual for ice hockey!) and the veteran Dave Randall was in goal. Randall had seen far better days on the ice!

I realised publicity and sponsorship were the only answer. I did not pay the players but funded equipment, food and travel (I said the players were no longer allowed to bring family on the team coach, but the local press were still permitted access to travel and the dressing rooms ten minutes after the match had finished).

You were allowed three overseas players. I reckoned we could afford two Canadians. Steve had a tip-off about a 21-year-old from Saskatoon called Chuck Taylor. A brilliant defence man who was in the Edmonton Oilers farm team. But he was being transferred to Germany because, in one game with 10,000 spectators, someone in the crowd spat at Chuck and he went into the stands to sort him out!

We intercepted Chuck and his colleague Barry Skrudland. I met them at the studios and took them next door for a local news conference. It was Beaujolais Nouveau Day, and I thrust a glass of French wine into their hands. Then I took them to Lorenzo's restaurant and tried to get them to sign. I could only offer them £100 a week, free digs, a sponsored car when I got one, travel to and from their Canadian homes at the end of the season, a free holiday with me in Spain if they got promotion and a good time! This was early 1982.

Chuck was not keen. He was being offered far more in Germany, but Barry wanted to have a go. Eventually, they signed. Ironically I had to sack Barry the following season after he was banned for nine months by the British Ice Hockey Association for trying to decapitate Rob Carnegie at bitter rivals Peterborough Pirates.

Once onboard, Chuck and Barry made sure that the Barons won every game and were promoted to the second tier of the three leagues. We had a great and lively holiday in Majorca at Cala Millor.

I found the council-owned rink difficult to deal with. One rink official clearly did not want us there. He was all for figure skating, not ice hockey. I did have a spy in the camp and she kept me one step ahead. Eventually as the crowds increased I got a 50 per cent attendance deal and the 'spy' made sure I got my full amount.

Derrick Richardson of Glynwed International became the generous club sponsor and after taking advice I changed the name on the players' shirts to GI Solihull Barons. Alan Blackwell represented the sponsors and we were in business. The players and officials off the ice wore the red Glynwed Jerseys. I had a chairman's bar to feed the players after each game and invited guests including the players' families, plus the individual sponsors.

We still had the netminder problem. British players were amateurs. Chuck wanted the England netminder David Graham from Whitley Bay, who were in the top league. The Northern rinks and the Smith family took an instant dislike to this upstart from the Midlands – me! – and dubbed me 'Mr Big', so I put a cartoon full-page advert out to inflame them even more, inviting top English players to join the Barons and be paid!

By now we had been joined by two more Canadians to replace Skrudland: we had Dean Vogelgesang and top goal scorer Mark Budz.

The crowds were growing rapidly and soon we had full houses. We reached the quarter-final of the national knockout cup and were drawn at home to Streatham Redskins, the premier team in London. Thames TV decided to cover it, and there were also highlights for ITV's *Midweek Sports Special*. We won, and now as the minnows were up against the mighty Durham Wasps in a two-legged semi-final.

We were nervous about stories of biased refereeing up north and we were drawn away in the first leg. I insisted and argued long and hard for neutral referees. Eventually after threatening to withdraw and go public we were allocated Rob Naylor and his team from Grimsby. They were great and the Wasps funnily enough kept skating offside! We were trailing in a hostile atmosphere 3–2 with ten seconds left. Chuck then equalised with a terrific shot from a short corner. Three-all.

I was full of hope for the return leg. It was a sell-out. We crammed almost 2,000 in – way over the limit with a disappointed trail of queuing people outside, waiting in the hope of returns for this all-ticket match. Even the local Birmingham ticket tout, Paul Docherty, came to see me for tickets, without luck of course.

Sadly on the day the English players for once froze, and we were beaten 11–6.

The team was often ill-disciplined. I missed the worst two instances. In protest at what they perceived as bad refereeing at Nottingham Panthers they threw all their sticks across the ice. Then while losing 6–1 at Crowtree, our players abandoned the game. Netminder Graham broke the news to me on the phone. I resigned the next day.

It had been difficult at work. Every time Jimmy Greaves and I discussed violence in football on air, Greavsie would ask: 'Well, what about the Solihull Newbons, then?'

My bosses advised me to quit the Barons and after the Crowtree walk-off, it was time to go as the national press picked up the story – especially *The Times*!

I fixed Chuck up with the Telford Tigers franchise and he became a new hero there. Then he joined Nottingham Panthers in his late thirties. He was a beautiful skater for a big man and a terrific player.

Then after a spell with Granada TV, Chuck joined my production team at Central at the request of my production sports chief, who at that point was Mike Inman.

Chuck Taylor, a great person with a big personality, married a Birmingham lady called Carolyn (Cal), and they have two grown-up sons. These days he is a football ground floor manager for two TV stations, a host broadcaster's man in big tournaments as well as a UEFA venue manager.

He remains a valued 'adopted' member of the Newbon family.

CHAPTER TWENTY-NINE

EXTRAS

Freddie Starr was a good mate and in his time a very funny comedian. He was introduced to me by a Leeds businessman called Martin Goldman. Freddie wanted a plug for his local cabaret show, but he turned out to be a nightmare on the set of Central News.

First of all he had the newsroom playing cricket. Then five minutes before the live six o'clock show went on air, we lost him.

It was a particularly heavy news day with several bad stories. Central had a coloured moon shape symbol behind the news desk, and the show was being presented by David Foster and Liz Pike. Suddenly, to my horror, Freddie appeared behind the news desk and began polishing the 'moon' with a handkerchief.

Our floor manager, Stan Harding, had to go on the set to drag Freddie off.

We had decided that Starr should be interviewed by Bob Hall. We told Freddie that Bob liked to be called Bob or Robert – not Bobby. When it came to it Freddie called him Paul. Bob then suggested Freddie came from a sporting family, to which he was told: 'Yes, my uncle John was a boxer, but my uncle Stan was an Alsatian!' After a few more quips the interview was abandoned and Bob started to introduce a football item, only to find Starr ramming a finger up Bob's nose!

When I came out of the studio, the tannoy greeted me with: 'Would Gary Newbon please report to Terry Johnston's office?' I arrived and was threatened with the sack if that occurred again.

The next incident was in front of 1,000 people at the Stardust cabaret/dinner club in Ashby-de-la-Zouch. The venue unfortunately no longer exists. I had taken two people I was doing corporate work for to see Freddie, but I had asked the owners not to tell him I was there.

They obviously did, because halfway through his act, he had everyone singing a very rude song about me.

Against my wife's advice, in an attempt to rescue our shocked guests, I led everyone to Freddie's dressing room. I could not see him there, but suddenly he flattened me to the floor. He had been on top of his wardrobe knowing I was coming in and had jumped on my back. It was a disaster.

My favourite Starr story was when he lived in Windsor. He was keen on big powerboats, and one day he had picked up his latest and put it on a trailer. The latter had speed limits of 50mph. He was going far faster than that driving down a deserted M4 motorway when he was suddenly stopped by a policeman.

'You're Freddie Starr, are you not?' Freddie replied: 'Yes,' hoping he would get off. Instead, he was told that he would be booked and anything that he said from then on would be taken down and may be used in evidence against him.

Freddie's response was: 'Well in that case, officer, will you please stop hitting me?'

What a comic.

The guitarist Tony Iommi, founder of Black Sabbath and heavy metal, has become a close friend after first being introduced by Trevor Francis. But Tony is a real wind-up artist.

A few years ago, I did a sell-out 800-seater with him titled 'An Audience with Tony Iommi' at the Birmingham Town Hall. Six minutes before we went on stage, Trevor and my wife came to my dressing room to say that Tony had been taken really ill. He was suffering from cancer at the time. I really believed it because my wife had never wound me up in our many married years.

My first thought was purely selfish: 'What the hell am I going to do? These 800 people have come to hear Tony, their legend, not me! Oh, God – what a situation.'

Then I went to see Tony, who was retching into a basin. But suddenly one of his party laughed and gave the game away. He was fine!

I inadvertently got my own back. The interview was split into two sessions of seventy-five minutes each. Two minutes into the second half, I remembered I had left some important notes in my dressing room. I gave Tony one more question and then walked off stage to retrieve my notes. Tony thought I was getting revenge by leaving him out there to dry, which was not true of course, but he said he was so relieved when I returned!

I told the crowd my favourite Iommi story that night, and it got a huge laugh. When his band started to be big, they were in Germany in a town that did not speak a lot of English. They came down for breakfast in their black leathers and were surrounded by German businessmen, suited and booted. This was long before mobile phones. Tony saw a non-English-speaking waiter going round the dining room ringing a bell to bring attention to his notice board, which said in German: 'Phone call in reception for Herr Smicht.'

Tony then approached the waiter when he left the room, gave him money and wrote a message on the board while teaching the waiter to read it in English. The waiter kept repeating: 'Phone call for Mr Hairy Bollocks. Phone call for Mr Hairy Bollocks.'

Prime Minister John Major and his wife Norma were close to my late parents, Jack and Preeva. We still swap Christmas cards. I remember having dinner with John and Norma when he was Chancellor at No. 11 and then attending a cocktail party with my mother and my wife at No. 10 when he became PM. He had a lot of class. My mother asked for a photo with John and me. John said: 'First I will go and find Katie.' He searched the crowded room and brought my wife to join us. Then he said: 'Now we will have that photo taken.'

Later, John broke up a Cabinet meeting to grant me a football interview. He did it outside, because as it turned out they were contemplating the Iraq War or some crisis like that! My mother had arranged my chat.

Chelsea's Ken Bates tried to introduce us once. Major, now Sir John, said: 'I know Gary, but I know his mother better! Preeva is a formidable lady, but I like her very much.' He was right. She usually got what she wanted!

I had been to Clarence House several times while making the film on the Queen Mother. I used to drive past Buckingham Palace and wonder if I would ever enter that great building.

Then I did about four times in just a few years. The first time was the 125th anniversary of the Grand Order of Water Rats. The Duke of Edinburgh and the then Prince Charles were members of this showbiz charity.

We were invited on another occasion to the Palace for a reception as a sponsor for the Birmingham Royal Ballet. There was a special ballet performance and dinner at the Palace. Prince Charles was the Ballet's patron.

I wore my Water Rat emblem as is the rule and when being introduced Prince Charles exclaimed: 'You are a Water Rat! Oh, it's such great fun.'

The dinner, by the way, was quite incredible. One of the best I have ever eaten, with lovely wines.

I have been to a royal garden party at the palace, but the best of my visits was my investiture when I was awarded the MBE in the 2019 New Years' Honours list for services to the media, sport and charity. The citation also acknowledged my role in promoting women's roles in TV sports coverage.

I was very proud and thrilled to be accompanied by my wonderful family – my wife Katie, daughter Claire and twin sons Laurence and Neil. I wore my Garrick Club tie as the rest of my relations were waiting back at the club for a reception.

The Prince of Wales had been briefed about me as I stepped up to receive the medal, but he exclaimed: 'That's a Garrick Club tie!' which I was not expecting. After a brief chat I was on my way.

I was honoured to receive the award as a recognition of my long career. It was not expected but appreciated.

Previously I had won three gold awards from the Royal Television Society – one in 1996 for *24 hours – Barry's Blues*, and one in 1997 for *24 hours – Losers Limited*. The third was Sports Programme of the Year 1998 for the World Cup match Argentina v.

England by Central/ISN for ITV sport, which was led by me and Rick Waumsley.

I was voted as one of the 100 Great Brummies, which I accepted even though I had never visited Birmingham until I was twenty-six. I was convinced to accept it when I was told that Ed Doolan, the Australian BBC radio presenter, was going to have one.

Apparently I would be filmed on a BBC programme arriving in a Rolls Royce at the Council House with my great pal Jasper Carrott... Oh well, easily persuaded!

I was also honoured with a plaque as a member of the city's Broad Street Walk of Stars. The stone was dug up to make way for a tramline, but I hope it will be reset one day!

Finally, I accepted the Lifetime Achievement Award in the 2021 Birmingham Awards in Association with Aston University. I've been lucky enough to have a wonderful career.

CHAPTER THIRTY

THE FAMILY AND
THE FUTURE

As much as I've enjoyed my career, the highest priority in my life is my family, who have all made sacrifices to enable me to go flat-out at work.

My parents came from poor backgrounds but made their money and made sure my brother Ian and I had every opportunity to succeed with their generosity and support.

We both had a private education and were given every chance. Ian went to Leeds University and the Middle Temple going on to be such a successful barrister that he retired from the Broadway Chambers in Bradford at sixty, only to die at seventy from bowel cancer. I miss my parents and my younger brother so much. After Ian died, his son Peter, married with three young daughters, passed away in such sad circumstances. I feel for his own family, my sister-in-law Susan and her daughter Anna. It's times like this you wish for the magic wand.

I am so proud of my own family. By the time this book is published my wife Katie and I will hopefully have celebrated our fiftieth wedding anniversary. Katie gave up her own career in television to bring up our three children and support my career, during which time she ran the Sunshine Coach programme for the Variety Club of Great Britain; chaired and belonged to various arts societies; set up her own speaking agency and produced events for the Birmingham Film Festival.

These days she keeps fit. As a qualified speech and drama teacher she writes brilliant charity pantomimes for our neighbours and local residents, raising thousands of pounds for charities. She has also co-written a musical.

Katie and I are business partners in our television and film production company.

She is a remarkable person, having overcome malignant melanoma on four separate occasions. Katie has done a wonderful job bringing up our children and is now a much-loved granny to our three grandchildren and Laurence's partner's three children.

My father Jack wanted his two sons to pick their own careers – not be talked into anything. I have done the same with ours.

After attending boarding school, our daughter Claire read Italian and Art History at university. She spent several years working for Christie's auction house before deciding to pursue a career in journalism. She had stints working for different publications, including the *Independent*, the *Mail on Sunday* and worked for a brief period out in New York before returning to the UK to become news editor at *Grazia* magazine. After getting married and having two children, Claire decided to spend more time with her family and became a freelancer. She continues to be a talented writer.

The twins Laurence and Neil are close, but they are so different that they are on opposite sides of the camera. Both are very talented too.

Laurence is an extremely busy outside broadcast camera operator specialising in the steadicam. He is a regular on ITV's horse racing, covers football and a multitude of other sports, including cricket and motorsport as well as major events including the funeral of Queen Elizabeth and the Coronation of King Charles. His CV, like his brother's, is very long!

Laurence lives in the Sheldon area of Birmingham with his partner Stella and her family.

Neil had many roles as an actor, including being the waiter in that famous and often-shown clip from *Goodness Gracious Me* where the cast go for an English! He has had lots of parts in TV and movies.

But an inventive change of acting direction has paid off big time. He is now an actor, stuntman, director and consultant in motion capture in the world of animation/video games. Neil is the star of many of them including *Resident Evil Village*, *Baldur's Gate 3* and *Detroit: Being Human*.

Neil has his own academy producing future talent, which he runs with Saleta Losada.

Neil lives in London with his wife Saleta. They run and own Performance Captured Limited, which is a capture production company. Neil also works in Los Angeles. His daughter is from a previous marriage.

How long will I live? Well, at seventy-eight I am moving up the bench, but I hope I have plenty left in the tank. I have had some health issues – a stroke in 2002, I recently had a pacemaker fitted and have undergone operations on my back, hip, shoulder and toe. But I feel great and Steff Affleck, the highly talented pilates teacher, keeps me and my wife strong at the weekly sessions we attend with her. I was introduced to pilates by Andy Adamson whose own company is called Cool Pilates.

I suppose I do not need to work except to keep my mind active. As long as I am fit enough I will never retire because I enjoy working so much.

It has meant that after those fifty years in TV I have had to reinvent myself with a range of topics – writing this book, writing two newspaper columns a week – every Tuesday in the *Birmingham Mail/Coventry Telegraph* and another in the *Sunday Mercury*. Both are online. I am grateful to Jem Maidment and James Heyes of Utilita Energy for their support on the former.

My latest venture is consultant with Mackrell Solicitors in London and Birmingham. Their main office is based in Savoy Hill off the Strand in London. Mohit Pasricha, who was head of sport and entertainment, was responsible for my taking the role. I joined for a year. Mohit has since left and the founding partner Nigel Rowley has contracted me for another two years.

Nigel is the reason I stayed with Mackrell. I work closely with Nigel, Chris Lane and James McKimm. I love being in this new field.

I am still involved in the media and have a strong working broadcasting partnership with Chris Pritchard with whom I previous worked with at Sky.

I also do after lunches/dinners with Barry Hearn, who is a brilliant orator.

For the past fifty years, I have worked in many corporate roles alongside my broadcasting roles, for which I am very grateful. These have included eighteen years of speaking engagements for Ansells Brewery, six years with the West Bromwich Building Society with Tom Cardall, thirteen years with Warwickshire

Cricket Club, several years with my close friend Martin Ladbrooke at Smithfield Motors and many more.

I really enjoy all these roles. Got to keep dementia at bay! I could go on (I usually do!), but it is time to pull up stumps. Thanks for reading this book.

ACKNOWLEDGEMENTS

I would like to thank Chris Pritchard (and for his technical advice), Jem Maidment and Mike Lockley for their editorial notes and Richard Morgan and Graham Affleck for checking the script. My thanks to my wife Katie for her support and original collating.

Thanks to Biteback Publishing for their guidance, support and platform: James Stephens, Olivia Beattie, Ryan Norman, Ella Boardman and Suzanne Sangster.

Thanks to all my subjects, bosses, TV stations, sponsors and sports superstars for making my career possible.

Special thanks to my big pals Tim Watts of Pertemps and John James.

To my family past and present and my great friends, thanks for giving me a wonderful, successful and memorable life. I wake up every morning thankful for my lot… And I hope to keep waking up for quite a bit longer!

And finally, I have always needed an audience, so thank you for reading this book!

INDEX

317